THE BROTHERS GRIMM

The Brothers Grimm

RUTH MICHAELIS-JENA

PRAEGER PUBLISHERS

New York   Washington

Books That Matter

*Published in the United States of America
in 1970 by Praeger Publishers, Inc.,
111 Fourth Avenue, New York, N.Y. 10003*

© *1970 in London, England, by Ruth Michaelis-Jena*

Library of Congress Catalog Card Number: 72-109480

Printed in Great Britain

For
A. J. J. R.

Contents

CONTENTS

Throughout the text and with illustrations relating to the period the old spelling of Cassel has been kept, otherwise modern usage has been adopted.

Plates

Illustrations in the Text

THE decoration on the title page represents the ex-libris of Philipp Wilhelm Grimm, now in the *Brüder Grimm Museum*, Kassel.

Illustrations in the text, reproducing drawings of the contemporary scene by Ludwig Emil Grimm, are from his *Reisetagebuch in Bildern, 1850*, in the *Brüder Grimm Museum*, Kassel. The everyday articles and designs of the period are from records, and the collections of the *Bergwinkel Museum*, Schlüchtern.

ILLUSTRATIONS

PAGE

Preface

THE *Nursery and Household Tales* have spread the fame of the Brothers Grimm everywhere. Jacob and Wilhelm Grimm made their collection in Kassel.

It was England, however, that gave the world the first important translation. In 1823, following the rendering of a few stories into Danish (1816) and a translation into Dutch (1820), Edgar Taylor published his translations. In doing so, he introduced the Grimms to the English-speaking nursery where they have been firmly established ever since. But, more remarkable than that, Taylor's work formed the basis for numerous translations into other languages, so that today many children all over the world find enjoyment in the old stories. Adults recapture the pleasures of their own childhood in them, and increasingly attention has been focused on the folktale as a subject for serious enquiry.

Like a golden net these fairytales have drawn together people far apart in time and space.

The present book shows that the brothers deserve our respect and affection also for reasons other than the discovery of the *Märchen*. As scholars they laid the foundations for the study of Germanic language and literature, and many of their books are still indispensable to the student. As human beings they were lovable, possessed of a sense of friendship and fairness, of integrity and incorruptibility in politically difficult times.

I am happy that the *Murhardsche Bibliothek der Stadt Kassel und Landesbibliothek,* successor to the library where the brothers spent many of their working years, and the *Brüder Grimm Museum,* have been able to play a part in the making of this valuable and delightful book.

Kassel/Germany   Ludwig Denecke

Acknowledgements

INTEREST in the Brothers Grimm goes back to my childhood, fostered early by my mother who – like the Grimms – came from Hesse, and my patient story-telling father. Many years after I conveyed my enthusiasm to my late husband, with whom I translated some of the lesser known tales from the Grimm collections. He in turn supported my researches, and shared the initial stages of the work.

It is my pleasant duty to thank the many friends who have helped me over years, first and foremost Dr. Ludwig Denecke, emeritus Director of the *Murhardsche Bibliothek der Stadt Kassel und Landesbibliothek*, incorporating the *Brüder Grimm Museum*. I have benefited much from his wise counsel and his valuable suggestions during the preparation of my manuscript. The staff of his library have never tired in giving me their amicable assistance. On account of an unpublished letter in his possession, Kassel's archivist, Dr. Robert Friderici, let me into the secret of how the brothers met their Fairytale-Wife, and allowed me to use the information.

Bürgermeister Désor of Steinau, Dr. Karl Dielmann, Director of the *Kulturamt* in Hanau, Wilhelm Hansen, Director of the *Landesmuseum* in Detmold, Dr. Hans Hornung, Director of the *Stiftung Preussischer Kulturbesitz*, Wilhelm Praesent, of the *Bergwinkel Museum* in Schlüchtern, and nearer home, Dr. Katharine M. Briggs, of Oxford, Dr. Gotthard Guder, Senior Lecturer in the Department of German in the University of Glasgow, and the Curator of the Edinburgh Museum of Childhood, Patrick Murray, have all given encouragement and good advice.

A Grimm 'freemasonry' stretches across Europe, and I have been warmly welcomed, and guided by Professor Sandor Kozocsa, of Budapest, Professor Leopold Schmidt, of Vienna, and Professor Pavel Trost, of Prague.

I remember with gratitude the late Nora Hassenpflug, great-granddaughter of *die liebe Lotte*, the Grimms' beloved sister, who made me feel at home in the Grimm family circle, also the much lamented Dr. Calum

Maclean, of the School of Scottish Studies, with whom I was able to discuss many points.

The extract from the letter by Sir Walter Scott on pp. 173-5 is reproduced from the centenary edition of *The Letters of Sir Walter Scott* (Constable & Co. Ltd. 1932-7) by kind permission of the publishers. I am also indebted to Elwert, publishers, of Marburg, Lahn, for permission to reproduce my translation on pp. 131-2 of an extract from Isidor Levin's essay, published in the *Grimm Gedenken*.

There are many more who must remain unnamed, like the kind nursing sister who showed me round the Haxthausen manor house of *Bökerhof*, now a home for the aged, and the old Steinau innkeeper who felt quite close to the Brothers Grimm, and spoke of them as if they were among us now.

Mrs. Marie Muir lent an ever-willing ear during the work's gradual progress.

The Lang Hoose   Ruth Michaelis-Jena
East Saltoun/E. Lothian

Jacob and Wilhelm Grimm, 1843. Etching by Ludwig Emil Grimm (from a pencil drawing) Berlin, August 1843, Historisches Museum, Hanau

Dorothea Grimm, *née* Zimmer. Oil painting by K. G. Urlaub, Staatsarchiv, Marburg/Lahn

Introduction

JACOB AND WILHELM GRIMM have been compared with two trees, sprung from the same root, grown together, and developing a common crown. The comparison is apt, for the brothers from the beginning shared work and play, were seldom parted, and lived in rare harmony. Their extraordinary complementary talents were to exercise a strong influence, far beyond their own country and their own time.

To the philologist they are the founders of *Germanistik*: Jacob, the grammarian and formulator of the principles of consonantal changes in the Germanic languages, Wilhelm the sensitive editor of many old German texts, and both in later years committed to hard labour on that formidable dictionary of the German language which was finished only in our day. With the brothers' work in comparative philology and mythology the student may associate a picture of two elderly scholars, one stern-looking, his finely cut face surrounded by white curls, the other softer, more gentle, with the eyes of a dreamer and poet.

To some Jacob and Wilhelm are two of the *Göttingen Seven*, those German professors who, in 1837, had the integrity to protest against despotic authority, and in doing so, displayed a *Zivilcourage*, sometimes found lacking in their countrymen.

To the majority, however, the name of Grimm becomes a household word in childhood. Ever since the *Nursery and Household Tales* began their triumphant progress through the nurseries of the world, the name has been a symbol for an enchanted, if somewhat fearful, world, the world of fairytale.

There were and still are many who believe that Jacob and Wilhelm invented the tales they published, that in fact they set out to write a book for children. Others, puzzled by the brothers' unique relationship, have harboured vague suspicions that the *Household Tales* are the outcome of an 'unnatural' fraternal attachment, hiding under their innocent surface Freudian depths. The Grimms have been accused of excessive nationalism,

A

a nationalism that made them stress, consciously or unconsciously, certain German characteristics. It is maintained that they glorified in their tales particular qualities, and a scale of values which in an exaggerated form became the false and corrupting mystique of 'blood and soil'.

They have been charged with anti-Semitism, with attributing dubious qualities to the Jews in their stories and making them figures of public ridicule.

To get nearer the truth, we must consider the background and history of the folktale as well as that of the Grimms' collection.

The folktale is probably as old as man himself. Its images express man's hopes, anxieties and aspirations, his deepest desires and fears. In tales, ugliness may turn into beauty, poverty into riches, and the weak and neglected will triumph in the end. Horror and cruelty, violence, suffering and pain have their natural place in a world where benevolent and evil magic fulfil some profound subconscious longings. Observation and description of natural phenomena become interwoven with custom and religious belief.

As the innermost experience of man is the same everywhere, the same tales and tale motifs are found existing independently in places far apart, though tales have also spread by word of mouth and through the printed word, then taking on local colour, become acclimatized to their new surroundings. To quote Professor Tolkien, in his essay, *On Fairy Stories*:

'. . . the Pot of Soup, the Cauldron of Story, has always been boiling, and to it have continually been added new bits, dainty and undainty . . .'[1]

Opinions about the origin and diffusion of tales differ widely, and perhaps there is no hard and fast answer. Theories abound.

An entertainment for adults, when men were the chief storytellers, in the market place or around the camp fire, the folktale found its true home in dimly lit rooms, in the twilight, when men and women busied themselves with some household tasks, or just sat enchanted at the feet of the storyteller. The written or printed word seems to destroy the tale's magic. Still, collections were made early in the East and in the countries round the Mediterranean.

The *Gesta Romanorum* of the Middle Ages, though consisting mainly of legends and anecdotes taken from Roman history and tradition, contained a number of folktales. In the sixteenth century Giovan Francesco Straparola published at Venice the *Tredici piacevoli notti*. In this collection, according to the fashion of the day, a frame story presents a noble lady passing her time by listening to stories. Many derived from literary sources, but about thirty of them were folktales. In the seventeenth century Giambattista Basile, a Neapolitan, collected *Lo cunto de li cunti*, to become known as the *Pentamerone*. Though presented in a framework, and told in baroque language, his material, collected verbally in the Neapolitan dialect, has the true ring of the genuine folktale. All these collections were for adults.

Charles Perrault, in France, was the first to make a book for children. At the end of the seventeenth century his *Histoires ou Contes du Temps passé avec des Moralitez*, subtitled *Contes de ma Mère l'Oye* – and ascribed to his son, Pierre Perrault Darmancour – were folktales, cleverly adapted to suit contemporary taste. This was followed by Madame d'Aulnoy's *Les Contes des Fées*, and *Contes Nouveaux ou les Fées à la Mode*. The popularity of Perrault's and Madame d'Aulnoy's work encouraged a great many, mostly ladies, to take up their pens, and a flood of tales eventually made up the forty-one volumes of the *Cabinet des Fées*. In these sophisti- cated stories, elegant, witty, often moralizing and didactic, typical products of the Rococo, the ghosts and fairies of folk tradition were tamed and prettified. In France, too, originated Jean Antoine Galland's popular adaptation from a fifteenth-century Arabic manuscript of *A Thousand and One Nights*, which immediately caught the imagination of the reading public.

On the whole, the Enlightenment of the eighteenth century considered folktales silly, even dangerous superstition, fit perhaps for old wives and the nursery. Such tales as were published provided moral teaching, often mixed with satire. The climate changed towards the end of the century, and in Germany Johann Karl August Musäus, schoolmaster in Weimar, began to collect tales. Before 1782 he obtained about ninety, some from printed sources, but many told him by peasants, old soldiers, 'journeymen' and the goodwives of the Thuringian spinning-rooms. He manipulated his material, changed the language, and gave the stories a touch of wryness and a certain stiltedness, belonging rather to the Weimar schoolmaster than to the tales themselves. *Frau* Naubert's collection, published about that time, suffered from the same shortcomings. However, it was a beginning.

Then came the Romantics.

They saw folk literature as a product of natural evolution, distinct from the deliberate culture of their age, an expression of wisdom and funda- mental truth. Inspired chiefly by Herder, they interested themselves in songs and tales, mainly as raw material to be used freely for their own fantastic creations.

Not so the Grimms. Tales to them were the debris of myths, primeval beliefs, religion, early customs and law. They stood at the beginning of all their work, ancestral reminiscences, to be collected for the investigation of ancient German literature, and to be treated with respect. The brothers searched for the genuine tale which can be traced through the ages. Contrary to their friends among the Romantics, the *Kunstmärchen*, a story contrived or adapted, did not interest them.

It was their considered aim to take down stories straight from the teller. They were aware of the importance of exactness and truth, and did not wish to change the essential contents of a story. They saw the folktale as a document not to be tampered with. In their day this approach was revolutionary.

In his preface to the 1819 edition of the *Nursery and Household Tales*, Wilhelm explained that their main concern had been accuracy and truth, that they had neither embellished incident nor feature of a tale. The mode of expression, however, and certain details were their own, while they endeavoured to keep the storyteller's characteristic turn of phrase.

Only over the years, and with growing success from edition to edition, did the *Household Tales* change from pieces of oral tradition into *Buchmärchen*, tales to be read. There had, of course, always been some material, taken from literary sources. The transformation into *Buchmärchen* was performed largely by Wilhelm, who devoted himself to the fairytales after the 1819 edition, almost single-handed, as Jacob became more and more involved in his own work on language. The brothers were fortunate in that most of their storytellers and recorders had a perfect ear for tradition. Wilhelm, with his gift for the colloquial, was aware of the teller's ways, and could reproduce them in a true and poetic fashion. By the slightest touch he could develop a character or give motivation to a certain happening. He often replaced indirect speech by dialogue. He could make animals talk, enhance the beauty of the king's daughter by describing her long golden hair, or add a telling phrase on how the wind played with the leaves in a deep dark forest. In that way he turned flat pieces of narrative into enchantment. But he never lost sight of the original, preserved its tone, yet gave it new expression.

Much of Wilhelm's work was done under the eyes of his stern philologist brother, who may not always have approved. However, on checking the few remaining manuscripts and early notations with Jacob's own transcriptions, it appears that he, too, allowed himself a certain freedom in smoothing out the style, and making a pleasing whole of sometimes disconnected parts. The Grimms did not change motifs or add new ones, but they did combine variants, sometimes printed and oral ones, to obtain more detail or create a more unified story.

Modern scholarship is apt to disparage the Grimms' method. No doubt, the *Urfassung* of the *Nursery and Household Tales* is most valuable to the student of the folk-narrative, but there is equally no doubt that the masterly transformation, done in patient revision for nearly fifty years, made the *Nursery and Household Tales* a classic of world literature, a book loved by generation after generation.

One has also to remember that a story told has a different life from a story read. The storyteller's voice, his gestures, even his surroundings, play a great part which the printed word has difficulty in conveying. Somehow, the artist in Wilhelm overcame this handicap.

In his book, *Les Livres, les Enfants et les Hommes*, the literary historian, Paul Hazard, has this to say about the Grimms:

'. . . at the beginning of the nineteenth century in Germany, two brothers were busy with a strange task, so strange that many good souls found it unworthy of serious writers. Scholars, philologists, historians as well as philosophers, Jacob and William Grimm collected tales, much as though they were running after butterflies. As a matter of fact their first thought was to catch the tales while still alive . . . A taste for folk tales, as savoury as home-made bread, that is what children found in their work; that is the superb gift they received from the two German writers . . .'[2]

Many years after the first publication of the tales, Jacob was to refer to them as 'everlasting food for the young and every open-minded reader . . .',[3] providing, he said, at the same time, a divining-rod for the student of past ages.

So much for the background and history of the Grimms' collection. It becomes abundantly clear that the *Nursery and Household Tales* belong to an age-old tradition, and that all they owe to the brothers' unique relationship is their final shape, given them by Jacob, and to an even larger extent by Wilhelm. This relationship, often commented upon, was by no means 'unnatural'. When circumstances allowed, Wilhelm entered into a perfectly normal and happy marriage, while Jacob, the 'engaged' scholar, gave all his energies to work, and was devoted to the family around him.

The motivation for the brothers' researches into German language and literature was not provided by excessive nationalism but rather by the literary and political climate of their times which had witnessed the rise of a patriotism highly charged with emotion. The Jew – when he appeared in the tales – was the stereotype figure of folk literature, and, indeed, the characteristics attributed to him were founded in common belief.

The Grimms' notes on theories, variants, motifs and origins of tales, published as an appendix first, then grown into a separate volume, created a new science, *Märchenforschung*, the enquiry into the origin, significance and diffusion of tales. The 1856 volume of notes, the last edited by Wilhelm, supplies a solid mass of information. These notes, together with much unpublished material, handed over to Professor Johannes Bolte, became the basis of a five-volume commentary on the folktale. Professor Bolte obtained the collaboration of Georg Polivka of Prague, mainly for Slavonic material, and archives in many countries were successfully searched. Bolte and Polivka's commentaries, preserving as a nucleus the Grimms' investigations, are still the most important handbook for students of the folktale.

Jacob's and Wilhelm's theories that their tales were of Indo-Germanic origin, that similarities of motifs and incidents of tales in countries far apart were due, either to these tales having been carried by word of mouth, or to the fact of simple basic situations being the same with all peoples, have since been challenged.

The orientalist, Theodor Benfey, in notes to his translation of the *Panchatantra*, made India the source of all tales, believing them to be of Buddhistic origin, created mainly for instruction. Reinhold Köhler followed in his footsteps, and the Sanskrit scholar, Max Müller, identified links between European and Eastern tales. These theories became fashionable, and everybody tried to discover how tales migrated from Asia, via Africa, to the Mediterranean and farther north. Benfey had his critics, and eventually Edward B. Tylor and Andrew Lang introduced the anthropological school, maintaining that in essence and origin all tales were survivals of early and savage states of society, the same existing all over the globe. These ideas were, in time, expanded by the French scholar, Joseph Bédier, in an introduction to his *Les Fabliaux*, to the concept of polygenesis. Under the same circumstances the same tale may have arisen in a number of unrelated places.

Discussion continues to this very day. There certainly exists a basic unity of human nature, of fears, desires, hopes and longings. But, there has also been a continuous diffusion of tales by word of mouth, through wandering traders, scholars, minstrels, jesters, soldiers and sailors. Oriental material became intertwined with Celtic lore and the debris of Norse sagas.

Modern psychologists have added their theories of the collective subconscious, and have drawn attention to the close relation of dreams to motifs of myths and tales. In our century the Finnish school of folklorists, *The Folklore Fellows*, founded in 1907 by Kaarle Krohn and Antti Aarne, began systematic research into the many types of the folktale, on a chronological and geographical basis. Separate monographs deal with variants of one primary form of tale. Out of this, too, has arisen Stith Thompson's vast *Motif-Index of Folk Literature*, and Aarne and Thompson's *The Types of the Folktale*, both indispensable tools to the folklorist. The emphasis has shifted from the person of the collector to that of the individual storyteller, helped by the introduction of the tape recorder which faithfully reproduces the quality of the telling. Archives of material are being built up in many countries, often taken down from old men and women who may well be the last carriers of oral tradition.

Märchenforschung has come of age.

At a time when folk-life studies are gaining ever-increasing importance, the brothers' fame may well rest on the fact that they turned the amateur antiquarian into the professional folklorist. Through their initial insistence on 'genuine and true' recording, ballads, songs and tales changed their status. From 'sinful superstition' or, at best, material for prettifying they were elevated to documentary evidence of mankind's half-forgotten past.

This aspect makes the brothers unique in their own period. If many of their conclusions are now outdated, they did spark off a new beginning.

Though within the circle of the German Romantics, the Grimms were not quite of it. Their studies under Savigny taught them scientific method, and beyond their romantic enthusiasm for the medieval was a purpose: careful investigation, and application of their findings.

The brothers' span of life took in wars and revolutions: the French Revolution, Napoleon, the collapse of the Holy Roman Empire, Waterloo, and the Rise of the Common Man. They lived to see great changes in science and learning, in art and literature. Their childhood Germany, parochial and composed of many small states, was on the threshold of becoming the new united *Reich*, at the time of their death.

Through it all, Jacob and Wilhelm remained much the same, affectionate, simple in their tastes, staunch patriots, of utmost integrity and single-minded devotion to their chosen work.

Circumstances, often harsh and limiting, yet favoured the brothers in some strange ways. Their early years, close to nature, in a beautiful region where the accustomed lingered, set their pace for life, and made them sympathetic to tradition. Public and private disasters forced them into diligence, and strengthened their inborn love of quietness.

Wilhelm's son, the art historian Herman Grimm, considered quietness his father's and uncle's true element. As a boy in Göttingen, he had tiptoed through their studies, hearing nothing but the regular scratching of quill-pens, and he had retained a picture of Jacob, bent, writing very intensely and quickly, and Wilhelm slowly and more deliberately. Their favourite pot plants decorated the window sills while letters and manu-scripts were held down by stones and pieces of crystal, brought home by the brothers from their many walks. Herman also reports that wherever he went and was recognized as son and nephew of the Grimms, he was accepted as a friend.

Jacob and Wilhelm had identified themselves with the people, and the people in turn understood and loved them. Theirs was a humanity which turned mere knowledge into wisdom.

CHAPTER 1

Childhood in Hanau and Steinau

1785–1798

JACOB LUDWIG CARL – to be known as Jacob Grimm – was born in Hanau on 4 January 1785, and Wilhelm Carl – Wilhelm – a year later, on 24 February 1786. They were two of a family of nine, six of whom were to survive infancy, among them the only girl, Lotte, and the gifted painter, Ludwig.

The Grimms' ancestors had been settled in Hesse for centuries. In 1508 a Peter Grimm (or Grym) was a burgher of Frankfurt am Main, and his son, Lotz, became watchman of one of Frankfurt's guard-towers. Another Grimm owned a *Hofreite*, a farm, at the end of the sixteenth century, others again were bakers, millers and innkeepers, till in the seventeenth century the family moved into the professional classes.

Friedrich Grimm, Jacob's and Wilhelm's great-grandfather, seems to have been a remarkable man. He was born in Hanau on 16 October 1672, and died there on 4 April 1748. In his early twenties he had become chaplain to the Prince of Isenburg, and while still young he was called to the ministry in Hanau, and made inspector of churches. He held these offices for forty-two years. He was praised for giving the ministers under him 'scientific' stimulation, and this stress on the scientific must have been a family characteristic. Philipp Wilhelm, father of Jacob and Wilhelm, was born the tenth child of Friedrich's son, another Friedrich, and also minister in Hanau, who at the age of twenty-one was called to Steinau near Hanau where he remained for forty-seven years. His wife died at thirty-nine at the birth of her eleventh child. Philipp Wilhelm was then not yet three years of age. He was largely cared for by his eldest sister, Juliane Charlotte Friederike, who later on was to play a part in the bringing up of his famous sons.

Son and grandson of the parsonage, Philipp Wilhelm did not follow family tradition but read law, and became town clerk of Hanau. On 23 February 1783 he married Dorothea Zimmer. His bride's family was Hessian too, from Cassel. The name of Zimmer indicates that at one time the family's occupation may have been that of *Zimmerleute* – carpenters

9

or timber people – though they now belonged to the professional class. Dorothea's father had served in the Landgrave's chancellory, and as a retired *Kanzleirat* lived in Hanau.

His grandson Wilhelm was to write of him, in his autobiography:

'. . . our grandfather, the *Kanzleirat* Zimmer . . . was in retirement. During the Seven-Years-War he had been with the Landgrave, William VIII, when the prince was forced to leave his country, and, it appears, that in this position he acquired his even friendliness, mildness and forbearance . . . I remember well how our grandfather – later on when we visited him from Steinau – often sat with us for hours, putting his trembling hands on the table, and watching us copy the copperplates from Niebuhr's *Arabian Journey*. Up to his very end, when he could hold a quill only with difficulty, he continued giving us most affectionate advice in his letters . . .'[1]

Over the centuries Hanau had grown from a small mainly agricultural community of humble low-roofed, often timbered houses, into a prosperous little town extending beyond the bounds of its medieval walls. Its carefully laid-out *Neustadt* was an example to German town planners. It owed much of its prosperity to being a Protestant stronghold which had given shelter to successive waves of refugees, the Flemish, Dutch and Huguenots, all bringing with them their native skills. Cloth-making, dyeing, printing and particularly the craft of the silver- and goldsmith became firmly established. Hanau had survived the ravages of wars and invasions, and was in the late eighteenth century enjoying a period of peace. New houses, new bridges and new roads were built, while the town's rulers, like other German princes, followed the French fashion in creating 'Turkish' gardens, grottoes and follies around their spacious residences. The burgher's course of life was slow and measured, with everyone having a settled place in a firmly established social order.

The Grimms' home was a typical German *Bürgerhaus*, roomy, comfortable, unpretentious. Tastes were simple, and family ties close, even by the standards of an age which accepted emotional display and strong sentimental attachment to one's kith and kin. Relations were happy, and Jacob and Wilhelm were to remember their childhood affectionately in copious letters and notes, and in the autobiographies which they prepared in middle life for Karl Wilhelm Justi's biographical dictionary of Hessian scholars.

From them a picture evolves of security and domestic bliss.

In 1814 during the Napoleonic campaigns, Jacob, then thirty years old, and 'not suited to diplomatic life', lonely and disgruntled, found comfort in writing down some childhood memories:

'. . . I can quite well remember the house where my parents lived, in the long narrow street in Hanau. It was painted light red. To the left, looking out of the window, was another house, its stone a little darker . . .'

10

'...there was a large courtyard with a green where I played sometimes...
Opposite us lived a glove maker, called Femel, and in his place I sometimes
was given pieces of leather or leather balls. Next to him lived *Mamsell*
Stapfern, seamstress, washer-woman, upholsterer or something like
that...'[2]

These neighbours were typical in a town where shops were few and
simple, and where most things for daily use were made by craftsmen in
their workshops. Only the seasonal fairs supplied, apart from everyday
things, the special and the 'exotic', silks perhaps, and lace, fine linen,
leather goods from the Tyrol, cribs and toys carved in Berchtesgaden or the
Thuringian Forest, amber beads from the Baltic, and the latest chapbooks and picture sheets. There, too, one would see puppet shows and
tight-rope-walkers, and hear all recent scandal from *Moritat* singers who
illustrated their gruesome tales with large gaudy posters. Somewhere
a quack would loudly praise his mixtures, pills and ointments, a panacea
for every conceivable complaint.

These fairs were occasions for much feasting, with the inns putting
out their traditional wreaths or green branches to show that new wine
was for sale, while the scent of frizzling sausages and freshly baked bread
made old and young hungry. Big and small bretzels would hang, strung
up, from booths, with shelves full of honeycakes, peppernuts, gingerbread-
men and large baked hearts to take home to one's love. For a while the
town seemed very quiet when all the booths were packed up again and
the fiddlers and brass bands had gone on their way. The houses then
resumed their staid appearance, with their pointed gables and huge wooden
doors with polished handles.

The Grimms' 'rented house' was entered from the street by a large
door, painted yellowish-brown. On the ground floor was the drawing-
room – *die gute Stube* – kept mainly for visitors, and not in regular use.
Its wallpaper, a sign of elegance, when walls were mostly painted, was
decorated with pictures of huntsmen. There was a narrow courtyard
where wood was sawn, and where the weekly washerwoman reigned over
her steaming laundry. Sometimes she would put a drop of *Schnapps* from
the bottle she carried, on the boys' hunks of brown bread.

Towns were still closely linked with the country – where the bulk of
the population lived – and many townsmen were *Ackerbürger* who, in
addition to their gardens, owned or had leased land outside the city walls.
Many kept cows on the common, and most had a few hens. There were
hens in the Grimms' courtyard, and Jacob remembered going down with
his father to attend to a hen sick with the pip.

Above ground floor and courtyard was mother's realm, the sitting-room.
Here she sat sewing or knitting while Marie and Gretchen, two Hessian

11

peasant girls, busied themselves about the house. Father had his own room on this floor, and to the back was the nursery. Through its windows one could see the fruit trees in the neighbour's garden. The usual large German stove stood in a corner of the sitting-room:

'. . . my mother often washed me by the stove', Jacob remembered, 'with warm water to which a little wine had been added. It smelt sweet, and was only annoying when it got near the ears, and made them sore . . . I remember well sucking a baby's tit, and playing with small baking tins. The tits were made of fine brown sugar and bread, put into a cloth . . . Near the front door, close to the wall, I made a little garden of grass, but my parents didn't like it . . .'[3]

Jacob recalled no playmates at that time. Outside the window of one of the rooms was a little mirror, and after all those years a vision flashed through Jacob's mind of maids, carrying on their heads wooden tubs filled with water at one of the *Brunnen*, the morning sunlight flooding every corner of the street below.

Wilhelm, too, liked to conjure up pictures of early childhood, himself '. . . in a white dress with a red sash', lost in the shrubbery of a park where 'the green twilight' had frightened him. For a party at Grandfather Zimmer's his and his brother's hair 'had been curled'. He recalled carriage drives to the Landgrave's parades and manoeuvres, with much martial music and 'the thunder of guns'.[4]

The brothers were keen observers, and both showed great anxiety to learn. They were fortunate in having a patient instructor in their father's widowed childless sister. Juliane Charlotte Friederike Schlemmer – *Tante* Schlemmer – told the boys their first Bible stories, and taught them to read and write from a little book:

'its covers were made of wood, with painted pictures, on one side was a cornet, painted red, on the other children blowing bubbles, and some allegorical figures. From a fan our aunt had made herself an ivory pointer which was used also as a bookmark after lessons. Usually she took a pin, to be able to point more finely, and eventually all letters looked pierced . . .'[5]

This aunt, with her 'blue-ribboned bonnet', sensible, well meaning but serious, made a strong impression on her two nephews. Jacob was to prove a particularly good scholar, and this made him his aunt's favourite. He in turn loved her dearly and spent much time at her house.

Aunt Schlemmer's lessons were the brothers' first step in education. Dancing and French they learnt from an old teacher who lived near one of Hanau's churches. Hand in hand the brothers would set out for their tutor, then stop to admire the church's gilt weathercock, turning in the wind. Once on a visit to a real school Jacob saw a boy writing with yellow ink, and was thrilled to be allowed to use a penful.

Much of the boys' time was spent with their Grandfather Zimmer, and he was to prove always a very good friend to them both.

In 1791 Philipp Wilhelm Grimm was made *Amtmann* – justiciary – at Steinau, and this little town in the Kinzig valley became the Grimms' true childhood home. The move was a great event for them. There were now five children: Jacob six years old, Wilhelm, Carl and Ferdinand, with a year between each, and the youngest, Ludwig, a year old only.

With chairs wrapped in straw, glasses and cups in tow, and the removal carefully prepared, everything was ready for the journey. During it Wilhelm sat on a box in the small carriage, or slept on his aunt's knees. After selling her house at Hanau, *Tante* Schlemmer moved with the family to Steinau. Wilhelm always remembered the hedges of flowering black-thorn they had passed. They looked as though they were covered with fine snow, and the driver had stopped to break off a branch and let the children touch it.

It was only a short distance to Steinau *an der Strasse*, on the great trade-route from Frankfurt to Leipzig, and though parting from Hanau had caused pain, it was something of a coming home. In Steinau the name of Grimm was highly respected. Father was born there, where grandfather and great-grandfather had occupied clerical positions. Relatives still lived in or near the town, and the floor of the parish church held the mortal remains of many ancestors.

'There was rain, the day we arrived', says Jacob in his notes of 1814. The first night was spent at the house of friends, and a boy there wore a white pointed night-cap. In the room, Jacob remembered a 'yes-nodding man and a no-shaking woman', most likely two of the then very popular 'nodding figure' ornaments, made in the nearby highlands of the Rhön.[6]

Soon the family was established in one of Steinau's old houses, the *Amtshaus*, official residence of the *Amtmann*. It was a handsome half-timbered building, surrounded by gardens and a walled courtyard. The façade had consoles and rafters, finely carved with scrolls and fantastic figures. One irregular beam ended in a little squinting devil which both fascinated and frightened the children. There were stables and outhouses, a turret stair and a huge lime tree at the front door.

They settled happily into their new home: Philipp Wilhelm, a loving father, busy, well-respected, and aware of his new and more important position, Dorothea, now thirty-five, filling the house with cheerful bustle, supervising the maids, looking after the house and garden, baking bread, making preserves, adoring her husband, and caring affectionately for her five boys.

13

Jacob's notes make it easy to picture what these boys looked like. Under the heading, *Clothes*, he says:

'... mornings and evenings still smocks, tied in the back, wide shirt collars turned out, the smocks made of brown and grey floral cotton. During the day, shorter or longer jackets, made of purple linen. In winter, coats of heavy grey cloth, with white buttons . . .'[7]

To begin with the boys wore their hair loose, cut to shoulder length, but soon enough they adopted the Steinau fashion of pigtails, the more tightly plaited, the better. If a boy, unfortunate enough to have poor hair, wore a false pigtail, he risked having it pulled by the other boys. Hats were round, coats red on Sundays, and trousers tight and short, worn with low-heeled slippers.

Ludwig Grimm, too, has described Steinau life vividly in his memoirs. There was comfort and a certain amount of stateliness. Father, in keeping with the dignity of his office, wore a blue frock coat, with red velvet collar and gold epaulettes, leather breeches and boots with silver spurs. There was a coachman to lift the excited boys on to his horses. Flowers, fruit and vegetables grew in plenty, and there was room to keep rabbits.

Soon happiness was increased by the arrival of a sister, Charlotte Amalie, affectionately called *das Malchen*, and later on *die liebe Lotte*. Everybody fussed over the new baby. She was good-tempered, and only cried when too many wanted to kiss her at the same time. Life was just that little bit grander in Steinau, due to the *Herr Amtmann's* new station. On Sundays meals were taken in the large dining-room, with stucco work on the walls. The coachman acted as butler, complete with livery. The sledge for winter outings was decorated with a gilt Hessian lion. There were journeys in the snow to neighbouring villages where Papa had to conduct some legal business with peasants crowded into small overheated rooms.

Steinau itself was a democratic little community where everybody knew everybody else, and people took an interest in each other's joys and sorrows. Its brown and yellow half-timbered houses clustered round the old moated castle of the Counts of Hanau, enclosed by the crumbling ivy-covered town walls. The Gothic church of St Catherine's and the baroque *Reinhardskirche* were the burghers' pride. Gardens were full of flowers which in high summer burst over the garden gates and walls into the narrow and crooked streets and lanes. Most of these seemed to lead to the *Stadtborn*, the little stream that flowed through the town. Its banks were a natural haunt for the townsfolk: burghers taking the air, the potter carting a load of clay for his wheel, the tanner carrying a hide for drying, or the town musician passing on his endless visits to inns and other places to play for dances and weddings. The people of Steinau loved their holidays. Seven times a year fairs were announced by the roll of drums. Easter eggs were hidden and searched for on the green, and apples were painted silver and gold during the weeks of Advent. Christmas was looked forward to with excitement. The grown-ups prepared 'the Christmas room' in the true German fashion, decorating the tree, and laying out the presents, while the children listened anxiously for the sound of the bell to summon them. They would find the tree shining with candles, with apples and nuts in plenty. Under it would be dolls and doll's clothing, painted lead soldiers in matchwood boxes, and, a great favourite, picture sheets with gilt animals for cutting out.

There were many callers at the *Amtshaus*: a friendly postilion might raise a child for one wonderful moment to the height of his seat on the post-chaise, or the forester call after dinner and give the boys a ride on his leather-trousered knees.

The year fell into seasons naturally, a time for sowing and for reaping, and a time for gathering in the lamp-lit room where the linen was spun. In the spinning-rooms of Steinau, perhaps, but certainly from the lips of their mother, Jacob and Wilhelm heard the first Hessian tales. The countryside was full of old traditions. White ladies, fairies, elves and witches were real, and the Grimms' very home was haunted by a former *Amtmann*. It was a world, too, in which animals held a part quite as sensible and ordained as humans. Every spring the swallows returned, and the Grimm family almost had a private pair of storks which nested year after year on the tower outside the *Amtshaus*. In the evening the cows came back on their own from the common grazing, while the goose girl brought her flock home from the green. Even the rare black lamb had a special purpose, for from its wool could be made without dyeing the black socks and stockings coveted by everybody.

Steinau held a wealth of simple magic for children. The gates, guard-rooms and disused towers of the defences, the rambling stairs and passages within the painted houses, the yards and alleys around them, made fascinating playgrounds. Woods, hills and fields were there to be explored, and on autumn excursions acorns were collected to be marshalled as soldiers, the double ones being officers. Fallen apples could be mounted on sticks, and catapulted over incredible distances, baking ovens were made from sand, and tiny wagons out of chestnuts.

But even in these early days Jacob and Wilhelm recognized in themselves a sense of purpose. They showed an interest in collecting and drawing plants, cock's feathers, stones and marbles, and there was much bartering with other boys. They also drew the things they saw around them, corn-fields, people and houses, with much attention to little doors and windows. School was patriarchial. The *Amtmann's* boys mixed with the *Bürger-jungen*, sons of the peasants and artisans who paid their school fees in logs,

15

while wealthier folk paid in money. The children of woodcutters, millers, tailors, weavers, innkeepers and potters were the Grimms' companions and playmates. The ordinary folk of the Hessian countryside were their friends, and their ears became used to the people's way of talking. It was forthright with at times a telling phrase of earthy coarseness.

Learning began in earnest under the guidance of the preceptor Zinckhan who came to the house every day. This strange and pedantic old man took his task seriously, so much so that little Jacob, who had learnt to read in Hanau and had, in fact, read whole articles from the newspaper to his grandfather, often became bored. By his own account, he used to sit through the lessons, watching the hands of the clock, anxiously waiting for the hour of release. The severe dominie set great store by careful writing, and the brothers never forgot his insistence on diligence and attention. They learnt their first Latin from a small grammar with rhyming jingles, and added to the French they had started earlier, according to the German fashion of the day which made a sound knowledge of French a necessity in polite society. *Tante* Schlemmer continued her Bible lessons.

Jacob, in particular, spent much time with Aunt Schlemmer who was now in poor health, and he later remembered:

'. . . her room was painted yellow (with a flower basket, made by Master Eirich, above the door). Under the window were two stone seats, covered with green cushions. Next to them stood a wash-hand basin, green, and yellow inside. There was a wicker-work trunk for the dirty linen, between cupboard and wall. I often sat on it in the dark, as it was hidden by a curtain. Above our aunt's bed hung the picture of a woman praying, with two smaller pictures below. One was of a man, sitting reading, surrounded by trees, the other showed a soldier carrying a girl on his shoulder, in the moonlight. The windows in the picture were painted a glowing red to give the effect of a genuine night scene . . .'[8]

As a boy Jacob had been aware of just the slightest uneasiness between Mother and Aunt. With her adored brother the only surviving relative, Aunt Schlemmer was apt to overcompensate on the Grimm inheritance, rejecting a little everything that was Zimmer, and on the mother's side. Jacob, so much like Grandfather Grimm, was therefore a natural in her favour.

Jacob vividly recalls the peacefulness of a Steinau day. He and Wilhelm would wake up in the green-and-white-striped bedroom, next to their parents' four-poster, with its grey-and-dark-blue-striped curtains, to hear the tea urn hum in the sitting-room next door. In his dressing gown of Polish cotton, Papa would say prayers, and then have a smoke. His toilet finished, wig attended to and powdered by a servant, he would go upstairs to work. The boys spent the mornings in the schoolroom, with

Philipp Wilhelm Grimm. Oil painting by K. G. Urlaub, Staatsarchiv, Marburg/Lahn

Juliane Charlotte Friederike Schlemmer, *née* Grimm. Privately owned

the stern preceptor, often in Mamma's presence. After the midday meal, coffee had to be ground for an afternoon cup, a task Jacob enjoyed. Sometimes he would even be allowed to wash the precious blue-and-white Dresden china, and be given some coffee in return for his services. School over, at four o'clock, the boys were free to roam in house and garden. Father often took a walk round the gardens after lunch, cutting bunches of grapes for the evening's dessert, inspecting poultry-yard and pigeonloft, and having a look at the horses. There were sheep, too, and cattle, and Jacob recollects how he fed the cows, and saw them being milked. He also had to gather the eggs, and watch for new chicks. The boys were made to help with many household tasks, some to their taste, some not. Jacob liked 'sausage making time', when, according to the German custom, a whole animal was prepared for winter food, some parts salted, others smoked, and the rest made into various kinds of sausages. He also liked baking and the 'cooking' of electuary, considered a cure-all for many ills. Washing-day, however, was a nuisance, and so were boring slow tasks, such as cutting beans or cabbage for preserving, or sorting out hop cones. Mother was a good cook, but even then there was a soup, not favoured by the children, and therefore called 'headache soup' as only the pretence of a headache might save one from having to eat it!

Steinau evenings were spent sitting round a large table, with much chatting and receiving visits from neighbours and friends. The men drank beer and smoked, while Father often checked the strangers' registration slips which the inns had to send for the *Herr Amtmann's* perusal. There might be a game of Lotto before the children were sent to bed.

It was a tranquil life, warm and secure, ruled by parents, loving but strict, sternly Protestant and devoted to duty. They were not given to compromise, and considered their country, their prince and their religion the best in the world. In a Germany split into many small states, there was no feeling of nationality. One's own principality was the Fatherland, and everything outside it *die Fremde* – abroad.

This quiet world was fated not to last, either in the national or private field.

The Steinau idyll was cruelly shattered when in the winter of 1795–96 the *Amtmann* Grimm fell seriously ill. He was devotedly nursed by wife and sister, while in a series of touching letters, Jacob kept Grandfather Zimmer informed about his father's state.

On 5 January 1796 he wrote:

'. . . our dear father is very weak . . . and this is not surprising, as during the last few days he has been bled five times, and three large blisters were raised on his chest. With violent stinging pains at every breath, and having had nothing but medicine and drinks for a week, he is completely

B 17

exhausted, while worry about us has also increased his suffering. O, my dear grandfather, Mother, Aunt and we two oldest ones will never forget this last Christmas as long as we live. Our doctor did not want to take on the responsibility alone, and we were forced to call in *Hofrat* Wagner. But, shortly before he arrived, God blessed our own doctor's medicines, and granted a little relief. It was fortunate that the two doctors agreed on everything which we thought was very good, giving much comfort to the patient and to ourselves. Now we must go on trusting in the Lord whose goodness is overflowing. Our dear father feels his appetite returning, and has been thinking of baker Schürko's special bread. Mother would therefore be very grateful if you could use an opportunity to send a small loaf. It must be freshly baked the same day, as Father cannot eat anything dry . . .'[9]

Grandfather Zimmer sent a freshly baked loaf at once, assuring the family of his loving conern and his hope that things would now take a turn for the better.

Alas, the improvement did not continue, and on 10 January 1796 Philipp Wilhelm Grimm died of pneumonia, just over forty-four years old.

All happiness was gone.

The black coffin, and the bearers carrying yellow lemons and rosemary, marked the end of childhood for Jacob and Wilhelm. Suddenly they had grown up, helpmates of their distressed mother, and with a firm hand the eleven-year-old Jacob noted the father's death in the family Bible.

The widow Grimm soon had to leave the *Amtshaus*, and within a short time the family moved twice. Life with six young children was not easy.

So far the wars raging since the execution of Louis XVI had not affected the family directly. In 1796 a French army under General Jourdan was defeated by the Archduke Charles, and forced to retreat across the Rhine. This brought the war close to the Grimms' own door. Grandfather Zimmer sent sympathetic messages, hoping Steinau would not suffer too much from roving soldiery. He also sent the children cherries.

That year, too, the good *Tante* Schlemmer died. Her place was taken by another affectionate aunt, Henriette Philippine Zimmer, Dorothea Grimm's sister. A maiden lady, she was in the service of the Landgravine at Cassel. She cared most warmly for the bereaved family, sending comfort, advice and gifts: money for the household, toys for the children.

'. . . I wish you could have seen little Lotte's joy over her beautiful doll and the other things', wrote Jacob to Aunt Zimmer. 'Mother will have a kitchen made for her to put all the pretty things in . . .'[10]

The Steinau joiner would be sure to make a fine 'Nuremberg' kitchen, that famous toy upon which the careful Dutch and German mother began her daughter's domestic education.

18

On 29 December 1797 Wilhelm wrote to their aunt:

'. . . I hope you will not be displeased if I, too, send you a few lines. I have my share in the books you so kindly sent, and it is my duty to thank you most loyally. My brothers and sister are grateful to the Lord who has given us such wonderful support in you . . . Our nasty hooping-cough is better. Several children here were suffocated with it . . .'[11]

Aunt Zimmer continued her loving care, and some two years after her husband's death *Frau* Grimm was pleased to accept her sister's offer to look after Jacob and Wilhelm, now thirteen and twelve years old. Jacob had already shown signs of impatience with his schooling, protesting that he could learn no more from Zinckhan, and seeking compensation in the books of his father's library. Now the boys were to go to Cassel, and continue their education at the *Lyceum Fridericianum* there.

Within earshot of wars and bloody revolutions Jacob and Wilhelm had experienced an idyllic childhood, loved and cared for, in harmony with the countryside and people around them.

These early years were greatly to influence their future tastes.

Decoration on the consoles of the Amtshaus.
Drawing by Otto Brinkmann

CHAPTER 2

Schooldays in Cassel: Students at Marburg University

1798 – 1805

AT the end of September 1798 Jacob and Wilhelm took a sad farewell from their family and the loved home of their childhood. The journey to Cassel was quite an enterprise. They had to travel to Hanau, and continue by boat on the river Main to Frankfurt, by the very *Marktschiff* Goethe had watched in his youth, conveying the most varied cargo and sometimes strange figures to the old Imperial City. From Frankfurt the boys were to take the diligence to Cassel. This involved a stay and a night's break.

Grandfather Zimmer eased the way by recommending his grandsons to a Frankfurt friend, and sending 'old Johann' to see them safely there. From an account of their adventures, Jacob later sent to his mother, we know that Grandfather's introduction to *Herr* Rüppel, Head Postmaster in Frankfurt, had been successful.

'. . . We arrived here safe and sound', Jacob wrote from Cassel, 'yesterday at noon, and I must now give you some news of our journey . . .'[1]

Jacob then relates how he and his brother had arrived in Frankfurt, had walked around its cobbled streets, and then gone to see *Herr* Rüppel. He was not at home, but they waited undismayed, and were eventually invited to lunch and afternoon coffee. Then the hospitable postmaster took Jacob and Wilhelm 'to see all kinds of wild animals: elephants, tigers, parrots, monkeys and many others which just happened to be on show in Frankfurt. It cost money, but he paid for us too.' Here speaks the responsible eldest son who had been warned to watch expense, now that life was so different, without a father.

In Frankfurt the boys also saw 'some fifty wax figures which looked quite natural, all dressed. They were present-day emperors, kings, generals and others. It was very nice.'

The postmaster could not put the boys up for the night, and, after sleeping at an inn, they took an early coach to Cassel. Aunt Henriette Zimmer received her nephews lovingly. She had found lodgings for them with the Landgrave's cook. They were to share one room and even one bed.

Jacob and Wilhelm, united in everything, were very different in appearance: Jacob small, slender and nimble, with a finely cut face, curly hair and keen penetrating eyes, Wilhelm taller, with a round, softer face, his eyes large and sensitive. All through life the brothers were to keep their strong individualities which in some curious way heightened their common achievements.

The *Lyceum Fridericianum* in Cassel had seven classes. The four upper served to prepare for the university while pupils of the three lower ones did not aim at further academic studies. Unfortunately Preceptor Zinckhan's lessons had not done enough for Jacob and Wilhelm. Jacob was admitted to the lowest form only while Wilhelm had to get further private tuition before entering the High School.

This was a disappointment, but the family kept counselling and encouraging in many affectionate letters. On 6 October 1798 Grandfather Zimmer wrote from Hanau:

'. . . I cannot repeat often enough that you must remember your goal, the reason for being where you are. This means diligence during lessons and away from them, so that you may lay the foundations for your future good, do yourselves credit, and give pleasure to your mother, to me and the whole family. Therefore, keep away from company which might lead you into temptations, but associate with sensible men from whom you can profit, and, above all, fear the Lord, which is the beginning of all wisdom. It will give your old grandfather great pleasure at all times to have good news from you . . .'[2]

From Mother, at Steinau, Wilhelm received this special letter, dated 27 October 1798. Perhaps her son had been a little restive.

Street scene, Steinau. Drawing by Ludwig Emil Grimm

'. . . I remind you, my son, to be diligent, particularly at home. You must do without many pleasures just now. Do not look for company of other young lads around, or you will become too distracted, and also be a nuisance to your good landlord. Wilhelm, do use this heaven-sent opportunity, and remember that, if it pleased the Lord, to call me or your good aunt, everything would be finished at once, and you would be forced to do something else. Also, remember how you and your brother have advantages, not granted to your brothers and sister on whom not the same amount of money can be spent. You must not compare yourself to other young people of your age who may go out and enjoy themselves. Perhaps they still have both their parents. But you have no longer a father, and that counts for a lot. Jacob can help you with anything you do not know in your home work, as you are still much behind him . . . God keep you both in health, and may He bless your work . . .'[3]

These promptings fell on fertile ground.

The two country boys worked hard to catch up with the Cassel children. Apart from six daily lessons at school, they received four to five hours' tuition from the pages' private tutor, Dietmar Stöhr, a kind and sympathetic man, helpful, if somewhat unconventional, well-liked by the boys.

Some years later Ludwig Grimm benefited from Stöhr's instruction, and he has described the informality of this schooling, in his memoirs:

'. . . summer or winter, we had to attend lessons in the cadet school at six o'clock every morning. Sometimes he [Stöhr] was still in bed. I then took pleasure in putting a match to his light, but the matches were very bad, so that I often had to use a whole packet before getting one to burn. The smell of sulphur was awful, and made one cough. As soon as he was up, he splashed his head with water, put on straw-coloured trousers and waistcoat, white cotton stockings, shoes with large silver buckles, and an old red dressing gown, which trailed after him. There were holes at the elbows.

'Stöhr was a very kind man, about sixty years old, with a round, healthy, and very friendly face. He wore his hair powdered, with a pigtail. He was not tall but portly, and kept himself neat and tidy. His room, however, was very untidy, dust everywhere and thick layers of powder. I do not know whether the room or the large round window were ever washed or scrubbed. About once a month an old woman from the *Elisabethspital* cleaned the place very roughly. The same old woman brought him hot water in the mornings. He then took a sheet of thick blotting-paper, made it into a bag, poured ground coffee into it, and happily brewed his morning drink. If the milk had gone sour, or if there wasn't any, he put the yoke of an egg into the coffee. He then sat down comfortably in his easy-chair, covered with red velvet, but gone shabby. The chair showed an indelible white mark in the place his head rested. Every time he sat down or when the cushions of the old chair were touched, clouds of dust and powder rose into the air. The floor of the room was very uneven, and the old table, not very steady, wobbled all the time. We used to put a book or something else unsuitable under the legs, which would soon slip out again with a bang. By the time he had drunk his coffee and eaten his roll, it was usually after seven o'clock. Only then lessons started. At half past seven the wig maker arrived, which never failed to amuse me vastly. Stöhr sat down in the middle of the room, enveloped in a huge mantle. First his head was rubbed with pomade, then the wig maker poured nearly a whole packet of powder into the pocket of his apron, took the large puff, turned it in the powder, and began to work on the good man who, closing his eyes, enjoyed it all. Terrific clouds of powder wafted through the room, morning after morning. The wig maker was an artful dodger, and we noticed that every day he cheated the good Stöhr out of half of the stuff, and took it away with him. We told our tutor, but I do not know whether he did anything about it. Later he prepared his shaving knife, soaped his face, and shaved himself. He remained like that until he dressed at noon to go to court with the pages. The pages and cadets whom he taught, came between nine and ten, but usually we just had a lot of fun. When the papers arrived, he read out aloud stories and anecdotes, joining heartily in the general laughter . . .'[4]

Through inborn gifts and diligent application Jacob and Wilhelm soon moved to the top of their classes. In the autumn of 1799 Jacob found this remark in his report: 'The teachers have pleasure in commending him as one of the ablest, most diligent and well behaved pupils'. Wilhelm was similarly praised soon after entering the school. The boys were spurred on by natural keenness and curiosity but also by a feeling of responsibility. Responsibility as sons towards their much-loved mother whom they hoped to be able to support early; responsibility also towards Aunt Zimmer whose kindness was making their present schooling possible.

In their scarce leisure hours Jacob and Wilhelm found time for drawing, an activity they had always liked. Some examples of greeting cards and fine small drawings have survived. They show how efficient the two became without the help of a master. They haunted second-hand bookshops, read widely, and made excerpts in little notebooks from books they could not afford. This habit was to remain with them through life. Yet, with all their interest in the academics they enjoyed nature study, made many drawings of living plants, and collected butterflies and bird's eggs.

Ties with the family in Steinau remained close. Regular dutiful letters were written to Mother, but there were also very special little notes to the brothers and sister Lotte, then called Malchen.

On 2 January 1801 Wilhelm wrote from Cassel, in the careful neat writing of a schoolboy:

'To my dear little sister Malchen,

'I have found in my chest a pretty little sheet of paper, and so I thought to myself, you must congratulate dear Malchen on being very good, knitting diligently, being obedient to Mother, and keeping me in her affection.

'Dear Malchen, will you not soon learn to write letters? Once you are able, you must write to our good aunt, and thank her for the beautiful *Polonaisgen* [Polish-type fur coat]. Do write to me, too, and I will send you some little notes which you can put into your knitting bag.

'Farewell, and keep in your affection your loving brother
Wilhelm Grimm'[5]

And, on 20 February of the same year:

'Dear Malchen,

'You cannot imagine how much I enjoyed getting your little letter from which I can see that you can now write correctly. You must endeavour to learn to do it by yourself, for I can see that this letter was traced out for you. However, that does not matter meantime. Are you busy knitting and learning to spin? How much will I enjoy some day a pair of stockings beautifully knitted by you.

'This is a little sheet I have found. I'll be glad if you like it.

'Keep in your affection your brother who loves you well.
Wilhelm Grimm'[6]

There is also an undated note:

'Dear Malchen,

'I believe your last little letter was written during the old year, and in order that you should not forget me altogether, I must now begin to remind you of myself – And how are you? Are you diligent and good? All little girls have to be that, or nobody will like them; but when they are obstinate – well, I don't need to tell you, my dear little sister, because you love our good mother, and will obey her readily. Now you will learn to sew, to draw and to embroider; for if you are attentive, and ask Mother nicely, she will teach you to do all these things. And that you should remember the one who loves you, this little band for your head comes from
Your affectionate brother
Wilhelm'[7]

If the letters to Malchen were moral in tone and slightly didactic, the brothers, particularly Ludwig, mostly received teasing notes. Ludwig liked painting and hanging around the potter's workshop, better than lessons at school. He was the gayest of the family, and at that time inclined to soldiering and picturing himself of high rank.

Without date, Jacob wrote:

'Dear Louis, [scratched out]
'Your Excellency,
'Right Honourable gentleman, highly esteemed gentleman, also good friend, dear protector, and most generous patron!
   'The undersigned takes the liberty of sending your Excellency these five and a half lines, although it appears that your Excellency has deigned to forget him.
   'For further protection recommends himself
                    Your Excellency's most humble servant
                              Jacob L. C. Grimm'
'(Enclosed a few paints for you, dear Louis. More another time. Regards to Lotte)'[8]

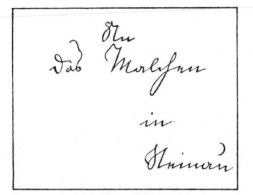

One of Wilhelm's letters to his young sister, 1802
By courtesy of the *Brüder Grimm Museum*, Kassel

Then, on a more serious note, also undated:

'Dear Lui,
   'I must send you my good wishes for the new year, which I do herewith. It is my wish that you will be very diligent.
   'I thank you very much for the nice little pictures we received all along, and I will send you something in return as soon as opportunity offers. I can see that, if you had something to copy, you would do it very well.
   'Keep me in your affection
                         Your faithful brother
                              Jacob L. C. Grimm'[9]

   It had been the *Amtmann's* intention that his sons should follow his career in law, and he had early prepared them for it by discussing legal matters with them, and writing down for their benefit cases from his own experience. That the boys would be of note whatever career they followed had been apparent from the start of their school days, and both

Rector and teachers in the *Lyceum Fridericianum* had, with considerable foresight, stated that they would in time take an honourable place among scholars.

There was no final examination, and pupils could go to university when they were ready. Some initial difficulties, however, had to be overcome.

The need for catering to the limited number of seats at the universities had led the Hessian princes to the arbitrary ruling that only some of seven well defined social categories could be admitted. Justiciaries, like the elder Grimm, and even the burgomasters of Marburg and Cassel, fell within the eighth. To get her son into Marburg *Frau* Grimm had to apply for a *Dispensation*, and this was actually obtained on 6 April 1802, when Jacob was seventeen.

At first he found his new situation strange. He was lonely, being away from Wilhelm, with whom he had always shared the same room and the same bed, and he thought Marburg ugly and its steep lanes and endless flights of steps tedious to move about in. But there were compensations: the beauty of the town's natural situation, with a fine view into the valley of the river Lahn, and, above all, the wide fields of mental discovery now becoming open to the young student. To get over the initial loneliness he threw himself into academic work. He attended many lectures, taking endless notes which he later, in his little room, copied out carefully. He read widely outside his own subject. With its two hundred students the university had the intimate atmosphere of a High School, and it was easy to make friends. Jacob was perhaps a little precocious, and this gave him the nickname – *der Alte* – the old man. He had the family gift for mimicking others. He tended to mock his fellow-students, and was critical, even sarcastic. He could not refrain from scribbling scathing remarks into his autograph album about the little pieces of verse or the friends who had contributed them. He hated pomposity, and expressed his dislike in footnotes: 'extremely stupid' is typical. Apparently very few found favour, and this is only implied by their not being commented on.

In the summer of 1803, the Landgrave having given his consent, *der Kleine* – the little one – Wilhelm joined his brother. Again they shared the same room. The more gentle Wilhelm was also the more sociable of the two, though neither took part in the more boisterous manifestations of German student life, beer-drinking bouts and duelling. There were, however, ample parties and pleasures. They attended concerts and dances, were entertained by Marburg families, played in amateur theatricals, and were regulars at the *thé dansant*, a very fashionable innovation.

They visited Marburg's old castle, and were impressed by the beauty of the great Gothic church of St Elisabeth. They crossed the river into little villages, and enjoyed walks through the countryside. Jacob's craving

26

for literature increased all the time, and he is reported to have refused to take part in a walk, saying 'I take walks into literature'!

There was one memorable excursion, on the occasion of the Landgrave being made Elector, in 1803. A number of students were keen to attend the celebrations in Cassel, but were hampered by lack of time and money.

A friend provided the answer.

Fritz von Schwertzell, son of an estate owner in Willingshausen, between Marburg and Cassel, suggested that the party take the six hours' walk to his home. They would spend the night there, and his father's coachman would convey them to Cassel the next day. The proposal was enthusiastically accepted. Another student friend of the Grimms, Paul Wigand, has left an account of the venture.

'our friend's parents were in Cassel, and when we arrived at the estate, he was himself the lord and master . . . We rode into the woods, and explored the sights of this beautiful region; we shot at the butts, and had much fun and games . . .'[10]

They were invited to tea by a kind lady, and dined at the Schwertzells' *Schloss*. Then a deputation of peasant lads arrived, asking the young squire's permission for a wedding party to dance at the big house. There wasn't enough room at the bride's own home. The people being highly respectable, permission was given, and soon the hall was filled with merriment. At first the young gentlemen merely watched from a distance, but soon enough the pretty girls drew them into the gaiety, and the young master displayed proficiency at the dances of his own countryside.

The celebrations at Cassel the next day were also enjoyed but the youths were somewhat disgusted at the unctuous oratory appropriate to such occasions. It appears that Wilhelm was not of the party. For him – less robust than Jacob – the Cassel régime had proved a little too rigorous. After a short and sharp attack of scarlet fever, he had shown signs of strain, perhaps the first indication of a heart weakness which was to trouble him in later years. He was still under medical care, and even on short walks had to take the arm of his friend, Paul Wigand.

Whenever there was enough money to pay for the journey, Jacob and Wilhelm went home in their vacations. Ludwig Grimm, in his memoirs, remembers how much Jacob impressed the younger ones, used to simple home-made clothes, by his student finery: a scarlet-coloured frock-coat with black velvet collar and facings, leather breeches and high, polished boots with spurs.

Jacob and Wilhelm were given no academic endowments or scholarships. They had to live on a small sum provided by the family. But their meagre income never worried them.

Later, in his autobiography, Jacob was to write: '. . . privation is a spur to diligence and hard work, it protects from many a distraction, and inspires a not ignoble pride, maintained by the consciousness of one's own merits, in contrast to those bestowed on others by rank and wealth . . .'[11]

Somehow the brothers found money to buy books and have them bound to their liking. They diligently attended lectures, Wilhelm often in poor health, and depressed by it. Many lectures were still held in Latin, or half in Latin and half in German. Jacob and Wilhelm found some of them dull, and the professors uninspiring. There was one exception: Friedrich Karl von Savigny. For this young lecturer the Grimms had the greatest admiration.

Savigny, born in Frankfurt am Main in 1779, into a highly cultured family which originated in Lorraine, was orphaned early. He was brought up by a friend of his father who sent him to Marburg University. He completed his course of studies brilliantly, obtained a doctor's degree, and in 1800 began to teach as a lecturer in law. Three years later he was made professor, and published a treatise on the Roman Law of Property, *Das Recht des Besitzes*. Savigny took a special interest in the Grimms. It was a case of a great teacher recognizing two gifted pupils.

He taught them scientific method and the advantages of the historical approach, but more than that, in giving them access to his rich library and introducing them to his particular circle of friends, he provided one of the decisive factors in their lives. They spent much of their time among his books, and one day Jacob got hold of Bodmer's collection of the German Minnesingers.

His interest in these romantic travelling poets of the Middle Ages had first been kindled by Ludwig Tieck's collection, *Minnelieder aus dem schwäbischen Zeitalter*, and the editor's stirring introduction. Like Tieck, before him, Jacob became 'intoxicated with joy and delight'. Enthralled by both rhythm and content of the old poetry, Jacob and Wilhelm surrendered themselves completely to the medieval, and, in doing so, they showed their awareness of the spiritual life and needs of the Germany of the early nineteenth century.

In reaction against the rationalism and sophistication of the Enlightenment, the Romantics were turning to the heritage of the common people, to things that they believed to have evolved naturally, not made by a deliberate act of creation. They idolized Germany's medieval past. Their national consciousness had been stirred by the impact of the French Revolution and the Napoleonic Wars. They were inspired by Bishop Percy's *Reliques of Ancient English Poetry*, and by Macpherson's Ossianic writings which, forgery or not, superbly suited their susceptibility.

In his autobiography Wilhelm states: '. . . the ardour with which the

28

studies of Old German were pursued, helped to overcome the spiritual depression of those days. Without doubt, world events and the need to retire into the peace of research, contributed to the re-discovery of this long-forgotten literature; but not only did we seek some consolation in the past, it was natural, too, for us to hope that the course we were taking, would add something towards the return of better days . . .'[12]

Johann Jakob Bodmer in Zürich, Johann Georg Hamann in Königsberg – the *Magus of the North* – and, above all, Johann Gottfried Herder, had discovered 'the folk', believing that ballads, songs and tales embodied a nation's genuine culture. *Volkspoesie*, the poetry of the common people, became the only true poetry.

This Romanticism was marked among Savigny's friends. He himself was more than sympathetic, believing that law was not made by ratiocination but by a natural evolution from the growth of society itself. Professor Philipp Friedrich Weis, a close friend and neighbour of Savigny, often entertained members of the gifted Brentano family. Through this connection the Grimms met the Brentanos, themselves sons and daughters of a wealthy Frankfurt merchant of Italian ancestry. They became specially friendly with Clemens Brentano, who had come from Jena where he had hungrily absorbed the new mood in German writing. He was a keen collector. In 1801 he had met Achim von Arnim, a young nobleman from the Mark Brandenburg. Both were animated by a love for the German past, and had struck up a friendship at once. It was to find concrete expression in their collaboration on the collecting of a great number of old German folksongs.

Clemens's interests were close to those of the Grimms. Jacob and Wilhelm now studied Tieck's *Minnelieder* in detail, and the dream of discovering some day forgotten treasures of the German past took firm possession of them. Their energies were directed more and more to the study of old manuscripts.

When Clemens married Sofie Mereau, the divorced wife of a Jena professor, and settled for a while in Marburg, and when a little later Gunda Brentano married Savigny, closer friendships developed, drawing Jacob and Wilhelm into this lively young group. They admired Brentano almost as much as their professor. Their horizon widened, and windows to the world opened.

There were social evenings at the Brentanos' home where the Marburg literati met, reading, conversing and drinking tea laced with red wine. Pleasant profitable evenings ending with Hulda Mereau, Brentano's step-daughter, seeing the guests down the stairs, carrying a heavy silver candlestick.

In the summer of 1804 Savigny decided to go to Paris for further research on a proposed *History of Law of the Middle Ages*. He approached Jacob, his most gifted student, asking him to come to Paris and help him in his work at the *Bibliothèque Nationale*. Jacob was immediately attracted, and at once sought his mother's permission to go. She gave it – with secret fears – France being a country outside her ken.

Late in January 1805 Jacob was on his way, via Metz and Châlons.

The Savignys made him very welcome, and tried to draw the retiring young scholar into their social rounds. Jacob was grateful. He had a special admiration for *Frau* von Savigny, and together with other friends was looking forward to a 'happy event' in the family quite soon. In April of that year he was able to announce to Wilhelm:

'. . . this morning *Frau* von Savigny was safely delivered of a healthy girl. I was rather anxious about this event, as she is not one of the strongest. In fact, everybody was anxious, and the joy is all the greater. Most likely the child will be called Bettina, and you can guess who will be the god-mother . . .'[13]

Paris was a great experience, and the library a treasure house, with its many manuscripts and rare books. Jacob was in his element. Every day after finishing excerpts from legal documents for Savigny, he devoted himself entirely to the study of medieval manuscripts.

There, too, was the wonder of coming face to face with art.

So far the brothers' knowledge of art had come mainly from reproductions and descriptions. Now Jacob saw with his own eyes the works in the *Louvre* and other galleries. He went back again and again. Raphael, Titian, Dürer, van Eyck and Bellini deeply impressed him. The cool and quiet young man became rhapsodic in writing about them to his brother.

Jacob explored the city though work at the library remained his greatest excitement. On 2 April 1805 he reported to Wilhelm that he knew the old parts of Paris, the *cité*,[14] pretty well, the suburbs but little, that he had visited the *Palais du Luxembourg*, and much admired the paintings there. He was impressed with the life of the big city where he saw 'Moors, Turks and Greeks',[15] quite familiar sights to him now. In August of that year Jacob wrote:

'. . . I now go often to the gallery. There are few Dürers but beautiful Eycks and Bellinis. Apart from Raphael I look mainly at the Leonardo da Vincis and Titians, much less at the Corregios . . .'[16]

Jacob joined the Savignys in visits to the theatre, and developed quite a taste for it. He told his brother:

'. . . twice recently I have been to the Italian theatre (*opera buffa*). I have enjoyed the music which was very Italian, and very different from the less vigorous French kind. The first time I heard *Il Matrimonio segreto*, music by Sarti (in this piece there was the most ridiculous misproportion I have ever seen – between the persons of the actors and those they were to represent. An old very fat and ugly actress played the youngest pretty daughter, because she had the biggest singing part, and she did sing truly beautifully. The elder daughter was played by the youngest and most agreeable actress. All this contrives to make people not look but listen only.) The play itself is fairly simple – the second time, there were two plays, *La Passione* by Paesiello, rather wearisome, and *Stabat Mater* by Pergolese, which, one or two things excepted, I liked very much . . .

'*Au français, La Prise de Jericho* will be done today, when presumably only the walls of Jericho will fall, but the other walls nearby will all tremble in sympathy, and to make the illusion more complete. They are doing more spectacular pieces here, for example, *Le Vaisseau Amiral*, which includes a regular sea battle, where the thick smoke of the gunpowder hides the pitifulness of the whole thing . . .
. . . then there is *Le Tremblement de Lisbonne* . . .'[17]

Wilhelm kept encouraging his brother to look for old German manuscripts as they might be useful for their researches. In fact, Jacob now handled for the first time the *Manesse* manuscript of the minnesingers, and made excerpts from it. The brothers continued to exchange news about the books they read and bought. Goethe, Schiller, Bürger, Kotzebue, Schlegel, Tieck and Novalis came under discussion. Wilhelm reported from Marburg about new additions to their 'library', just arrived from the bookbinder. He got pleasure out of arranging them, and did not forget to mention that on a table near the bookcase stood a wallflower plant in a pot, Jacob's favourite flower.

The brothers' first longish separation had increased their love, and they eagerly reassured each other of it. Already in February 1805 Wilhelm had written:

'...there is nothing to tell you about the first few days (after parting from you) except that I was very sad . . .'[18]

On 1 March 1805 Jacob wrote from Paris:

'. . . please God, you are in good health, and no longer too sad about my absence. To go by my own feelings, you must still be very sorry, sorrier even than I am, as, with more distractions here, I do not think of it all the time . . . do write me about everything. For, whatever may seem very trivial and small at home, abroad it becomes something to cherish, and of significance, as one loves to re-visit home in one's thoughts. In this process every detail makes the illusion more real. What I would give, for example, just to see the curtain in your room, or hear you sing, badly as you have done it at times . . .
'. . . that on your birthday I have congratulated you warmly – in my

thoughts – you can well imagine, more easily than I care to or can express in writing . . .'[19]

And in July of that year:

'. . . we do not want to separate ever, and if at any time one of us should be sent away, the other must give notice at once. We are so used to being together that the mere thought of separation grieves me deeply . . .'[20]

Wilhelm returned the sentiment, and assured his brother of his affection.

With her younger boys now at school away from home too, and since his death in November 1798, bereft of her father's benevolent presence in close-by Hanau, *Frau* Grimm had become very lonely in Steinau. Encouraged by her family, she at long last decided to move, with her young daughter, to Cassel, the home of her own childhood. All alone she prepared the removal, settling her affairs, and selling the much-loved meadows and gardens. She took time to have her pig – 'weighing two hundred and fifty pounds' – killed, to supply a lot of sausages, welcome provision for life in the town.

Aunt Zimmer once more helped, and obtained a comfortable house in Cassel's *Marktgasse*. It pleased everybody, and the return of Jacob and Wilhelm was eagerly awaited.

Jacob, often worried about their mother's isolation in Steinau, was glad and relieved to picture her in Cassel, near her loving sister, and with many old friends at hand. On 7 September he wrote from Paris:

'Dear Aunt and dear Mother,

'With truly childish and at the same time childlike joy did I receive your letters last week. What could have given me more pleasure than the news that my good mother and Malchen have had a happy journey, and are now safe and sound in Cassel. This was a thing I was worried about, and now I feel much easier and happier. I hope to arrive in Cassel at almost the same time I used to come to you, dear mother, at Steinau. If at all possible, the greater distance this time will increase the gladness of meeting again. I really do not know what else to write, and most likely you are not expecting another letter from me. However, I wanted to write, even if only to acknowledge gratefully the receipt of the money. I shall be able to convince you by word of mouth that it has not been spent unnecessarily. Our departure from here has not been definitely fixed yet, only that we shall not stop at some provincial towns, as originally planned, but travel straight to Germany. Whether we go by Metz, Strasbourg or Brussels, depends on several circumstances, as distances do not vary much in the three directions. My trunk has gone off with the *rouilliers* [sic] or carriers, but will be on the way for thirty days. I myself will hardly be with you before the beginning of October, but then for certain. And now a hundred greetings to everyone who loves me. I expect to find my sister Malchen, a female, no longer showing many traces of Steinau associations, much as

Henriette Zimmer. Etching by Ludwig Emil Grimm. The original pencil
drawing in the Historisches Museum, Hanau

Birthplace of the Brothers Grimm in Hanau. Pencil and crayon drawing.
Artist unknown. Staatsarchiv, Marburg/Lahn

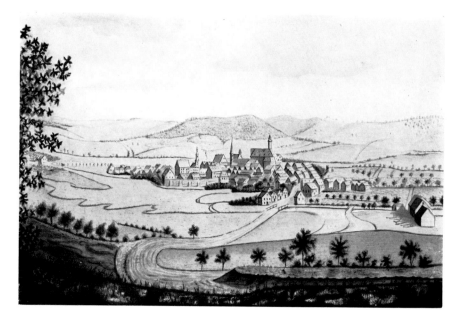

View of Steinau. Sketch—not signed—from the *Nachlass* of Ludwig
Emil Grimm. Brüder Grimm Museum, Kassel

I wish she may always shun the way of life of Cassel girls which tends to be rather silly and ordinary. From Ferdinand and Louis I have not had news for a very long time, neither bad nor good, but hope to receive the latter.

'I embrace you, dear Aunt and Mother,

Ever your obedient son,

Jacob'[21]

Departure from Paris was delayed longer than expected.

At length Jacob and the Savignys arrived in Metz on 24 September. They were unable to travel to Strasbourg as Napoleon was actually setting out from there on his campaign against Austria.

They reached Frankfurt at the end of September, where Jacob spent a week. He continued his journey to Targes near Gelnhausen, the family estate of the Savignys, to attend the christening of his professor's little girl. He then collected Wilhelm in Marburg, to go to Cassel with him.

Arriving in the evening, and finding that their mother had gone out to visit her sister, they impatiently went to meet her. They came across her in the dark street, walking home slowly, carrying a lantern. There was a happy reunion.

Jacob's stay in Paris had served him well, and he in turn had been a loyal help to his professor. In 1815, in his preface to the first volume of his great work on Roman Law, Savigny was to acknowledge Jacob's exactness and care which he had since lavished on his own work, but had then given generously to his – Savigny's – cause.

Frau Grimm now had her six children around her: Carl was articled to a bank, the younger ones, Ferdinand, Ludwig and Lotte, went to school, while Jacob and Wilhelm were planning their future, tentatively groping the way to their true selves.

Jacob Grimm's seat-ticket for Savigny's lectures
By courtesy of the *Brüder Grimm Museum*, Kassel

CHAPTER 3

Settling in Cassel

1805 – 1810

THE brothers now looked for employment.

The thought of a legal career had become less and less attractive. The brand-new *Code Napoléon*, and application of the law according to it, could not appeal to disciples of Savigny.

Jacob had made this clear in a letter to Aunt Zimmer, written in Paris, in July 1805, adding:

'. . . my decision is made. I want to remain in Hesse, and be employed there . . .'[1]

Wilhelm felt the same way. They hoped for appointments with sufficient leisure to allow them to continue their researches into the older German literature. Examinations were not obligatory but Wilhelm prepared for one. The family in Cassel were hopeful that Jacob's stay in Paris would improve his chances of obtaining a post. Rumours had reached Aunt Zimmer's ear that the Elector had been favourably impressed by an official letter Jacob had written from Paris, for the Hessian Minister, *Herr* von Malsburg, away from office through illness.

However, things did not move quickly.

The brothers read, and copied carefully, whole books and manuscripts. Their notebooks were filled but, in spite of their efforts, no appointments came their way. Early in 1806 Jacob at long last obtained a clerkship in the Hessian War Office. It was boring work, and very different from the stimulation Paris had afforded. But one hundred thalers a year meant a small income, and there was still time for private study.

Jacob's interest at that time was focussed on the chapbooks of early popular literature, and he used every opportunity to obtain material. A friend, still in Paris, was asked to try and buy some cheap reprints. He might find them, said Jacob, in the *faubourg St Antoine*, where a dealer kept them pinned on a wooden board. Poor copies they were, still they served their purpose, and his collection lacked *Les faits de Charle-*

magne et des douze pairs de france, le roman de Mabrian roi de Jerusalem, and *Morgan le géant occis par le comte roland.*[2]

There was zest in tracing even the smallest object helpful to the brothers' researches.

In the spring Wilhelm passed his final examination, and in less troubled times he too might have been placed. But the political horizon was darkening, and soon the war was to draw very close.

On 14 October 1806 Napoleon totally defeated Prussia in the battles of Jena and Auerstedt. The Holy Roman Empire collapsed. Napoleon was at the peak of his power. Disregarding a separate treaty the then Landgrave had signed with France in 1795 securing Hesse's neutrality, French troops marched through Hessian territory to Cassel. One army under General Mortier approached from Frankfurt, and one corps, belonging to the troops of King Louis of Holland, marched towards Cassel from the region of Paderborn. The Elector was forced to leave his elegant capital and flee to Denmark, to live later on in Prague. The Electress went to Gotha, where her youngest daughter was married to the Hereditary Prince of Saxe-Coburg. Aunt Zimmer accompanied her.

On the last day of the month Wilhelm anxiously watched the French bivouacs in the distance, still unable to believe that his country would come under foreign domination. The next morning the victorious regiments moved into the town. Everything changed: foreign people, foreign manners and a foreign tongue invaded Cassel. The Hessian War Office was transformed into a commissariat for the French troops. Jacob's good knowledge of French proved useful, but he soon resigned from an exhausting and unsatisfactory position.

Again the brothers were without income. Modest in their wants, and undemanding, they continued working in their study.

Slowly the troubled year of 1807 passed.

Then fate dealt the family another blow. On 27 May 1808 Dorothea Grimm – in her early fifties – died after a short illness. Not one of her six children was settled in life. Good neighbours, the family of *Herr* Rudolf Wild, owner of the *Sonnenapotheke*, took the shocked Lotte into their home for a while. The others, stunned but given strength in mutual affection, carried on as best they could. Jacob, at twenty-three, became the head of the family, a position he held all through his long life.

At the end of July Wilhelm accepted an invitation from Aunt Zimmer, lonely in her enforced exile and distressed about the loss of her sister. They were comfort to each other, and the Gotha library, rich in medieval manuscripts, encouraged investigation. Wilhelm stayed for some weeks.

In a Germany divided and powerless at his feet, Napoleon set out to establish a new order. Members of his family were to occupy several thrones. His youngest brother, Jerome Bonaparte, was made king of the new Kingdom of Westphalia. He chose Cassel for his residence. A friend of the Grimms, the Swiss historian Johannes von Müller, then Minister of Education, suggested to the secretary of the King's Cabinet, *Monsieur* Cousin de Marinville, that Jacob would make a good administrator of the royal library. The recommendation was successful.

Jacob – who had previously tried unsuccessfully to obtain a position in the Elector's library – was made librarian to King Jerome at the castle of *Wilhelmshöhe*, now called *Napoleonshöhe*, in July 1808.

It was a welcome appointment, and not too onerous. Jacob recorded that the only instruction given to him was: '*Vous ferrez mettre en grands caractères sur la porte: Bibliothèque particulière du Roi*'.[3]

The position carried a good salary, and very soon the king made Jacob *Auditeur au Conseil d'Etat*, the only German on the council. This meant advancement and a still better salary. The king treated his librarian well, and there again was leisure for private study. The most hated duty was the attendance – in fancy uniform – at the State Councils, but this was a small enough inconvenience for the greater security Jacob's position gave to the family. He now earned four thousand francs or one thousand thalers, a small enough sum at a time when prices for all the necessities of life were rising steadily.

It is interesting to note that about King Jerome, so much maligned for his excesses, Jacob had this to say in his autobiography:

'. . . I cannot speak ill of the king; he behaved to me in a friendly and decent manner.'[4]

In fact, there was possibly little to choose between him and some German princes.

Jacob, now a Westphalian subject, might have had to serve as a private soldier, but by good luck he drew a 'free number' in the military service lottery, and so remained a civilian.

With the help of a faithful maid, Lotte Grimm was bravely and earnestly endeavouring to become a good housewife at the age of fifteen. From Aunt Zimmer, still in Gotha, came comforting letters, advice on domestic matters, food parcels and financial help. Under the Occupation life was expensive, and taxation high. Jacob and Wilhelm, feeling their joint responsibility for the younger brothers and sister and drawn still closer together by the death of their mother, kept reassuring their aunt. On 27 June 1807 Wilhelm reported that everything in their household was done with care: '. . . Lotte irons and mends all that is necessary . . .'. Sometimes a woman had to be engaged to help with the mending; Lotte just wasn't strong enough to do it all. The woman was given her meals and two *Groschen* a day! Even that was luxury, and so was wine. Still, '. . . a little wine is always needed . . .', and a cask of Rhinewine was shared with a neighbour. This brought the price of a bottle down to two *Weisspfennig*.[5]

On 3 August of the same year Wilhelm told Aunt Zimmer:

'. . . we keep a careful note of everything . . .'

Butter was being ordered from Steinau, as it was cheaper there than in the town, and foresters were written to for supplies of winter fuel.[6] The little family was forced to economize in food, and to cut out all non-essentials. In another report Wilhelm says touchingly:

'. . . in all tribulations, however, we shall remain united in love . . .'[7]

Ludwig Grimm's gifts were turning more and more to drawing and painting. Achim von Arnim and Clemens Brentano, always anxious to give tangible proof of their friendship, invited him to stay with them in Heidelberg. He was to do some illustrations for their paper, *Zeitung für Einsiedler*. The two men gave Ludwig every help and support, but he was lonely and very homesick. He wrote in his memoirs:

'. . . I went to Heidelberg to join Achim von Arnim and Clemens Brentano. We lived on the hillside below the castle, in a beautiful garden full of vines; but nothing could cheer me. I was homesick, and thinking only of my dearest mother and sister Lotte, I was very unhappy. Arnim took me on walking tours to the Odenwald, and we looked at the Mannheim gallery. There were outings to the old castle, but I could not bear it anywhere, and liked best to stay in my little room. They could not make me go to the park in Schwetzingen, as I told them I didn't want to see stage sets. A squirrel was my sole pleasure, and sometimes I went to the open-air market to see some peasant faces . . .'[8]

Ludwig longed for the simple and familiar, and shrunk from the sophistication of baroque parks. He was restless and unhappy.

Jacob and Wilhelm tried to cheer him by loving letters, particularly Wilhelm, whose own nature was closest to Ludwig's.

On 8 August Wilhelm wrote a long and understanding letter, showing himself very patient with Ludwig's often difficult and impetuous moods. Wilhelm also expressed interesting and, for his time, very modern views on the way an artist should work:

'. . . I have heard with much pleasure that you are now working on landscapes. This is excellent, as it gives you a true feeling for living things which you get also from doing portraits . . .'[9]

Wilhelm then advised Ludwig to change his method of working. His work is stiff, he says, because, though doing each part of a picture carefully, he does not consider the composition sufficiently as a whole. This may make for good likenesses, but these likenesses lack life. It would be better to look at an object carefully, and then paint the impression afterwards.

37

Ludwig worked on in Heidelberg without much zest, but recognizing his talents, Savigny and the Brentanos eventually helped him to go to Munich and continue his studies at the Art Academy there.

Both Ludwig and his brother Ferdinand, who had also left Cassel, still needed financial help. The four remaining members of the family kept reducing their expenses. They only had one full meal a day. Tea was no longer drunk in the evening as it involved the use of dear sugar. Lotte made neckerchiefs for the brothers from a white dress grown too short for her. But in spite of rigid economies, it was difficult to make ends meet, and again and again good Aunt Zimmer had to lend a helping hand.

Perhaps through the very Spartan life, perhaps through the sorrow of his mother's death, Wilhelm's health declined steadily. He found breathing difficult, was easily exhausted, and complained about pains in his chest.

Years after he was to describe these symptoms in his autobiography:

'. . . after my mother's death (1808) the poor state of my health became increasingly worse; to the shortness of breath which made climbing even a few steps a terrible burden, and constant fierce pains in my chest, there was now added a heart condition. The pain which I could only compare to the sensation of a fiery arrow being shot through my heart from time to time, left me with a constant feeling of anxiety. Sometimes I experienced violent palpitations, appearing suddenly without obvious cause, and ending the same way. Several times this state lasted, uninterrupted, for twenty hours, leading to extreme exhaustion; a feeling of imminent death seemed not unjustified. Many a sleepless night I sat upright, without moving, waiting for the dawn to provide some comfort. A quail, hanging in a cage, outside a neighbour's window, was often first to announce the break of day, and even now I cannot hear that bird's strange call with indifference. It is incredible how much one can endure physically for years, without losing the joy of life. The feeling of youth may have helped; I was not completely cast down by my illness, and when things were bearable, I continued working, even with pleasure . . .'[10]

In the spring of 1809 it was decided that Wilhelm should travel to Halle to consult the famous Professor Reil.

While Jacob's early admiration was for Schiller, Wilhelm's idol had always been Goethe. He was determined therefore to break his journey in Weimar, and call on the great man. However, when he arrived there and went to see Goethe, the *Herr Geheimrat* had gone for a drive, and Wilhelm continued his journey to Auerstedt. In a letter to Jacob he described the strange feelings he experienced when, in the moonlight, he saw the battlefield 'where more than twenty thousand are at rest'. The Auerstedt postmaster gave him an account of the battle.[11]

In Halle Professor Reil examined Wilhelm, diagnosed a heart condition, and advised him to 'take the cure'.

This soon started in earnest, and in May Wilhelm reported to his brother:

'. . . I have not had any baths so far, Reil has not mentioned them during the last few days, perhaps because the bathing establishments are not yet ready. I have, however, to take a lot of medicine. On getting up in the morning, about half past seven, I rub my neck with a strong black mercury ointment. Then I wash my heart with spirit, and at nine o'clock I take a powder which I much dislike as it makes me sick. I have to take it every month when the moon is on the wane. Half an hour later I take some bitter essence which is to restore the stomach and appetite. At eleven o'clock I take Conrad's pills, and between twelve and two o'clock the region of the heart is washed once more, then again pills and essence which give me an overwhelming feeling of hunger. This is soon overcome by a little food. At four o'clock again pills and washing, and more powders and washing before going to bed. The medicines cost a lot, some twenty-five to thirty thalers so far, as the spirit is expensive, one single prescription often as much as half a *Louisdor*. Reil, by the way, takes great trouble. A few days ago he sent me a book on the influence of the magnet on the heart. I am to make excerpts from it. I saw him this morning, and he thought that if I could get one, I should try wearing a magnetic amulet on my heart . . .'[12]

Meantime Jacob, left behind in Cassel, felt lonely and miserable, though glad that Reil's interest in Wilhelm's condition might prove helpful. He offered to pay for anything his brother required, but Wilhelm assured him that, the actual journey paid for, he could manage, and was careful over all unnecessary expense. He met old and new friends, and spent much time with the family of Johann Friedrich Reichardt, writer, composer and for a time *Kapellmeister* to King Jerome in Cassel. The Reichardts had encouraged Wilhelm to come to Halle, and their hospitable home in Giebichenstein on the Saale was a congenial meeting-place for writers, artists and musicians. Wilhelm enjoyed musical evenings there, particularly when Reichardt's own family performed his *Lieder* to words by Goethe. He liked the quietness and the pleasantness of Halle's surroundings. On 21 April he had told Jacob:

'. . . I have been to Giebichenstein [on the Saale]. The countryside is glorious. The clear river runs between beautiful rocks. There are gardens on the heights from where one can enjoy a lovely view of the river and the distance beyond. The whole is extremely serene and comforting . . .'[13]

On 18 June he could report that he felt 'somewhat better'.

'. . . I know again what I have not known for two years: what it feels to fall asleep without fear, and then to sleep without interruption. At home, going to bed every night had become torture, as I lay awake and listened in the stillness to the strange flow of my own blood while anguish crept to my heart. Lying like that, without moving, it took hours before my eyes would close. It seems a wonderful thing that now I can lie down, tired, and find sleep quickly, and can even turn on my side. It makes me think of my childhood when it was just like that. I dream a lot here, long, strange and continuous dreams. I will tell you about them some day. Nearly all of them have a sad ending . . .'[14]

Potter's workshop, Steinau. Drawing by Ludwig Emil Grimm

One of his dreams Wilhelm had reported in detail on 28 May:

'. . . yesterday was the anniversary of our dear mother's death . . . As so often, I dreamt about her end . . . The same day I had a strange dream about you. I only know vaguely and in a confused way what happened before. I wandered through many rooms with all their doors open. I took things from chests and cupboards, wanting to pack them as for a journey. When I had taken the stuff from one place, it lay again in another, in some curious order. Somebody unknown helped me, and I was in constant fear of touching his hands. Suddenly I was somewhere else, on the way to a high mountain. Now you know that on the St Gotthard in Switzerland there is a wire cage where they put people who have perished in the cold . . . I then stood in front of a wired cavern, and in it you sat . . . As I stood beside you, you turned gently. Your eyes were blood-shot, and in a weak voice you said: "Why have you not come sooner, I have sat frozen here for two nights". This made me cry bitterly with dreadful anxiety . . . and I woke up . . .'[15]

Jacob was delighted about the improvement in Wilhelm's health, and sorry only that everything was being done for his brother by strangers, and not by his nearest and dearest who loved him best.

Jacob's unease continued. He was unsettled, wondering whether Cassel was the best place to be in, and whether a smaller town of some two or three thousand souls might not be more agreeable. Young as he was, he wished for nothing but a quiet life, devoted to study, and not overmuch concerned with 'serving for money'. Social life did not interest him greatly, believing, as he did, that more complication meant less sweetness of existence, and that everything outside quiet domesticity tends to corrupt. This did not involve staying at home all the time, Jacob thought; travel, for example held the joy of returning. All the same, with many the wish to travel was but something vague, and often a hundred miles or a hundred steps might provide the same result, just as a glutton for books would not be more satisfied after reading a hundred than he was with the very first book he ever read. Travel would certainly be helpful to their studies, and he hoped that Wilhelm would in time be able to move about a little.[16]

In July a letter from Wilhelm brought further news about his treatment. He had now begun taking the baths, very hot, with a cool sponge over his heart. He agreed with Jacob about travelling, hoping that eventually he might be well enough to stand journeys, adding:

'... could I not obtain a position as tutor to a wealthy *Graf*, without being obliged to teach, merely there for prestige . . .'[17]

Later that month he discussed Jacob's ideas about leaving Cassel. He did not agree that a smaller town would be pleasant. A village, or, better still, life on an estate would be preferable. Yes, an estate would be fine, just think of the joys of a garden![18]

Aunt Zimmer, too, was given news about Halle when Wilhelm wrote on 17 July:

'. . . Dearest Aunt,
'I am astonished that my letter has been so long in reaching you. Some others do not seem to have arrived at all, as you do not mention them. Your kind letter came only yesterday, and so has also taken six days. It is not really astonishing during this war, when the actual theatre of it is getting so close. We see troops of all kinds passing through every day, in bigger or smaller numbers.
'Yes, dear Aunt, I have already taken the baths. A fine building has been specially fitted for the purpose. There is a long corridor in the centre, with small cabinéts on both sides where one takes the baths. Everything is comfortable and pleasant, with sofa, mirror etc., quite elegant. In the

front of the house are two large rooms where people assemble and wait. There are already some forty families here . . .'[19]

War was certainly on the doorstep, and Wilhelm now saw the Duke of Brunswick's volunteer corps pass through Halle. On 2 August he reported to Jacob:

'. . . last Wednesday, during the night, the Brunswick Corps entered the town. About nine o'clock in the evening a few men came, forming the avant-garde, then, at three o'clock in the morning, the whole corps marched in, their band playing. At daybreak one could see them in the streets, infantry, cavalry and a few riflemen. Their uniforms are black, with light blue collar and facings. They wear felt caps, decorated with a metal skull. Some had put red cloth and glass underneath this, to make death look quite horrifying. The infantrymen wear a kind of Polish jacket and long trousers. The cavalry consisted of hussars who carried carbines, not pistols. On the whole, they did not look well, especially when their black uniforms were dirty. Then, the men were rather like chimney sweeps. Some were handsome, others small and plain. They were quiet, asked for nothing, and left again in the afternoon. I saw the Prince ride, all by himself, in the market square. He could be recognised only by the star he wore. His expression is stony and rigid, somewhat Cossack-like, his long snow-white eye lashes and white beard forming a strange contrast to his tanned face . . .'[20]

Wilhelm remembered the Duke's stony face brightening a little, when he stopped his horse to shake hands with an old friend.

Late in August Clemens Brentano arrived unexpectedly in Halle, a pleasant surprise to Wilhelm. On von Arnim's invitation he decided to accompany Brentano to Berlin. Clemens offered to pay Wilhelm's expenses, to which he agreed on condition that this was an advance payment on some literary work he was to do for Brentano.

In September he could write:

'. . . Dearest Aunt, This is to tell you that I reached Berlin safely, the day before last [18 Sept.], and was very well received by Arnim. On Sunday we, Brentano and I, left Halle, to arrive safe and sound the next evening. It is pleasant to be here, and this beautiful city is imposing to anybody who sees it for the first time. Arnim takes us about everywhere, and I have already made a lot of interesting acquaintances . . .'[21]

Wilhelm enjoyed Berlin and the many new contacts. But he never forgot Jacob nor their common interests. Each day he sat for many hours copying from borrowed books. He then took time off to admire Berlin's 'elegant streets'. Elegant they were, but not full of life.

The capital of a defeated Prussia was deserted and depressed, and there was much poverty, the flat sandiness of the city's surroundings did not appeal to Wilhelm, though he admired the *Tiergarten*, its great park, and the lively salons stimulated both his sociable nature and his ever-active mind. His admiration for the Romantics, particularly for von Arnim, increased, but the longing for home was always with him.

The king of Prussia, Frederick William III, and his court were in exile in Königsberg and the Berlin palaces empty. Only the king's daughter, Princess Augusta, married to the Hereditary Prince of Cassel, and later to become Electress, occupied a wing of the Berlin *Schloss*. Hessian loyalties prompted Wilhelm to pay his respects to a lady he greatly admired. She never forgot, and always favoured him during her future residence in Cassel.

The busy social life of Berlin was taxing Wilhelm's limited wardrobe, also the weather was getting colder, and a cry for help was sent to Jacob. On 10 October Wilhelm wrote:

'. . . today only a few words to you, dear Jacob, as an enclosure to my letter to our dear aunt. I want to ask a favour: please enquire, or let somebody ask at the posting house how much it would cost to send my brown woollen coat here. It would serve me very well, particularly on the journey, and be almost necessary then. I am assured the cost could hardly be more than one thaler, as the weight won't be much. Talk the matter over with the official at the post, because much depends on his decision, and I am willing to spend a thaler. Also, have you had a new pair of black silk breeches made, and could you send me your old ones? I have nothing but my woollen ones, and they are not in too good a state . . . as all the rest of my clothing . . .'[22]

Jacob obliged and sent the good woollen coat, informing Wilhelm at the same time that the unmentionables had long since been worn out and discarded, and that he, Wilhelm, would be well advised to have a new pair made for himself. Jacob changed his mind last minute and enclosed a pair of woollen trousers.[23] In a letter of 28 October, Wilhelm thanked him for the coat and the breeches, the latter now being his 'finest piece of clothing', which, of course, he would bring back, either to return to Jacob, or to keep if his brother felt inclined to let him have the breeches.[24]

In November 1809 Wilhelm set out on his return journey, well wrapped up against the cold and the rigours of travelling, sometimes in open coaches. About the journey from Berlin to Halle he wrote:

'. . . I left Berlin at 4 o'clock in the morning. Arnim was kind and friendly as usual. Brentano was still asleep and I did not want to wake him. The journey which took three nights and two days, without break, was wearisome, and though I had taken good precautions against the cold, I was well knocked about in the true coach manner . . .'[25]

This was common experience in a country where roads were very poor, coaches badly sprung, and passengers' accommodation often separated only by a sheet from heavy chests and valises which kept falling forward in every curve.

After more tough travelling in open coaches, while a cold wind was blowing, Wilhelm arrived at Naumburg where he had to wait for two days for a covered diligence. He made use of this break to visit *Frau* Naubert, who had published a collection of fairytales. He found 'a small hunch-backed woman, hard of hearing, with a pale, good and finely cut face'. The two enjoyed their meeting.

Wilhelm reached Weimar at last, and called at Goethe's house, this time with a letter of introduction by von Arnim. Goethe was recovering from an illness, but Wilhelm was received after a day's delay.

He was impressed by the beauty and orderliness of Goethe's handsome *Haus am Frauenplan*.

On 13 December he reported that after calling at the library he made his way to Goethe's at noon. He entered the house, passed through a hall decorated with fine statues, to come to 'a broad staircase which looked elegant and comfortable'. He then reached another hall where the word *Salve* was marked in black letters on the floor. A tall lamp stood at one side, and the room was full of pictures. Then followed a smaller room with drawings and old German woodcuts on the walls. The walls were painted a soft brown, and the gilt door handles were in the shape of a lion's head. Everything Wilhelm thought was 'quite special'.

Then entered 'Jupiter', dressed in black, wearing two medals, his hair slightly powdered. 'Now I have often seen pictures of him, and I knew them all by heart, still I was much surprised by the nobility, perfection, simplicity and kindness of his features. He asked me to sit down, and began talking in a friendly manner . . .'

Though Goethe had been the force which drew the early Romantics together, to him the study of the German past and the older literature was not an end in itself. It was a background only to his own creations, and part of world literature. But his brilliant art of conversation soon led the talk to matters familiar to Wilhelm. For almost an hour they discussed the *Nibelungenlied* and the ancient Norse sagas which were of particular interest to Wilhelm, who was busy on a translation of the Danish *Kaempe Viser*. Goethe had managed to put him at his ease.

The next day Wilhelm was favoured with an invitation to lunch – 'a very splendid meal' – consisting of a number of courses and some 'very good red wine' of which Goethe partook freely, 'better still his wife'. Lunch lasted from one to four o'clock, and there was more lively talk.

Madame Schopenhauer, mother of the philosopher, invited Wilhelm to one of her enormous tea parties where all Weimar gossiped, and twice he was taken to the theatre by Riemer, tutor to Goethe's son. He sat in the great man's private box, and found the theatre 'agreeable and of good proportions'.[26]

But, most important of all, Wilhem's access was eased to the Weimar and Jena libraries. He found two manuscripts of interest in the Weimar library, but to his disappointment was not allowed to take them to his rooms. In Jena a huge codex, beautifully written on parchment, was chained to a desk. It was opened for Wilhelm, and he was shown another manuscript on paper, a story of the crusades. Neither could possibly be taken to Cassel, and Wilhelm returned to Weimar 'vexed'.

Eventually a formal application from Jacob, the librarian, obtained the Weimar manuscripts for detailed study in Cassel. It also brought a letter from Goethe himself, dated Weimar, 19 January 1810:

'. . . the pleasure I have enjoyed through making your brother's acquaintance here, is not little increased by the honour of your letter. I am pleased to send the manuscripts which I have borrowed under my name from the Ducal Library. I enclose a copy of the form I have filled in for the purpose. I shall be delighted if you will find some important pieces in the two volumes, and as you will interpret and publish them, you will increase the merits you have gained already in this branch of German literature, and earn all our gratitude . . .'[27]

Obviously Goethe had taken to the talented young man.

About to pay another visit to Aunt Zimmer in Gotha, and under the vivid impression of seeing Goethe, Wilhelm wrote to her:

'. . . Dearest Aunt,

'I enclose my letter to Jacob, left open, as it is also meant for you. Please read and then kindly forward it. You will see how I have fared, and that I am now in Weimar, only twelve hours' distance away from you. I will use the library at Jena before continuing my journey. I want to mention particularly that I am in excellent health and spirits, my old experience proved once again, namely that the vibration of travelling is beneficial to me. You will see from the letter how kind Göthe (sic) has been to me. I shall bring with me a very fine picture of him – a good likeness – which, I am sure, you will enjoy. He has one of the most beautiful heads in the world.

'The weather is very favourable, clear and healthy, without being cold. The surroundings and the park here are extraordinarily charming, the park finer than any I have seen.

'I hope to find letters from Jacob with you, and that all is well there. I am very sorry that I can do nothing for you while I am here. I should be delighted to have the chance. Keep me in your affection. I kiss your hands, and remain,

Ever Your
Wilhelm G.'[28]

After a short stay at Gotha Wilhelm rejoined his family in Cassel, mentally and physically refreshed. No longer 'pale and emaciated', he felt blessed with a new lease of life.

'Nodding Figure'
ornament

CHAPTER 4

The *Nursery and Household Tales*

1806 – 1812

IN the autumn of 1805 von Armin and Brentano had published the first volume of their collection of folksongs, *Des Knaben Wunderhorn*. In a postscript Arnim had appealed for tales as they were still current among the common people. The Grimms were sympathetic. They had become keener and keener on their country's oral tradition, and about 1806 they began writing down popular tales, realizing that this 'buried gold' was in danger of being lost, and that it was time to preserve an important heritage. Jacob and Wilhelm encouraged each other in their zeal. They infected many friends with their enthusiasm, and slowly the work which against all expectations was to make the name of Grimm known all over the world, began to take shape.

Clemens Brentano had first kindled the brothers' interest in fairytales. He himself intended to publish some, and was indeed busy on a translation of Basile's *Pentamerone*, of which he possessed a Naples edition of 1749. During a visit to Cassel in 1807 he was much impressed by the material the Grimms had accumulated in such a short time. He praised their diligence in glowing colours to von Arnim.

Shortly after, Arnim arrived in Cassel, and could only confirm all Brentano had said. The brothers generously handed over to Arnim their collection of folksongs, and became ardent collaborators on the second and third volume of the *Wunderhorn*. Their brother Ludwig designed the frontispiece for the third volume. A little later Brentano asked for a loan of the tales collected so far which he wanted to compare with his own store. It is typical of the Grimms' unselfish scholarship that they did not hesitate for a moment to grant the request. In 1809 Wilhelm wrote to Brentano: '. . . all we have is as much yours as ours . . .'[1] Jacob agreed, particularly as he knew that Brentano would treat any material in a manner completely different from their own. This would certainly have been so, as Brentano was content to take short notes, fill in the gaps later, and make up his own tale. This is not true recording, and far from the *Echtheit* – the genuineness – the brothers aimed at.

Knowing Brentano's volatile temperament, the Grimms took the precaution of making a copy of their original manuscript. Their foresight was justified, for without it there might have been no *Household Tales*. Brentano never returned the original manuscript. That was in 1810, and only some hundred years later it was discovered in the library of the Abbey of Oelenberg in Alsace. It is now in the possession of the Geneva collector, Dr. Martin Bodmer. This manuscript was edited by Josef Lefftz, and has provided useful information on the early stages of the fairytale collection. Brentano's own stories, which were not published till after his death, are a strange mixture of recorded material and his own brilliant fancy.

Jacob and Wilhelm received further stimulation from two fairytales taken down from fishermen in Low German by the painter Phillip Otto Runge. Runge had sent them to Arnim – via his publisher Zimmer in Heidelberg – stressing that such tales were first and foremost for telling and not for reading. One was *The Fisherman and his Wife*, an ancient tale of a fisherman and his discontented greedy wife, the other, *The Juniper Tree*, was the tragic story of the child who, slaughtered by his mother and eaten by his father, comes back as a singing bird to take revenge. Arnim had published *The Juniper Tree* in his *Zeitung für Einsiedler*, and of the other the Grimms had made a copy during one of Arnim's visits to Cassel. Runge's rendering was perfect. He, too, believed in faithfulness to oral tradition, and was an example to the brothers. They kept searching for tales, taken down verbally, and only noted few from literary sources.

Gradually a mass of material assembled on their desks, mostly from Hesse, their immediate surroundings, and from memories of the Kinzig valley. Jacob and Wilhelm had become the centre of a crowd of young people, all anxious to help with their collecting. Many were friends of Lotte Grimm, particularly the Wild family from next door. Among the six daughters – *das Dortchen* – Dorothea, years later to become Wilhelm's wife, was an excellent storyteller. Gretchen, Lisette and Mamma also recorded tales, and especially the source of them all, *die alte Marie*, the Wilds' old nanny. From her came *Snow-White*, *Little Red-Riding-Hood* and *The Sleeping Beauty*. Karoline Engelhard, a friend of the Grimms, of whom Jacob had said that she herself did not know much about tales, made contact with the sisters Hassenpflug. Jeannette and Amalie became keen contributors. *Frau* Hassenpflug was of French descent, and *Blue Beard* and *Puss in Boots* appear to go back to memories of her own childhood. These tales the Grimms omitted in later editions of their collection as they were too close to Perrault's stories.

Friends in the countryside were successfully approached, and we find their names pencilled in the Grimms' own copy of the first edition of the

Jacob Grimm, 1817. Pencil drawing by Ludwig Emil Grimm. Privately
owned

Wilhelm Grimm, 1822. Pencil drawing by Ludwig Emil Grimm.
Original missing since the War

Household Tales, often with the dates of the stories' recording. *The Singing Bone,* for example, is marked: 'Dortchen 19 January 1812 by the stove in the summer-house', conjuring up a charming picture of German *Gemütlichkeit.* Dortchen was then sixteen years old. Like most Cassel citizens the Wilds had a fine garden outside the town. These large allotments, enclosed by hedges, had often been in the family for many generations, and on the gateposts might be seen the carved initials of a far-off ancestor. Their straight paths were bordered by box, and the good earth supplied masses of flowers and fruit and vegetables for the pot. The gardens were a paradise for the young who tramped out to them, summer and winter. Coffee could always be brewed in the *Gartenhaus,* or potatoes and apples baked on the stove's glowing top.

The brothers found a picturesque collaborator in Johann Friedrich Krause, an old soldier, a former sergeant of dragoons, who bartered his tales for gifts of discarded trousers. He wrote the most delightful letters of thanks to his 'dear gentlemen benefactors'.

There were disappointments too. Jacob and Wilhelm had heard of a woman in an almshouse in Marburg. She had told Brentano a number of tales, and he had, in his usual manner, taken short notes, hoping to be able to reconstruct the stories later on. This was not possible, and sister Lotte, on a visit to Marburg, was commissioned to go to the *Elisabeth Hospital* and see the old lady. However 'the source' would not talk, neither

In the courtyard of the castle, Steinau. Drawing by Ludwig Emil Grimm

to Lotte nor Wilhelm who tried a little later. She feared repercussions in the almshouse, people might laugh about her. Eventually a tale or two were obtained through the intervention of the warden's wife.

At this time Jacob gave much thought to a publication, possibly a journal, which would concern itself with material collected from oral tradition. For a while Brentano was enthusiastic, proposing that collectors might be appointed in different regions. The contributions might even be made into a book. On 22 January 1811 Jacob sketched an appeal for material – *Aufforderung an die gesamten Freunde deutscher Poesie und Geschichte erlassen* – with ideas on the recording of oral tradition, much in advance of his time.[2]

He asked for authentic material only, expressly excluding 'made-up' or 'embellished' versions. The main interest was to be in local tales, legends and traditions, sad or gay, instructive or just fun, prose or rhyme. Of particular interest were tales told to the children, or in that great storehouse of folklore, the spinning-room in winter. All was to be taken down faithfully, nothing left out, nothing added, the turn of phrase of the teller was to be carefully preserved. Even what appeared to be nonsense should be recorded and not changed to make sense. The aim Jacob had in mind was not a book to entertain though it might accidentally do so, but one to provide documentary material for a history of German literature.

This attitude was typical of the Grimms. In opposition to many of their contemporaries their preoccupation with folksongs and tales was not a mere escape into a romantic past. Songs and tales were basic to their study of philology. They were evidence of the ancient 'poetry of the common people' demanding conscientious treatment. Jacob and Wilhelm, from the beginning, were keen observers of the colloquial, the simple vivid phrase of the people, and this gift of observation was to be largely responsible for the true ring of the tales in their own collection.

The Grimms' scientific approach did not hold Brentano's attention. The matter drifted, and their appeal, sketched out by Jacob, remained unpublished. A certain tension seems to have developed between Brentano and the brothers. The steadier Arnim, however, now married to Brentano's sister Bettina, continued to show a most sympathetic interest in the Grimms' work.

In January 1812 he came to Cassel and inspected their collections. He was impressed. Twenty-five years later Wilhelm was to describe the occasion: '. . . it was he [Arnim] who drove us to publication . . . of our collections he liked the fairytales best. He thought we should not hold on to them for too long before publication, because striving for completeness, the job might be given up altogether in the end . . . Pacing up and down the room, he read sheet after sheet, while a tame canary, keeping its balance with graceful movements of its wings, was perched on his head, and appeared to be quite at home amidst his thick locks . . .'[3]

Arnim set out to find a publisher for the Grimms, and he succeeded in interesting Georg Andreas Reimer, of the *Realschulbuchhandlung* in Berlin, whose firm was to go on publishing for them thereafter. An old friend, Ferdinand Dümmler, was then working with Reimer, and it may well be that his advice weighed the scales in favour of accepting the fairy-tales. Wilhelm remarked in a letter of June 1812 that 'the good Dümmler' was now in Berlin, and that 'perhaps he has put in a word for us'.[4] These were not good or easy days for publishers, and the acceptance of a manuscript meant much to an author.

In the autumn of the year the collection was completed and sent off to Reimer. It contained mainly recorded tales, with only a few taken from literary sources. In a letter to Arnim, Jacob stressed how he was increasingly convinced of the importance of oral tradition for the history of literature as a whole:

'. . . since your visit here our collection has grown considerably, always from oral tradition, and I believe it will make a rich and delightful book. Every day I see more clearly what an important part these ancient tales play in the evolution of literature. If we overestimate their influence, let people reduce our statements by a little. Enough will remain to make up for the injustice these tales have suffered by being overlooked for so long . . .'[5]

Wilhelm had expressed similar views in the preface to his translation of the *Kaempe Viser – Altdänische Heldenlieder, Balladen und Märchen –* published by Zimmer of Heidelberg in 1811. Originally, Arnim had tried to interest Reimer of Berlin in the Danish ballads and tales, who had, however, been only willing to publish if distinguished patronage could be found, in the form of a preface by Goethe. But Goethe remained aloof, and eventually Wilhelm provided his own introduction. In it he said:

'. . . these tales deserve better attention than they have received so far, not only because of their poetry which is of a peculiar charm, and bestows on those who have heard the tales in childhood a precious lesson and a happy memory throughout life, but also because they belong to our national literature . . .'[6]

The Grimms were fully aware of the tales' magic world for children, but they were anxious to lift them from an atmosphere in which they were only considered fit for children – old wives' tales – at best, raw material for prettifying. To Jacob and Wilhelm they were a strong and vital part of mankind's half-forgotten past. They firmly believed in the great ancient-ness of these tales, and took their survival as proof of the eternal delight in listening to a story.

Now, and in the notes and appendixes to the many editions of their fairytales which were to follow, the Grimms insisted on the tales' close relationship to ancient myths, and the great heroic epics of the past. Was not the Sleeping Beauty, who had fallen asleep after being pricked by a spindle, another Brynhild, thrown into sleep by a thorn? To set the Sleeping Beauty free, her Prince had to fight his way through a thick hedge of thorns, surrounding the castle. Brynhild slept, surrounded by a wall of flames, which Sigurd had to pass. Snow-White was likened to Snäfridr, the fairest of all women, over whose coffin her husband Haraldr watched for three long years. And did not King Mark of *Tristan* have a bird bring the golden hair of the princess, the king was to love, as in the fairytale the king is having search made for a bird that dropped a golden feather? They found remains of the Osiris and Orpheus legends in *The Juniper Tree*, and there were shades of Thor himself, who collected the bones of dead goats to revive them by shaking.

The witty and playful approach of fashionable writers, particularly Brentano, antagonized the Grimms, and they insisted that their collection must have an introduction and an apparatus of notes. Thus they did not aim at a book for children, it became one by accident. Their approach was purely scientific within the limits of their time. In this first edition they wrote down the stories as close to the original as possible, including peculiarities of the teller's turn of phrase and speech. This gave their stories authority, and made them genuine documents.

The *Household Tales* were finished before 20 December 1812, ready to go out, with the dedication: 'To Frau Elisabeth von Arnim, for the little Johannes Freimund'.

Jacob and Wilhelm had known Frau Elisabeth – Bettina Brentano – for years now. The newly married Arnims had visited the brothers, and had been well received in Cassel. Bettina's sister Ludowika – Lulu – was married to the Cassel banker Karl Jordis, to whom Carl Grimm was articled earlier on.

Delighted, Bettina acknowledged the Christmas gift. There it was, after six years of collecting, a fine book, bound in green leather, with gilt edges, under the Christmas tree, for their young son.

In the introduction, a beautiful piece of romantic prose, the brothers likened their gathering of tales to the gleaning of forgotten ears of corn: '. . . when the heavens have unleashed a storm, or when some other natural disaster has battered down a whole harvest, we may well find that in some sheltered corner by the roadside, under hedges and shrubs, a few ears of corn have survived. When the sun begins to shine again, they will grow, hidden and unnoticed. No early scythe will cut them for the cornhouses. Only late in summer when the ears are ripe and heavy with grain, some poor humble hand will glean them, and bind them carefully, one by one. The little bundles will be carried home, more cherished than big sheaves, and will provide food for the winter, and perhaps the only seed for the future . . .'

'It was just time to preserve these fairytales, for those who keep them in mind are getting fewer . . .'

Speaking about the nature of tales, the brothers have this to say:

'. . . their world is confined, it contains kings, princes, faithful servants and honest craftsmen, above all, fishermen, millers, charcoal-burners and herdsmen, in short, all who have stayed closest to nature. All else is alien. The whole of nature is animated, as it is in the myths of a golden age. Sun, moon and stars are our fellows. They give presents and even have garments woven for themselves. Dwarfs work the ore in the mountains, nymphs sleep in the waters, birds, plants and stones can talk and express their sympathy. The very blood can call and speak . . . This innocent communion of great and small things is of inexpressible sweetness. We would rather listen to the stars talking to a poor child, lost in the wood, than to the music of the spheres . . .'

'. . . we have endeavoured to present these fairytales as pure as possible . . . No circumstance has been added, embellished or changed . . .'[7]

And so the brothers' first major work went out in search of readers. And what was the reader's reaction? It was mixed.

In some places the collection was considered a dangerous work of superstition.

The Romantic poets, especially Brentano, did not care for the 'un-improved' stories, and called them boring and slovenly. Even Arnim thought that there was too much erudition, and that it would have been better to have neither preface nor appendix. He deplored the lack of illustrations, suggesting that Ludwig Grimm should make some drawings.

In time, the 1819 edition of the tales was to have a frontispiece by him.

The newspapers were cool, and from the beginning there were those who considered many of the tales unfit for children.

Others were enthusiastic. The Savigny children enjoyed the tales, and from Koblenz the Grimms' friend, Joseph von Görres, patriot and editor of the German chapbooks, wrote on 27 January 1813:

'. . . the Fairytales, longingly expected by my children, have now arrived, and we have not been able to tear them from the children's hands. My youngest girl, Arnim's godchild, can already tell some of the stories, particularly those with rhymes. My eldest girl has spread them among children in the town . . .'

Görres went on to say that only three days after the book had arrived, a boy came to borrow it, and that his wife had to read seven tales every night, and that, judging by appearances, they were well received.

Görres had the perception to conclude that with the *Nursery and Household Tales* the brothers had built themselves a lasting monument with children. He also believed that much more material would now be coming forward.[8] He was proved right on both accounts.

In spite of criticism, the triumphant journey of the *Nursery and Household Tales* through Europe and the world had begun. Nothing could stop it now. The children had taken the book to their hearts. By chance, and through allowing the public a peep into their workshop, the Grimms had hit on a masterpiece. It was to become an example and encourage collectors of tales everywhere. It gave folktales a status, and made them for the first time the object of serious enquiry.

Material, too, began to accumulate in the brothers' study, and early in 1813 they began planning a second volume.

Wrought iron decoration from the Reinhardskirche
in Steinau

CHAPTER 5

Westphalian Friendships: The Fairytale-Wife

1812 – 1815

DURING his stay in Halle in 1809, Wilhelm had seen a great deal of Werner von Haxthausen, who was then studying at the university there. Jacob and Wilhelm had known Werner and his brother August, sons of a Westphalian landowner, for some time. They were drawn to one another by a mutual interest in folksongs. The Haxthausens intended to publish a collection of Westphalian songs to which the Grimms were to contribute in return, it appears, for tales. The friendship grew, and the Haxthausens invited the Grimms to visit them at the family home of *Bökerhof*, in Bökendorf near Paderborn. When in the summer of 1811 Wilhelm stayed with his friend Paul Wigand, who now held a legal position in Höxter, he decided to call on the Haxthausens, not very far away.

Werner unfortunately was by this time on his way to Sweden, where he was to seek refuge. His anti-French activities had made him unsafe in his homeland, and he was eventually to spend three years as a refugee in London. Somehow, Wilhelm's letter reached him, and he recommended Grimm warmly to his family, praising the brothers' most wonderful collection of folksongs, tales and proverbs. He also said that Wilhelm was 'a little shy to begin with' perhaps because of his poor health, and not getting away much from his desk. 'Otherwise he is a very decent and able fellow.'[1] He wrote to Wilhelm, regretting his absence from the estate, and assured him that the family would be pleased to see him.

From Höxter Wilhelm hired a carriage to convey him the short distance to Bökendorf. However, the Westphalian roads lived up to their bad reputation, and after the vehicle had turned over twice, he thought it better to continue on foot. He reached *Bökerhof* eventually, found the place pretty and the family most agreeable. There were eight sons and six daughters. The youngest daughter, Anna, then ten years old, met the visitor, and while they were walking up to the house through an avenue of old lime trees, she told Wilhelm his first fairytale.

In those remote parts of Westphalia tradition was still alive, and

Wilhelm was to find a rich store of songs, tales and legends. The 'pleasant and dainty' sisters sang in the evening from collections they had written down themselves. Wilhelm admired the sweet airs of their songs. He stayed one day, and walked back the whole way to Höxter. That night he suffered from palpitations and discomfort on account of the undue exertion.

This visit to *Bökerhof* was the first of several which gained the brothers unexpected and faithful collaborators among members of the Westphalian landed gentry. Recorded tales were sent by the Haxthausens, and acknowledged early in 1813.

That summer Wilhelm returned to the estate to spend happy weeks in the temperate gaiety of this small contented world. There were walks in the park and the nearby woods, musical evenings and much recording of tales. The *Bökendorf Fräuleins*, particularly Anna, were well liked in the countryside. They had a way of getting stories out of old people when others had failed.

Life of the Westphalian gentry was unpretentious. They still were close to the soil, the men actively supervising their farmyards, barns and stables, leaving the finer arts of life to their womenfolk, who also busied themselves in kitchen, stillroom and garden.

During his stay in 1813 Wilhelm met the eighteen-year-old Jenny von Droste-Hülshoff and her slightly younger sister, Annette, the poet. The sisters often spent the summer at *Bökerhof*, the home of their mother, the eldest Haxthausen daughter. They enjoyed the company of their aunts, who were about their own age. Jenny and Annette's home, *Hülshoff*, in the Münsterland, was in a region of vast moors and scattered crofts where generation upon generation clung to the old ways. The sisters were keen on tradition, and, as Wilhelm was to report to his brother, 'knew most'. Both became collectors of fairytales. It is a matter of speculation whether Annette's preoccupation with the folklore of her native region, which shows so strongly in her work, received stimulation from her contact with the brothers Grimm.

Wilhelm took to the Hülshoff ladies. The temperamental and difficult Annette both interested and terrified him. On 12 January 1814 he was to write to Ludowine von Haxthausen:

'. . . I recently had a strange and frightening dream about *Fräulein* Nette. Enveloped in dark purple flames, she pulled single hairs from her head, and threw them into the air towards me. They turned into arrows and could have easily blinded me, had it all been in earnest . . .'[2]

In time Wilhelm found the 'gentle and quiet' Jenny more congenial. A tender attraction developed between them which might have blossomed into more had it not been for the difference in social standing. Their

Under the lime-tree in the Biengarten, *Steinau. Drawing by*
Ludwig Emil Grimm

friendship became vocal in an exchange of letters which covered a period
of some twenty years, up to Jenny's marriage in 1834 to the much older
philologist, *Freiherr* von Lassberg, a friend of Jacob Grimm.

Apart from their common interest in songs, legends and tales, Jenny
and Wilhelm shared a love of nature, particularly flowers and birds.
They both had a fine sense of humour, and in spite of Jenny being a devout
Catholic and Wilhelm a stern Protestant, they looked at things temporal
and spiritual in much the same way. Jenny became a keen recorder of
tales. They exchanged small presents, drawings and dried flowers, reassuring each other of their enduring friendship. In Wilhelm's letters
the formal *gnädiges Fräulein* soon changed to *Fräulein Jenny*. Then, for
over two years, between December 1821 and April 1824, the correspondence seems to have lapsed, perhaps for things left unsaid and feelings
which could not be expressed.

On 26 April 1824 Jenny took up the threads again:

'. . . though I have not heard from you for a very long time, I do not think
you have quite forgotten us. With neither inclination nor time to write,
you may not find it disagreeable to hear how we are. Spring in all its
beauty is with us now, bringing along new pleasures. I enjoy working
with my flowers as much as when I first began, and the pleasure remains
as fresh. How I wish you, too, could live in the country among flowers
and trees. You would be twice as happy, and spring would remind you, as

it does me, of old friends. Here we live very happily, and we are well. What more can one ask of this life. Indeed, the last two months have been specially pleasant. My eldest brother is with us again, and my good father is delighted to let him carry some of the burden. Time passes quickly with drawing and the care of my flowers of which I keep more than two hundred in pots, as well as two small flower gardens. And, I must not forget the joy my swans provide. So, I am contented, and if for a moment I am not, I soon feel that I would be wrong to complain.

'I wish with all my heart that this spring may bring you many happy hours also. I need not tell you how glad I should be to see you and your brothers and sister again . . .'[3]

In the summer Wilhelm thanked Jenny for her 'kind and friendly' letter, expressing his joy in seeing a few lines from her own hand. He then remarked that it is difficult to write when one can say but little, and even that in an imperfect manner only.[4]

In December of that year more dried flowers arrived in Cassel from the remote Westphalian manor house:

'. . . these flowers are from my garden, and I have dried them for you. During the quiet days of Christmas, they are to remind you of the new life which blossomed forth for us all in that holy night. May spring bring you lovely flowers, a happy and serene mind, health and the fulfilment of your dearest wishes . . . May you always have bright sunshine for your walks in the *Aue* [Cassel's park], and not meet wearisome acquaintances, bringing with them unpleasant thoughts, and so make you lose all relaxation . . .

'Now I have two more requests: I should like to know how large your theatre is. But the other is much more important. Clipping my swans' wings – which I had to do to the two young ones recently – is a long and sad business. I therefore ask you to enquire how this is done with the swans in the *Aue*. There is no hurry as I will not be able to use your information for some time. But, please, always regard swans with favour, and imagine that you are standing at the pond in *Hülshoff*, looking at mine. I will tell you what they are called: Beautiful Hans, Little-White-Foot, Long-Neck, and Snow-White. Do you like their names?

'It is hardly possible to live a more isolated life than we do at present; we are completely kept in by rain. You can't imagine how the wind blows while I am writing this. All morning we have had such storm and rain, it has made me feel quite weird. Apart from these few days, I have rather liked the rainy weather. Nobody can come to visit, and for once one lives really peacefully. Among all the summer visitors there is hardly ever one to give true joy. And if I did not feel that every human being deserves some attention and kindness, I would often just not appear . . .'[5]

In his reply Wilhelm gave the desired information concerning the size of the Cassel theatre, but had not yet been able to find out about the clipping of swans' wings. Concerning the birds themselves, he assured Jenny that he had always liked their noble tranquillity. He well remembered a night in early December when, in the falling light, he had walked in Cassel's great park. Swans were gliding on the water under the branches of weeping willows, the setting winter sun turning the few remaining leaves into pure gold. In the semi-darkness the swans had appeared whiter than ever, looking like some supernatural beings, so that water-sprites and swan-maidens had never been far from Wilhelm's mind.[6]

In a letter written on 28 May 1825, Jenny conveys a picture of life at *Hülshoff*, of the same quiet rhythm Wilhelm had enjoyed at *Bökerhof*.

'. . . I don't like getting up too early. Usually it is almost seven o'clock, unless I want to work before that with my flowers. Soon after seven we go to mass. After that we have coffee which I don't care for very much. My first concern then is to feed the swans. They are near my flowers. I see if the frame is warm enough, and I open the lights in my new little glass-house where I always find a lot to do. Often I don't get back to the house before ten o'clock. Then I do some needlework, play the piano or draw. It doesn't come to much during the summer, because visitors often arrive at 11 o'clock and stay till evening . . .'

The afternoon goes in happy activity till Jenny returns to her flowers and swans in the evening. She may take a walk with the family, but on the whole:

'. . . my garden is the place I like best. You will know yourself that one never tires of looking at one's own flowers, even if one soon gets weary of other people's . . .'

Dinner over, there might be some music or reading aloud, especially in winter. Walter Scott was all the rage.[7]

Jacob and Ludwig, too, became very friendly with the Westphalian circle, a friendship which was to last for some fifty years. There were repeated visits to the family homes, and return visits to Cassel, when collected material was exchanged, and the drawings admired which Ludwig had made of people and places.

Meantime the search for tales for a second volume continued, involving more and more friends. On a visit to Höxter Wilhelm made an excursion to the nearby hills, where an old shepherd told him stories and local legends. Another herdsman, however, obviously 'touched by enlightenment' as Wilhelm remarked, said he did not believe in 'spooks' and knew nothing.

Perhaps as early as 1812 Jacob and Wilhelm had a lucky encounter. They met with a genuine storyteller, *Frau* Katharina Dorothea Viehmann, their Fairytale-Wife.

Born in 1755, the daughter of an innkeeper, Pierson, who had come to

Hesse from Metz, she had married a tailor, and now lived with her children and grandchildren in the village of Niederzwehren, near Cassel. From there she set out, once or twice a week, carrying butter and eggs for sale in the nearby town. Among her regular customers was the family of Charles François Ramus, pastor to Cassel's French community. His daughters, Charlotte and Julie, friends of the Grimms, used to treat the good eggwife to a plate of soup or a cup of hot coffee, and in turn were told some old tales. Aware of the genuineness of her stories, and delighted with the discovery, they tried to persuade *Frau* Viehmann to include the Grimms in her round. Persuasion was needed because the Grimms lived a long way from the *Frankfurter Tor*, the region closest to the village of Niederzwehren. However, she eventually went, was well received and given a cup of coffee 'with a silver spoon'. The result was worth it!

Frau Viehmann told the brothers some twenty new tales, and a good few variants of others. She was unequalled for retaining the ancient stories firmly in her mind, pure and unspoilt. She died on 17 November 1815, not quite a year after the publication of the second volume of the *Household Tales*. It was fortunate chance that saved her treasure trove from oblivion.

Altogether, collecting now went well, so that, on 29 May 1814, Wilhelm could write to Ludowine von Haxthausen:

'. . . you cannot believe what pleasure the collecting for the second volume gives me, especially through the encouragement and collaboration of others; for the first volume the two of us collected alone, quite by ourselves, and therefore very slowly, over a period of six years. Now things are going much better and more quickly . . .'[8]

On 30 September 1814 Wilhelm had finished the preface to Volume II of the *Household Tales*. In it he commented on their collector's luck which had eased the work on this volume, at the same time thanking all friends who had supported their collecting. He made particular mention of the tales recorded in Low German, in Westphalia and the Münsterland where listening to the storyteller was still a popular form of entertainment. Referring to their Fairytale-Wife, Wilhelm continued:

'. . . it was one of those lucky chances through which we made the acquaintance of a peasant woman from the village of Zwehrn, near Cassel. From her we got a good number of the genuinely Hessian tales, published in this volume, as well as some supplements to our first volume. This woman, still vigorous, and not much over fifty, is called Viehmann. She has a strong and pleasant face, and a clear sharp look in her eyes. In her youth she must have been beautiful. She retains these old tales firmly in her mind, a gift, as she says, not possessed by everyone, as some cannot keep anything in their heads at all. She recounts her stories thoughtfully,

Bretzel

accurately, with uncommon vividness and evident delight, first quite easily, but then, if required, over again, slowly, so that with some practice one can take them down. In this way much has been left exactly as it was told, and its genuine ring will be unmistakable. Those who believe that, as a rule, tradition is easily tampered with, that there is carelessness in preservation, and that therefore tales cannot possibly survive in the same form for long, should hear how exact this woman is in the telling of a story, anxious to keep it right. In repetition she never changes anything, and should she make a mistake, she will immediately correct it while still talking . . .'

Wilhelm refers once more to their belief in the great ancientness of the tales, living remains of much older myths. He expresses the hope that with the recording of more and more tales a foundation will be laid for the study of the evolution of literature as a whole.

He then turns to the eternal controversy whether these tales are fit reading for children. They may not suit some children, he believes, but then, surely parents can make their choice. On the whole:

'. . . our best defence is Nature; flowers and leaves grow, of certain colours and certain shapes. Those to whom they are not suited – and Nature is quite unaware of this – can pass them by. They can, however, not demand that Nature should colour or shape them differently. Or, take for example, rain and dew. They are a benefit for everything on this earth. There may be some who dare not put their pot plants in the rain, for fear they might suffer as they are delicate. They prefer to water them indoors. But, surely, they would not demand that rain and dew should cease altogether. Everything that is natural is wholesome . . .'9

Reimer was willing to publish the second volume, and the manuscript was sent off to Berlin. The book was ready for distribution late in December 1814. There were again a few tales from printed sources, but the bulk came from oral tradition, the rich harvest from Westphalia and from the Fairytale-Wife.

Wilhelm had worked at the tales all through the vicissitudes of a difficult year, and remarked to a friend that some stories were written down 'while

Russian soldiers were singing in the room next door'. One story, sent by August von Haxthausen, had been told to him while on outpost duty near the Danish frontier. The teller, a hussar, was killed a day or two after, a fact which deeply touched the sensitive Wilhelm.

The *Nursery and Household Tales* were now safely established, and not without reason could Wilhelm say in a letter to his brother, then in Paris: '. . . the fairytales have made us known everywhere'.[10]

CHAPTER 6

Living in Turbulent Times

1810 – 1814

EVER since the dazzling but futile Erfurt Conference, in September 1808, of Napoleon, the Tsar and the *Rheinbund* princes, patriots had noticed with secret satisfaction cracks in the structure of Napoleon's vast empire. Discontent was coming to the surface, under the pressure of financial distress. There had been uprisings here and there, and though in the hard-won victory at Wagram the fortunes of war had been on the Emperor's side, the Treaty of Schönbrunn that followed it was to contribute to his downfall. By giving some of the territories newly ceded to him to Poland, Napoleon had offended the Tsar. Further friction with Russia led to war.

In June 1812 Napoleon assembled a new Grand Army and marched into Russia. This disastrous venture, involving half a million soldiers, including Germans, Austrians, Italians and many Polish patriots, changed the European situation. Early in 1813 Prussia rose, to be joined by Austria later, and in October of that year Napoleon suffered a crushing defeat in the Battle of Leipzig, the Battle of the Nations.

The citizens of Cassel, bent like their compatriots on the liberation of Germany, found in a strictly local disaster a portent of the impending ruin they heartily wished on their foreign overlords.

This was the great fire of November 1811 which devastated the Electorial Castle, then occupied by Jerome and his court. Unfortunately Jacob was concerned in this, the greater part of the library entrusted to his care having been moved there shortly before. Wilhelm has left a lively description of the event in a letter to Aunt Zimmer.

Cassel, 26 November 1811

'Dear Aunt,

'You will have heard of the terrible fright we had, through the night from Saturday to Sunday. There was a fire alarm at three o'clock in the morning, the bells rang, and up and down the streets people were called from their beds. I woke at once, and from the windows of our front room, looking down the *Marställergasse*, I could see the flames rise above the

63

castle. It was our first cold night, with the streets frozen hard, and icicles hanging from the gutters. Everybody was sound asleep, so it took a little while before people came out to help. However, a regiment of cavalry, stationed in the former *Marstall*, soon appeared on the scene, and then there was a terrible hustle and bustle all over the town. Jacob had dressed at once and gone to the scene of the fire . . .

'. . . several times I was awfully worried about Jacob, specially when a gentleman on a stretcher was carried past by soldiers . . . However, heaven be thanked, he came home at five o'clock, safe and sound. The fire had started near his library, and while everything around him was in flames, he packed a lot of books, and saved them. Eventually he was forced out by the smoke. I thank God that he has not suffered injuries. The acrid smell of burning was in all his clothes. He was very very tired, and rested for about quarter of an hour while I had coffee made, so that he could refresh himself a little. After half an hour he left again . . .'[1]

The fire got worse, a huge column of flames rose, and the wind, unfortunately blowing towards the town, carried waves of sparks everywhere. It had become impossible to save more from the burning building. The citizens were warned to have water in readiness in the attics. Soldiers collected fire buckets, all Cassel's bells were ringing, there were shouts and noise everywhere, terrifying in a town of many timbered houses. The Grimms took water to their attics, Lotte put keys into all cupboards, so that things inside could be reached quickly, and Wilhelm collected some valuable papers together. However, frost on the roofs prevented sparks from getting a hold, and when morning came, a relief in itself, the worst was over. The castle was burnt out but the houses in the old town were safe. The family rested while Jacob was still busy taking the treasures he had rescued to temporary safety. He was troubled for months after, sorting out the muddle of salvaged books, often driven by the impatience of his superiors.

During these years of turbulence and chaos, with Germany overcome by a foreign power, their own private lives complicated and insecure, Jacob and Wilhelm worked quietly at their desks, without haste but with great steadiness. Their thoughts turned to the Middle Ages, they did not indulge in patriotic nostalgia, but hoped to serve their country by careful research, and help to lay the foundations of a better future.

The balance and inner contentment the brothers achieved comes out in letters they happened to write on the same day – 29 October 1812 – to their friend von Arnim. They show clearly a difference in temperament. Jacob wrote:

'. . . I should be contented to sit for weeks, without going out, in a tiny study with a single large window without curtains, so that I could see the bright sky . . .'[2]

Charlotte Amalie Grimm. Oil painting by Ludwig Emil Grimm. Brüder Grimm Museum, Kassel

Dorothea Wild. Pencil drawing by Ludwig Emil Grimm. Staatsarchiv
Marburg/Lahn

And Wilhelm:

'. . . I take a walk . . . every afternoon . . . [to] where one has an open and beautiful view of the sun . . . the pure sky and the tranquil light are so pleasing . . . that I return home refreshed and cheered . . .'[3]

Since 1807 the brothers had become regular contributors to papers and learned journals. In 1811 the scientifically-minded Jacob had finished a study on the German Mastersingers while Wilhelm's more poetic nature had been employed on the *Kaempe Viser*. Goethe had now expressed his admiration of them, so had Scandinavian scholars. A year later there appeared an edition of an eighth-century manuscript from the Cassel library, the *Lied von Hiltibrand und Hadubrand* and the *Weissenbrunner Gebet*, under the signature of 'The Brothers Grimm'. To provide material for the study of the older German literature the brothers began publishing the journal *Altdeutsche Wälder*, giving excerpts from their own ever increasing collections. It received favourable comment at home and abroad.

When in 1813 war came close to the Kingdom of Westphalia, an order was given to pack the most valuable books and manuscripts of the Cassel library, and send them off to France. Jacob tried his best to keep manuscripts, especially those of Hessian interest, and he succeeded to a large extent.

Soon the short-lived glory of the Kingdom of Westphalia and its king was to vanish. After seven years of exile the Elector and his family re-entered Cassel, to the loud rejoicing of his loyal subjects. Aunt Zimmer returned with them.

Jacob went back to Hessian service. He was appointed secretary to the legation, and asked to accompany the ambassador to Allied Headquarters.

Slightly bewildered, Jacob left late in December.

Early in 1814, Napoleon having refused a peace settlement, the Allies marched into France. Carl and Ludwig Grimm joined the volunteers, while Wilhelm stayed behind with the responsibility of keeping the little household going. This he did with tender care, never failing to report to Jacob about all that was going on. Soon after Jacob's departure the job of second librarian at the Elector's library became vacant. Wilhelm decided to apply for it, but was advised by the head of the library, *Hofrat* Strieder, to apply for a job with the status of *Bibliothekssekretär*. Being fully acquainted with the situation at the court, Strieder assumed that the Elector, anxious to make economies, might not be willing to appoint again a second librarian, but would have no objection to a lower salaried secretary. Strieder was right, and Wilhelm obtained the position. He rejoiced. At long last he was earning a little money of his own, and in time, he believed, his status and salary would rise.

Moving west with the army, Jacob took every opportunity to visit libraries *en route*, always in the hope of finding ancient manuscripts. His and Wilhelm's joint interests were never far from his thoughts. He wrote regularly to his brother, news of war alternating with descriptions of people and places.

From Karlsruhe he wrote on 8 January 1814:

'. . . the journey has continued slowly. On Wednesday we only got as far as Darmstadt which looks pleasant, and the castle clock has a nice clarion . . . Thursday in Weinheim, a boring little Badensian county town; yesterday in Heidelberg – much better – I should have liked to stay for a few days. Boisserée . . . was very kind, but I could not see all his pictures before darkness fell. There are some very beautiful ones among them, particularly the ones by the old Flemish masters, van Eyk, and Hemmeling [Memling] . . .'[4]

In fact, Jacob liked Heidelberg, its old comely houses, and the pretty countryside around, so much, that he thought it would be a good place to be in forever.

On 9 January he wrote:

'. . . according to rumours the Austrians have reached Lyons, at least they must be pretty near it . . . I have called on Hebel [poet and writer, known for his work in the Alemanic dialect] who looks exactly as I thought he would. He walked up and down with me in his room which was very clean and orderly, smoking his pipe . . . He says he has read the Danish ballads three times but did not know anything about the fairytales. I said I would send him a copy, but then wondered whether I had been too forward . . .'[5]

Jacob saw Johann Peter Hebel again, who gave him a copy of the *Hausfreund*, a calendar which contained some of his stories. He kissed Jacob goodbye, and all was well.

Rastadt, 12 January 1814

'. . . Blücher has now reached Saarbrücken, and the French lines of communication to Mayence and Strasbourg are cut. The French are said to be concentrating around Metz . . . Every night in my dreams I am with you all, also during the day in the carriage when I usually sleep for ten minutes and am awake for the next ten. In spite of the distance I am in Cassel in the eleventh minute . . .'[6]

Among the five hundred manuscripts in the Karlsruhe library Jacob had to his great joy discovered the legend of *Titurel*, in a fine codex. He also kept an eager eye on the beauties of nature and art, describing in his letters the cathedral at Freiburg, the bluish-green colour of the Rhine, as well as the treasures of the Basle library, especially the Holbein drawings and an old manuscript which he 'had used as well as he could'.

Jacob continued his researches on French soil. It was cold, and he found looking on the snow-covered scene all day a great nuisance. Having been used to covered stoves the harsh light of open fires at night irritated him. That, combined with the constant whiteness of the snow, would harm his eyes, he thought. It was so cold, he would have liked a Russian cap, but had not bought one so far, because there would hardly be room for both his hat and cap!

Altogether Jacob hated the life forced upon him. There was no quietness, and the company was uncongenial. Having to keep up appearances was dear, daily expenses were high, and Jacob was worried in case he could not support the Cassel household. Seeing fine scenery and beautiful buildings provided some pleasure, and here and there he could buy books. But the disgruntled dedicated scholar did not lack compassion. He was filled with horror at the wretched-looking prisoners of war, the many wounded and dying by the wayside, and commiserated with the hardships of the rank and file.

Contacts with the family at home supplied steady comfort to both sides.

On 18 January Wilhelm thanked Jacob for his letters, giving much news himself, both topical and domestic. Jacob's desk, chair and papers stood ready for him to return to, as soon as the longed-for peace was there. The chimney had been on fire, and only through Wilhelm's quick action of putting a damp cloth into the stove had the family been spared greater trouble.[7]

'. . . the Russians have celebrated their New Year here. Standing in a circle in the street, their chorus leader in the centre, they all shouted loudly, to begin with in wild confusion. Then it all blended into a strange national song. Towards the end the man in the centre began to dance with regular movements, and gradually the others joined till there was great merriment. However, it was all measured, and came to a sudden finish, when they marched off in single file, to start all over again, somewhere else. It all took place in severe cold, with a blizzard blowing, which drove everybody else hurrying home. There is something powerful about national custom . . .'[8]

In Troyes, on 18 February, Jacob was surrounded by the horrors of war:

'. . . between Bar-sur-Aube and Troyes (twelve hours) the misery increased, specially after Vandoeuvre (not far from Brienne). Most villages are empty, and from time to time we saw naked corpses in the street, bivouacs and a village on fire . . .'[9]

The beautiful cathedral of Troyes gave some relief, and though the library was in a turmoil and of no use, Troyes had a depot for the sale of French chapbooks. A good place to purchase some.

On 24 February – Wilhelm's birthday – Jacob wrote that at exactly nine o'clock in the morning he would fold his hands, and think of his brother only.[10]

In far off Cassel Wilhelm longed for the family being together again. On 8 March he wrote:

'. . . I am very much looking forward to the days when you will all be back . . .'[11]

And Jacob wrote on the ninth of that month, delighted on hearing from the family after an interval of some ten weeks. He confessed that he was getting more and more tired of moving about, and complained that he could never find peace to do anything that really interested him.[12] Decidedly the services were not for him.

Meantime Wilhelm was anxiously checking the official lists of the dead and wounded, thanking God when there was no familiar name.

Early in April, on his way to Dijon, Jacob was relieved to be on a road not touched by recent fighting. For once there were no dead, man or animal. Villages were full of women, knitting or spinning, while the men were busy ploughing in the fields. In Dijon itself, Jacob heard the news of Napoleon's abdication and his departure for Elba. His joy knew no bounds.

On the morning of 5 April he wrote:

'. . . here the whole town was soon in an uproar, and full of white cockades. Urchins used saliva to paste bits of paper on their foreheads, and great swarms fought for money thrown to them. I shall never forget the suddenness and gaiety of the scene. I was deeply touched by it. Many a young and innocent heart in that crowd may have firmly believed in the Emperor, and now saw everything torn to pieces quite unexpectedly.

'. . . only the day before yesterday news of great victories was going about among the people. Our troops were totally beaten, a hundred cannons had been captured, and the Emperor and King were taken prisoners. For ten days we had been cut off, and without direct news. Even the Prussians themselves had heard nothing of their king since the 23rd.

'So you can imagine our jubilation . . .'[13]

That night Jacob went to the theatre where an excited audience demanded the removal of the imperial eagle from the curtain, with loud shouts of: '*à bas les armes du tyran*'. During the interval a large banner was hoisted, bearing the inscription: '*vivent les alliés*'. With standing applause and much noisy cheering, emotions rose to high pitch, till even the musicians in the orchestra were seen to weep.[14]

Soon Jacob was to find himself again in Paris. He worked at the familiar *Bibliothèque Nationale*, making many new discoveries, among them a Latin manuscript of *Reynard the Fox*. He was given the unrewarding task of trying to get back some of the books and manuscripts carried off to France during the war, but every free minute was spent copying for his researches. Again, the high cost of living in Paris worried him, and he applied to the Elector for a rise in salary.

While in Paris Jacob enjoyed a happy reunion with his soldier brother Carl. Carl and Ludwig had also managed to meet during the campaign, and Ludwig has left a touching and vivid account of this in his memoirs, another manifestation of the Grimm children's sense of belonging together.

Sitting at a bivouac, stirring beans in an army kettle, and waiting for them to soften, Ludwig felt hungry, and wondered where to find a piece of bread to eat with the beans. Then suddenly he saw another soldier carefully making his way over some men sleeping on the ground. Ludwig could not see the soldier's face because of the steam from the kettle. Then the soldier shouted: 'Good evening, Ludwig!'

'. . . Oh, what a joy, it was my brother Carl! We had not seen each other since leaving Cassel. He pulled a piece of stale bread from his haversack. It smelt of hay and leather . . .'[15]

And the two had a memorable meal.

Jacob kept longing for the quietness of his study but feared that he would not be free to return to it for some time. The new order in Europe had to be worked out, and the Congress of Vienna loomed large on the horizon. Jacob knew that he would have to attend it. If things dragged on in Paris, there was some consolation in the fact that there were still many manuscripts to make excerpts from. Jacob worked hard as he felt sure he would not be allowed to borrow the manuscripts later on. The Latin manuscript he was engaged on was in 'damnably small writing, with many abbreviations', but he persisted and completed some seven thousand verses in just over three weeks, on top of all his other duties.

In April 1814 Wilhelm had asked their Cassel landlord to reduce the rent. This was not done, and Wilhelm decided to move. The family was sorry to leave the home their mother had brought them to. On the other hand, there was the constant danger of fire in the old narrow streets. A flat in the *Neustadt* would be cheaper, and there would be more fresh air. Wilhelm obtained one at the far end of the town, at the *Wilhelmshöher Tor*. It is the only Cassel home of the Grimms to have survived the Second World War. Wilhelm conducted the removal, and arranged everything in the new house though he could not get leave from the library. The exhaustion showed in 'pains in the chest'. All the same, he took time to report to Jacob, hoping that he would approve of all that was being done. He remarked on the quietness and the 'almost country feeling' of the new abode. Jacob was grieved that he had not been there to help, and concerned that no books or papers should be lost in the upheaval.

In June he could at long last leave Paris and set out on his way to Germany, via Meaux, Château-Thierry, Epernay, Châlons and Verdun. He decided to break the journey in Metz to see the library there. Alas, the librarian, *Monsieur* Jaubert, was not available, nor was he there the next day. Annoyed, Jacob managed to obtain entry via an official, but after glancing over some six hundred manuscripts he found nothing to interest him or Wilhelm.

'. . . on Friday early I took the diligence via Pont-à-Mousson to Nancy where I arrived at one o'clock, among crowds of returning Russians. There was no room at any of the inns, and no diligence to Strasbourg before Sunday. So I booked a *patache*, a so-called *cabriolet acceleré*, which takes six passengers, their baggage and the driver. It is drawn by one single horse but is quicker than the diligence. After that I got some food at a remote inn, and the promise of a bed . . .'[16]

Jacob eventually reached Strasbourg where he

'. . . took a private room which can be obtained easily in a place where there are students and fairs. It means saving three-quarters of my usual expenses, and I am more quiet and comfortable. I have a poorly furnished old-fashioned room, with coarse linen curtains, and a view into an old monastery garden. It reminds me of our little room in Marburg. Strangely enough, the first place I enquired at, was the house of the university janitor and library attendant. I was not aware of this until I had taken the room. It means that I am under the same roof as the manuscripts for which I have come here, and I can have them sent to my room without any trouble . . .'[17]

This was a lucky chance indeed, and Jacob made the most of it. He admired the beauty of Strasbourg Cathedral of which 'he could never see enough', and was then ready to continue to Cassel.

During the few remaining weeks of summer the brothers worked enthusiastically. There was much to do, including *Altdeutsche Wälder*, the journal they maintained almost single-handed, and an edition of Hartmann von der Aue's *Arme Heinrich*, which was to be published in 1815. In keeping with this being a tale of sacrifice, Jacob and Wilhelm were to donate the royalties to the benefit of war volunteers. They worked on an edition of the *Edda*, also to be published in 1815. Jacob meditated on some Spanish romances, and there was an ever-increasing correspondence with scholars in their own country and beyond.

Early in 1814 Jacob had written to Walter Scott at Abbotsford whom he knew to be employed in studies similar to his own, and whose *Minstrelsy of the Scottish Border* had impressed him. He had asked whether he might consult Scott from time to time on questions concerning the older Scottish and English balladry. In 1813 Wilhelm had published three Scottish songs in translation. Two were taken from the *Minstrelsy* – *Lord Randal* and *O gin my love were yow red rose*, the third – *The twa Brothers* – came from Jamieson's *Popular Ballads and Songs*.

Wilhelm had made interesting comparisons between the old Danish songs and the ones from Scotland. The latter, he thought, were more tender and filled with a strange melancholy. Jacob complained to Walter Scott about the difficulties of exchanging books, due to the war. He was particularly distressed that two copies of Scott's edition of *Sir Tristram* had been lost on the way. The correspondence with Scott was to continue for some time, partly conducted by Scott's Russian born Anglo-German amanuensis, Henry Weber. They kept exchanging news on common literary interests.

Late in September 1814 Jacob departed for the glitter of Vienna.

*Penknife, belonging to the
Grimms' father*

CHAPTER 7

The Congress of Vienna

1814 – 1815

NAPOLEON defeated and believed safely out of the way on Elba, the monarchs and plenipotentiaries of Russia, Austria, Prussia, Great Britain, France and the minor German states were to assemble at Vienna to settle the new partition of Europe. Plans were laid, intrigues plotted, and after much delay work was to begin in earnest.

As secretary to the Hessian legation Jacob was one of the many making their way to the Austrian capital in the early autumn of 1814.

He took the chance of seeing old friends in Frankfurt, discussing literary matters, and picking up odd bits of gossip. He heard that Goethe was visiting the liberated town, and was being 'dined' by all the Brentanos. From the road he glimpsed the spires of his native Hanau. The Hessian party, including the ambassador, *Graf* Keller, the Count of Leiningen and the Hereditary Prince of Reuss-Greiz, travelled by Aschaffenburg, Würzburg and Nuremberg to Regensburg. From there the journey was to continue by boat on the Danube.

On 2 October 1814 Jacob sent his first letter from Vienna, starting what was to be again a constant flow of letters between the two brothers. He described to Wilhelm the journey on the great river. The Danube, he said, was greenish, and not often 'as broad as the Rhine . . . the boat was not very big . . . a small room with a solid table and seats along the walls . . .' There were two portholes, and the company of four filled the room to capacity. Another room, only half as big, housed three servants. There were also the ship's master and his mate, and some travelling 'journeymen' who helped with the rowing in return for a free journey. The blue-and-white Bavarian flag flew from a pole. Provisions were plentiful, and cooking was done on a small hearth covered with ashes.

It appears that Jacob did not enjoy himself. Travel was slow and sometimes wearisome. On land would have been better. There were neither bunks nor blankets, and as *Herr* Grimm had not taken an overcoat, he lay chilled and miserable on a hard bench. Finally he caught a cold!

Company and topics of conversation were boring, and obviously Jacob sulked.

There were some compensations: the antiquarian in him took notice of different types of houses in different regions, of the changing costume of women, the beauty of Passau's houses, and some 'strange old graves'. The scene became prettier when the mountains appeared in the distance, and once the water of the Danube looked like 'melting silver' in the moonlight. There was Richard Cœur de Lion's prison at Dürnstein, and – at long last – the arrival in Vienna, delayed for some hours by a high wind.[1]

Much to Jacob's regret the ambassador took quarters in the suburban Wieden district of Vienna. This meant a ten minutes' walk into town through dust and wind. Soon the official work of the chancelleries began, and Jacob did his job conscientiously but without much satisfaction. Aware of the futility of political discussions, and decisions which belied the lofty promises made, he remained unimpressed by the glamour. *Redoutes* and gay adventures did not interest him, and his feelings might have been summed up in the Prince de Ligne's famous bon mot: '*Le congrès ne marche pas, il danse*'.

Again libraries, particularly the *Hofbibliothek*, provided relief.

Here the secretary to the Hessian legation met Jernej Kopitar, librarian at the imperial library since 1810. He proved a mine of information on Slavonic tradition, and became the intermediary between Jacob and Vuk Stefanović Karadžić, whose collection of Serbian folksongs had just been published.

Again Jacob spent every spare minute reading, copying, or making excerpts from manuscripts. It was a great thrill to him to find that one of the *Hohenems* codici of the *Nibelungen* was in the hands of a Frenchman in Vienna. Access to it was difficult, but Jacob persevered and managed to borrow and handle the precious manuscript. He had contributed articles to the *Deutsche Museum*, edited by Friedrich von Schlegel. Schlegel was now in Austrian State service, and Jacob made a point of visiting him. His house had become a meeting-place for literary men, chiefly those German Romantics who had been attracted by the Catholic Church. The atmosphere of *Frau* Schlegel's salon – herself the daughter of the Jewish philosopher, Moses Mendelssohn, but an ardent convert to Catholicism – did not quite suit Jacob's Calvinism. He felt more at ease in a circle of men, open to him through Clemens Brentano's recommendation: librarians, scholars of all kinds, booksellers and publishers, all sharing Jacob's own interests.

This group met on Wednesday nights at the beer-house *Zum Strobelkopf*, and talked over 'a passable roast and poor beer and wine'. Here Jacob met the bookseller Mayer, and after years of search for a publisher, he found him willing to take on his translation of the Spanish romances, *Silva de romances viejos.*

Also there were people interested in fairytales.

'...I am setting everybody to work on contributions for the third volume...'[2]

Jacob wrote to Wilhelm, on 23 November 1814.

On 10 December he wrote:

'. . . I have got a fine tale of the *Krautesel* which we lacked entirely, and several people have promised to collect for the third volume. Also I have been told many stories and variants . . .'[3]

In Vienna Jacob realized his old plan of launching a *Märchengesellschaft*, an association for the collecting of folklore material. He sent out his *Märchenbrief*, a circular letter in which he incorporated principles, discussed at one time with Brentano, concerning the regional recording of oral tradition.

After some general information on the founding of the society, the letter points out the importance of oral tradition, and its significance to the student of history, language and literature. It goes on to specify the material to be collected:

'. . . (1) folksongs and rhymes, sung at different seasons, during holidays, in the spinning-rooms and dance halls, and while working in the fields . . .

'(2) legends in prose, in particular the many nursery and children's tales about giants, dwarfs, monsters, princes and princesses, enchanted and redeemed, devils, treasures and wishing-caps. Also, local legends remembered, and attached to certain places (mountains, rivers, lakes, marshes, ruined castles, towers, rocks and all monuments of the past). Animal fables, usually concerning the fox, wolf, cock, dog, cat, frog, mouse, sparrow etc, are of special interest.

'(3) jokes and anecdotes, tall stories; old-fashioned puppet plays, featuring *Hanswurst* and the devil.

'(4) traditional festivals, customs, usages and games; celebrations at births, weddings and funerals; old usages of the law, concerning strange tributes and rents, the purchasing of ground, the fixing of boundaries etc.

'(5) superstitions about ghosts, spectres, good and bad omens, apparitions and dreams.

'(6) proverbs, striking idioms, figures of speech and word compounds...'

The circular then emphasizes the importance of all material being taken down faithfully, 'without embellishment or addition, from the mouth of the teller, and whenever possible in his own words'.

Recordings in regional dialects are thought of particular value, and variants of the same tale should not be rejected because new and unexpected details might be found in that way. It is suggested that small towns yield more material than bigger ones, and villages, particularly remote ones, more again. Also, certain occupations are considered good 'sources': herdsmen, fishermen and miners, and in general, the old and the very young.

Jacob had not been able to resist adding a postscript in which he asked for information regarding books and manuscripts concerning the older German literature, such as might be found in archives or monasteries.[4]

The whole makes a perfect circular though it does not seem to have produced much new material. It is certain, however, that the activity connected with it made Jacob happier and less dissatisfied with his official duties.

On 10 February 1815 he wrote to Wilhelm:

'. . . I have been more quiet and contented recently . . .'

announcing at the same time that 'the circular' was now ready, was being sent out in numbers, and enclosing a few for Wilhelm's use.[5]

On 18 January Jacob had acknowledged the receipt of the second volume of the *Household Tales*. He was not entirely satisfied. Paper and print were not as good as in the first volume, and though the book was thinner the price was high. Why had Wilhelm not used all the available material for notes; there had been plenty of space

Enthusiasm for a third volume was, however, unimpaired:

'. . . I am now looking forward to the third volume, for which I have already three or four long, good and new tales, besides all sorts of fragments . . .'[6]

This proposed third volume was never published as such. It turned into a volume of notes and commentary, the basis of much future investigation into the folktale. It was to contain some fourteen pieces collected by Jacob during his stay in Vienna, or sent to him later by Viennese friends.

Like many patriots Jacob became more and more frustrated with a congress that ignored all revolutionary changes and liberal sentiments in favour of a rigid Balance of Power. The vision of greater German unity seemed as far away as ever. Vienna and the Viennese did not interest him greatly. As for diplomats, they were a race apart, and their way of life was alien to the scholarly recluse. Once again, Jacob worried about expense. Food and drink, though plentiful, were dear – 'a pear three or four *Groschen*'. Theatre tickets were a happy exception on the expense list. They were cheap, and Jacob enjoyed the theatre, particularly the popular farces, the *Hanswurst* plays. He also found some cheap books, welcome additions to the brothers' 'library'.

From Cassel Wilhelm reported faithfully all news, good and bad. Rumours had reached the Elector's ear that Jacob was devoting too much time to private study when he should live 'in society', getting to know about people and things. Wilhelm had loyally defended his brother, asserting that the way Jacob lived would gain him more useful acquaintances than would fruitless running from party to party. Jacob entirely rejected the accusations, calling them stupid and false.

The Cassel household had a constant struggle to meet all demands. The younger brothers were still unsettled and always in need of money. All the same, domestic life went on quietly.

In a letter of 14 December 1814 Wilhelm had told his brother that at long last Ferdinand had found a position with their publisher, Reimer of Berlin. He would be a clerk and also read proofs, receiving a salary of twenty thalers a month. This would make him independent. Carl's future was still uncertain, while Ludwig was back in Cassel, working in his old room, and being agreeable company. Wilhelm ended up by saying that during the cold winter, and perhaps through smoke from a chimney, he had lost some of his beloved pot plants, and could Jacob get seeds in Vienna of 'beautiful, strange, southern, perhaps Asiatic plants'.[7] Later on he described how the family had celebrated Jacob's birthday in his absence, and how Lotte had gone to a ball at New Year's Eve, while he, Wilhelm, stayed behind, mulling wine on the stove, but not drinking very much 'as it is not pleasant to drink alone . . .'[8]

In April 1815 Wilhelm had to convey the sad news of the death of their good Aunt Zimmer.[9] The Electress shared their grief and had said, with much affection, that she would try to take the place of their aunt. She had given Ludwig six hundred thalers from her private purse for his further studies.

Another relation of the Grimms, the seventeen-year-old Luise Bratfisch, from Hanau, entered the service of the Electress in the late *Fräulein* Zimmer's place. She appears to have been the only woman Jacob Grimm ever showed any serious interest in. Rumour has it that, as a young Hessian librarian, he proposed and was rejected. Luise stayed in the service of the Electress and later on that of her daughter for over fifty years. She never married but kept on friendly terms with the Grimm family.

In Vienna legitimacy was overruling the wishes of whole populations, awakened by the French Revolution's doctrine of freedom. Piles of paper work more and more disgusted Jacob, and to return to his own desk became an overwhelming desire.

When in May 1815 Napoleon once more landed on French soil, and the Congress hastened towards its end, Jacob saw his chance of escape. He asked the Elector to be released from his duties, and made plans for going home.

However, the quietness of the study was not yet for him. After Napoleon's final defeat at Waterloo, and his banishment to St Helena, governments again required representations in Paris.

Of this, Jacob says in his autobiography:

'. . . hardly had I returned to my brothers and sister in Cassel when I was once more required, this time by the Prussian authorities, to return to Paris, conquered for the second time. I was to trace manuscripts, taken from various parts of Prussia, and demand their restitution. Besides, I was to do some business for the Elector who then had no official representation there. My commission put me into an awkward position with the Paris librarians who previously had treated me with great courtesy . . .'[10]

Jacob again used all leisure for his own studies but the librarian Langlès whom Jacob had urged to return some treasures, one day remarked openly: '*Nous ne pouvons plus souffrir ce M. Grimm, qui vient tous les jours travailler ici et qui nous enlève pourtant nos manuscrits*'. At that Jacob closed the manuscript he was working at, and henceforth attended to his official work only. His task was thankless with obstacles at every turn. It was often impossible to find the people responsible for the confiscation of art treasures. In particular, a General Lagrange, who had carried off booty in 1806, could not now be traced, as there were a number of high officers of that name.

A letter, printed here as it remains in the Grimm manuscripts, bears witness to Jacob's efforts:

Paris, 20 Octobre 1815

'*Monsieur le Général*

'*Mon gouvernement m'a chargé de m'adresser à vous, pour vous demander les renseignemens necessaires relativement à plusieurs objets précieux et tableaux, qui ont eté enlevés de la Hesse, à l'epoque où vous en futes le gouverneur. Vous vous rapellerez, que deux caisses contenant des vases, coupes, gobelets etc. en partie antiques, mais tous d'une grande valeur, tomberent alors entre vos mains. Vous n'ignorez pas non plus, qu'une partie des tableaux placés au chateau de Cassel fut enlevée par votre ordre et independamment de ceux, que Mr. Denon venait choisir dans les collections de S.A.R. l'Electeur.*

'*S.M. Fr. Chr. a reconnu et admis en principe la restitution de tous les objets d'art et de science, que la France s'était appropriés aux depens de l'Allemagne. Elle nous a déja fait rendre ce qui se trouvait de notre proprieté au grand musée de Paris.*

'*Cependant les objets, dont j'ai l'honneur de vous parler et dont je pourrais vous présenter les etats détaillés, n'existant pas dans ce moment, à ce qu'il paraît, dans aucune des collections publiques de la France, il est de toute urgence, de constater l'autorité, qui a fait operer leur enlève- ment ainsi que celle, qui a dû les recevoir alors par ordre du ci devant gouvernement français. Veuillez bien, Monsieur le Général, vous expliquer la dessus et satisfaire le plutôt possible à une demande, dont vous ne pouvez pas méconnaître la justice. Veuillez, je n'hesite pas de l'ajouter, concourir à reparer une partie des maux et des calamités publiques, que pendant les années desastreuses de 1806 et de 1807 vous avez dû, malgré vous, infliger à ma patrie.*

'*Monsier le B^on. de Carlshausen Conseiller intime de l'Electeur vous avait déja anterieurement adressé sur le même objet plusieurs lettres, qui sont restées sans reponse. Je doute qu'elles vous soient parvenues, attendu, qu'il existe plusieurs autres officiers supérieurs de votre nom, ce qui a pu contribuer à confondre les adresses.*

'*J'ai l'honneur de vous exprimer l'assurance de ma haute considération . . .*'[11]

Jacob made a few good friends in Paris, but 'counted days and hours', longing for home.

During his brother's absence, in August 1815, Wilhelm enjoyed a journey to the Rhine. He spent some happy days in the Brentano-Savigny circle at Frankfurt where his painter brother, Ludwig, joined him. He again met Goethe, together with the Frankfurt burgomaster Guaita, who had married Meline Brentano.

Of this encounter Ludwig writes in his memoirs:

'. . . it was delightful to find Wilhelm [at the Brentanos' house]. He said: "Today Goethe and the Savignys will come for lunch, and you will see them". I was very curious to see Goethe whom I had never met before.

'At table he took the top seat between the ladies. I was presented to him by Savigny. There was a kind of solemn gaiety during the meal. We sat at a large table, as the von Guaitas and *Senator* Thomas were also there. An hour after lunch Wilhelm said: "Goethe wishes to see your sketch books, and take any drawings of Cassel you have with you". We went to him, and I then saw the famous man, from head to foot. He was not tall, but well proportioned, with a small Minister's embonpoint, dressed in black. He shook hands with both of us, and was very friendly, speaking slowly. Then, we all three sat down, and he first spoke to Wilhelm about learned matters. His face was still quite red because at table he had partaken freely of the *Johannisberger Eilfer*. When he noticed my books, he said: "Aha, now we'll see something of art!" He looked very slowly at all the sketches, portraits and studies of landscapes. I had the feeling that most of his remarks hit the nail on the head. He advised me to make more serious studies of some of my sketches; I should make a picture of some, he thought, etc. However, I must confess that many, he called most successful, were the ones I liked least. He did not think that the heads were well enough executed. "Of course", he added, "circumstances and time do not always allow for greater detail." But he was satisfied with the positions and the interpretation of character. He also suggested which head would suit which picture. He very much praised a life-size head of our beautiful cousin, Amalie Burchardi, and said very earnestly: "I should not know a more beautiful or more suitable head for a painting of Eve." etc. I was very astonished that he also liked my landscapes; I have had little practice, and have not what landscape painters call, a manner. I have painted trees, tree trunks, roots, leaves and plants without any special manner, but one can recognise nature in my drawings, and he may well have praised that. He also liked my conception of a whole scene. He spoke for quite a while about art, and gradually arrived at his favourite subject, mythology, which I have always disliked. However, it was most interesting to listen to him, and only then could one fully appreciate the radiance and spirit of his eyes. By and by more people came to the room, and conversation turned general . . .'[12]

From Frankfurt the journey was continued to Heidelberg, where it was now Wilhelm's turn to visit the brothers Boisserées' famous collection of Dutch and German Old Masters. The Boisserées cultivated Goethe's friendship, hoping that in time he would share their adoration of the medieval, and he too joined the party. He politely admired the pictures, but left it at that. To Wilhelm he talked about the older German literature, and enquired after the brothers' present plans.

Wilhelm paid a nostalgic visit to their home in Hanau, and everywhere enjoyed good talk and a gay social life. He was much impressed by the fine scenery of the Rhine valley where the vintage was in full swing, and by the old towns of Mayence and Cologne. Enthusiastically he wrote to Arnim:

'. . . I have much enjoyed this journey when I saw the Rhine for the first time. I cannot tell you how I felt when our boat began moving on the river's green waters. All the time we were favoured by a wonderful sky. In the morning the sun parted the mists like huge curtains, showing up rocks, vineyards and ancient castles in the purest light. Evening came with a gentle red glow, and at night there were the moon and the stars . . .'[13]

Wilhelm wished that all his friends could have shared this marvellous experience.

The year was nearing its end before Jacob could free himself, not without difficulties, from the service. He applied for the position of librarian at the Elector's library, a post that had recently fallen vacant, and returned to Cassel in December. He found peace at last, and a stronger Wilhelm, much improved in health. It was the beginning of thirteen happy years.

Decoration from a
house in Steinau

CHAPTER 8

Growing Fame as Horizons Widen

1816 – 1820

TOGETHER the brothers again settled in Cassel.

After the Napoleonic upheavals the peoples of Europe longed for peace. But things were not quite as before. The impact of the French Revolution had created a ferment which kept working, and everywhere opposition against the old order was growing. The Germany of many small states, the Germany of self-contained domesticity was changing. More and more people became aware of the world outside their own city walls, and their belief that their rulers could do no wrong was shaken. Politics, so far left to courts and chancellories, were engaging the man in the street. The word equality was heard more often, and citizens wanted to be consulted and play a part in their country's government. They asked for constitutions, believing that this almost magic notion would right all wrongs. A sense of freedom, a new patriotism swept the country.

The zeal and eloquence of Johann Gottlieb Fichte's *Addresses to the German Nation*, calling for national regeneration, stirred German intellectual life. Ernst Moritz Arndt's ardent patriotic poems and songs roused the imagination of the young. In Prussia *Freiherr* vom Stein was demolishing age-old privileges, assisting Gneisenau's and Scharnhorst's reforms of the Prussian army. Old institutions vanished to be replaced by the dream of a strong united Germany, democratic and national in conception.

Meantime autocratic repression prevailed, often harshly enforced on less and less willing subjects, but absolutism was on the wane.

The growing application of scientific knowledge was changing the tempo of life. In 1804 Trevithick had adapted Watt's steam engine to make the first locomotive, the steamship had arrived, and traffic was becoming faster. With improvements in printing and the exploitation of gas for lighting, vast changes lay ahead.

A new scientific approach invaded the humanities, influencing philosophers and historians, and creating a sympathetic climate for the rise of a new discipline: Germanic philology.

80

View from the Grimms' home at Cassel. Water-colour by Ludwig Emil
Grimm. Staatsarchiv, Marburg/Lahn

The Grimms' home at the Wilhelmshöher Tor in Cassel. Water-colour
by Ludwig Emil Grimm. Schloss Fasanerie, near Fulda

The wind of change was blowing into quiet Cassel. Following the example of Karl August of Weimar, first to give his people a constitution, the Hessian Elector, William I, incorporated certain constitutional clauses in the State legislation.

The Grimms took no immediate part in the controversies of the day. They were contented to work in slightly greater security. In these quiet hard-working and perhaps most fruitful years – as Jacob was later to describe their Cassel days – the brothers rose from publicists to European scholars.

On 16 April 1816 Jacob was appointed, and he, too, now worked regularly at the Elector's library, having filled the vacancy which otherwise might have been taken up by Wilhelm, who, in his autobiography, writes revealingly:

'. . . to me worth more than advancement was the hope that my brother . . . would obtain the position . . .'[1]

Jacob had refused the offer of a secretaryship with the legation at the *Bundestag* in Frankfurt. He was determined to free himself from official-dom. Short hours at the library allowed time for study and the leisure needed to bring the brothers' many plans to completion. Their income was small, but on 16 May 1816 Jacob wrote to their friend Paul Wigand:

'. . . when I consider how agreeable and free my position is, I would rather have a few hundred [thalers] less than a *Regierungsrat* who has to plague himself all day . . .'[2]

Freedom certainly meant more to the Grimms than money, and the little family continued to live simply. They had their 'home with a view', and the pleasantness of their immediate surroundings.

'. . . my balcony', wrote Wilhelm to a friend at Easter 1817, 'has been well prepared. By the time you come, there'll be sunflowers, sweet peas and convolvula in perfection. The wall flowers are out now in all their glory . . .'[3]

For a while the whole family was united once more, with sister Lotte strong and well after taking the waters at Wildungen spa.

During Jacob's absence the more sociable Wilhelm had started a *Lesekränzchen* where a number of young men and women met once a week at each other's houses. Most of them were interested in songs and tales, and had contributed to the brothers' store. With the Hassenpflug girls, Jeannette and Amalie, often came their brother, Hans Daniel Ludwig, then a junior judge at the Cassel law-courts. This learned young man, with the reputation of an ultra-conservative and reactionary, was steeped in German lore, and sympathetic to Romantic tendencies as opposed to rationalism. He was to play an important part in the Grimm family and

F

in the political arena of his day. Meantime antiquarian and literary interests became submerged by admiration for his young hostess, the pretty Lotte.

Reading aloud, talking literature and local gossip kept the young company busy. Wilhelm read specially well, and often the crowd listened to him into the small hours. Refreshments were simple: the poorer members of the *Kränzchen* served a glass of wine while the wealthier rose to brewing punch or bishop. Cakes and biscuits were home-baked, and only on a very special occasion was the court baker asked to supply one of his rich sponge and whipped-cream delicacies. Often as many as twenty-five young people were packed into one small room, and somehow managed to have music – even blow the trumpet – and dance! The serious and solitary Jacob was occasionally bored with it all, and when the reading was not to his liking he fell asleep. He was an outsider, and a later description of himself – to Lachmann in 1824 – as 'quiet, single-minded and often sad',[4] seems to have fitted him well.

The circle's favourite reading was the German seventeenth-century picaresque tale of *Schelmuffsky's Adventures;* its bragging hero's tall stories, with their often coarse humour, gave rise to much laughter. There was great fun at farewell parties for members ready to set out on a long journey. One was the young painter von Rohden who was given a special

The inn Zum Weissen Ross, *Steinau. Drawing by Ludwig Emil Grimm*

82

passport signed by everybody. He was about to go to Rome, a pilgrimage every German painter was then expected to make.

More elegant but perhaps less amusing were evenings spent at the house of Lulu Brentano, the wealthy *Frau* Karl Jordis. After the early death of his first wife Clemens Brentano, too, lived for a while in Cassel. Restless and unhappy, he often escaped to the Grimms' quiet domesticity, to forget, if only for a few hours, the distress of a hasty unsuccessful second marriage to Auguste Busmann. Through him Jacob and Wilhelm frequently saw Bettina, the sister Clemens had called 'the most sublime, most gifted, simplest and strangest creature'. Highly imaginative, extraordinary, as full of fancy as of sound commonsense and understanding, Jacob and Wilhelm came to love her. She and her husband remained trusted friends, even when later Brentano retreated into an alien world of mystical Catholicism and their friendship for him cooled off. Feelings of affinity tied them to Arnim, their *Herzbruder*, and they were grateful always for much early encouragement. In the spring of 1816 Arnim was recovering from a serious illness and longed for friends to be by his side. Wilhelm accepted Bettina's invitation, took leave from the library, and travelled to the Mark Brandenburg. He found Arnim a little pale and thin but well on the way to recovery. Life on the estate in Wiepersdorf was pleasant and natural, if a little Bohemian. Bettina cooked well, but was not an exemplary housewife. The children, like the peasants around them, ran about in home-made smocks, of material woven by Mamma. The spacious house, with a fine garden and birch plantations close by, was left to elegant decay, but nobody minded.

At Whitsun the Savignys with Clemens Brentano arrived, and the pace quickened. Clemens read some of his tales. They did not ring true to Wilhelm, and he did not think they would ever be a competition to the *Household Tales*.

On the return journey Wilhelm visited Leipzig and Dresden, admiring the beautiful scenery in the valley of the river Elbe. He then stopped at Weimar, and took rooms at the town's famous inn, *Zum Elefanten*.

During his journey Wilhelm had heard of *Frau* Goethe's death, and feared that he might not be received by Goethe. However, he appears to have been glad of the distraction, and Wilhelm was one of the first callers during his mourning for Christiane. Goethe talked with animation but remained distant, never showing a deep concern for what the Grimms were doing. His dislike for the excesses of the Romantics, their over-glorification of the past, often directed at rousing patriotism in the present, closed his mind to Wilhelm's real interests. He made polite conversation, asked about mutual friends, and even joked, but there was not the encouragement the brothers longed for. It would have made a great difference if Goethe had said personally what he expressed in a letter of 21 November 1816 to *Frau* von Stein when sending her a copy of the *Household Tales*: '. . . if you were to convey the title of this collection to your Mecklenburg friend, she would be able to give happiness to the young generation for many years to come . . .'[5]

Later in 1816 the Grimms published the first volume of *Deutsche Sagen*, legends collected from oral and printed sources. The plan for such a collection had been with Jacob and Wilhelm ever since their early contacts with Arnim and Brentano. The legends formed a natural complement to the *Household Tales* though they never gained the same popularity. The timeless *Märchen* has a greater appeal than the *Sage* tied to a definite time and place, and supposed to relate true events. The brothers made a clear distinction between the two types while earlier collectors had mixed them. They considered legends, too, genuine survivals of folk memory, the people's way of coming to terms with the strange and the supernatural. In them Christian and pagan thought mingled. Unlike some of their contemporaries who had published legends, the Grimms penetrated to the source, aiming again at exact documentation. They consulted manuscripts and early printed books, copying legends quoted by historians ranging from Tacitus to Gregory of Tours. Another source were the German chapbooks of the seventeenth century. Some orally collected material came from the brothers' circle of friends, outstanding once more stories from Westphalia particularly from the Münsterland, taken down by the von Haxthausens and the Droste-Hülshoff sisters.

Altogether, the two volumes, a second one was to appear in 1818, of *Deutsche Sagen* contain some six hundred legends, the first volume, those attached to a special locality, the second, the ones based on historical events.

A third volume for which the brothers had begun collecting material, and a projected volume of notes never appeared.

In an erudite introduction the brothers expressed their joy in collecting: '. . . the business of collecting, when one sets about it in earnest, soon repays the trouble, and is nearest to that innocent pleasure of childhood when it suddenly chances in moss and bushes upon a little bird, brooding on its nest. With oral traditions, too, there is a gentle lifting of the leaves and a careful bending aside of the branches, . . . to catch a stolen glance into the strange realm of nature which modestly nestles in itself, smelling of leaves, meadow-grass and newly fallen rain . . .'[6]

In the actual telling the Grimms again showed that mastery which is founded in sound knowledge of the people, their customs and speech. The work was the result of the brothers' complementary gifts.

More and more these gifts were to find separate expression. Jacob's enquiring mind began to concentrate increasingly on a historical approach to the grammar of the German language. The outcome was the appearance in 1819 of the first volume of his *Deutsche Grammatik*. Jacob was now convinced that a successful study of the older German literature demanded a solid knowledge of language and its historical development. For long German had taken second place, and had been considered barbaric and inferior to the classical languages of French and Italian. Little importance had been attached to its study since Luther's translation of the Bible. Franciscus Junius, seventeenth-century editor of Ulphilas' Gothic Bible, revived some interest in Germanic studies. But only when Sir William Jones pointed out the similarities between some European languages and the Indian group of languages did the discussion on origins become topical. Herder expounded his views, and Wilhelm von Humboldt made an investigation into the Basque language an occasion for the comparative study of languages.

In 1812, when reviewing Rask's *Icelandic Grammar*, published the previous year, Jacob had written on language and dialects. Now, in what was modestly called a German grammar, he supplied the first lengthy historical study of the Germanic languages. Work on the subject was to become a lasting interest to him. The four volumes of the *Grammar*, to appear over the next thirty-five years, laid the foundations of *Germanistik*, the study of Germanic philology.

By intelligently applied research and some daring combination Jacob traced the German language through all its dialects. Elaborating on the work of Rasmus Kristian Rask, the Danish scholar, he eventually worked out his system of 'sound-shifting', called after him *Grimm's Law*. Much of Jacob's findings has remained important to this day in etymology and phonetics.

It seems safe to assume that Jacob's greater concentration on scientific investigation was precipitated by a critical article August Wilhelm von Schlegel had published in 1815 in the *Heidelberger Jahrbücher*. Schlegel strongly opposed the view of creation by the 'folk', natural creation, being superior to creation through the art of a gifted individual. He attacked the Grimms' *Altdeutsche Wälder*, and made fun of what he thought was their uncritical acceptance and adoration of everything they considered to be 'poetry of the people'. He called their attitude *Ehrfurcht vor jedem Trödel* – respect for every bit of old rubbish. This sneer was reported to Goethe by Sulpiz Boisserée as the brothers' *Andacht zum Unbedeutenden*. Freely translated, this 'devotion to the little things of life' turned from the gibe it was meant to be into a perfect description of one of the brothers' most lovable characteristics.

In his critical article Schlegel had stressed the necessity for some scholar to prepare a historical grammar, and so provide a basis for precise textual criticism. It was this very work Jacob then took up. The fourth and final part of the grammar was not published till 1837, and there were several revised editions of the earlier volumes. It has been said that the grammar was his constant companion, the very basis of all his scientific activity. He valued work on it greatly, and treated his own copy as a friend. The four parts, separated into eight stout volumes, on thick paper with a broad margin, served as an archive of personal mementoes. Flowers, leaves, ribbons, feathers and pictures were put inside, often bearing dates. There were announcements, theatre programmes, political manifestos and cuttings from newspapers, spanning a period of nearly fifty years.

Jacob dedicated the grammar to his professor, Friedrich Karl von Savigny, whose legal teaching had accustomed him to scientific thinking. The publication of the grammar brought an immediate favourable reaction from scholars at home and abroad. Marburg University conferred honorary degrees on both brothers, and they were made members of more and more learned societies. Possibly for the first time a grammar became a best-seller. The first volume was out of print a year after publication. Ties to fellow-philologists became closer, particularly to the professors Lachmann of Königsberg and Benecke of Göttingen. Even Schlegel praised where he had formerly scorned. Jacob's work was giving Germanic studies a firm direction.

In the autumn of 1820 Jacob was busy on a completely revised edition of the first volume. In his eagerness, and absorption with the subject he made no concept but wrote down everything straight for the printer, sometimes only a sheet or two ahead of the text being set and printed. The volume was finished in the summer of 1822. Jacob had snatched every spare minute for work on it. Now, in his letter of 10 September 1822, to the von Haxthausen ladies, he was obviously pleased with himself:

'. . . the new edition of my grammar . . . [is] a thick book of one thousand and one hundred pages, horribly printed and on poor paper. I will take good care not to send it to you because you would be sure to say, why all this fuss about letters and words! But I will defend myself and answer; the Lord made small things as well as big ones, and everything man looks at closely, is full of wonder; language, word and sound. In a grain of sand we may see the sense and significance of large globes of which our world is one of the smallest . . . our concept of time and space is so narrow and obscure. You will have heard of the many ways in which man tries to conceive the idea of eternity. Say, for example, the globe consisted of grains of millet, and once in a thousand years a little bird came and picked one grain. The time it would take to carry off this enormous globe would mean nothing measured against eternity . . .'[7]

*Decoration from
a doorway in
Steinau*

Satisfaction with his work had made the sober Jacob rise to flights of fancy.

Growing fame brought the Grimms some brilliant offers, among them professorships at Bonn University. All were rejected because they wished to continue working together quietly. Lecturing to students, they feared, would mean distraction from their researches.

Fame, too, brought many visitors: professors, scholars, writers and the merely curious. All sought the honour of being received, and many entries in the Grimms' diaries recall their names: Wilhelm von Humboldt, the German statesman and philosopher, the writers August Wilhelm von Schlegel and Ludwig Tieck, Schleiermacher, the theologian, *Madame* Schopenhauer, and many others of their compatriots. From Copenhagen came the professors Molbech and Nyerup, Rosen from London, Schuster from Prague, Ampère from Paris, Ager from Lund, others from the Low Countries and some from as far away as America. They were received with courtesy, though often considered secretly cursed interruptions, most of all by Jacob who complains in his diaries that with visitors about nothing is accomplished and 'the whole day lost'. He hated acting the local guide but guests expected to be taken through Cassel's parks and galleries and up to Wilhelmshöhe, to admire its castles and follies, its splendid fountains and cascades, and remain in awe before the colossal statue of Hercules in whose club alone eight persons could stand upright.

Old friends turned up regularly. At Whitsun 1818 the von Haxthausens came, and as the weather was bad, had to be contented with museums, galleries and the theatre. They returned in August of the same year, and brought with them Annette and Jenny von Droste-Hülshoff. The fire of Jenny's feelings, always stronger than mere friendship for Wilhelm, 'one of the most interesting and handsome men', was newly fanned. Flowers he picked for her on a walk were jealously guarded to be made into a little wreath, and Wilhelm's farewell handkiss to her sister was seriously frowned upon. 'Nette' had made too much of it, and Jenny received hers silently. Much more becoming!

After that suitcases were packed 'with a heavy heart'. The two scholars, no doubt, heaved a sigh of relief, and returned to their studies.

CHAPTER 9

A Storm Gathers

1821 – 1829

SCHOLARLY success did not mean recognition of the brothers by their princely employer. He rather considered their scientific work an abuse of working hours due to him. When Jacob had handed the first volume of his grammar to the Elector William I, he was told it was the Elector's hope that *Herr* Grimm did not neglect his duties over such 'extras'. Things became worse when after the death of the old Elector, on 27 February 1821, his son, William II, came to the throne. Wrapped up in small power politics, and estranged from his people through his attachment to Emilie Ortlöpp, the beautiful daughter of a Berlin goldsmith – later to become *Gräfin* Reichenbach – the Elector was hardly the man to appreciate literature or the work of his librarians.

Jacob writes about this time in his autobiography:

'. . . after the death of the late Elector changes came about in the library's administration. While formerly the librarian could draw annually the funds set aside, and then give an account to the Elector's Treasury, the library now was put under the direct control of the Chamberlain's Office, which was to be in charge of all payments. I cannot judge whether these measures benefited the Elector's affairs, but it is certain that through them all payments were held up, and the librarian's hands tied. He could no longer make use of opportunities for purchase as they offered unless he was prepared to advance the money out of his own pocket . . .'[1]

It was also thought desirable to have a copy made of the library catalogue, and Jacob and Wilhelm with their old colleague, Völkel, after unavailing protests, spent some eighteen months on what they considered unnecessary drudgery. Tension was in the air, not lessened by the fact that openly the Grimms took the side of the Elector's wife, the Electress Augusta, who held court at the little castle of *Schönfeld*, called after her *Augustenruhe*, while the Elector himself was installed with his mistress at *Wilhelmshöhe*.

Both brothers, but particularly Wilhelm, became more and more drawn into the Electress's circle. They admired her stern Prussian qualities, and saw in her the wronged wife. They were apt to overlook her haughtiness, her caprices and her often difficult temperament, much at loggerheads, almost from the beginning, with her rash and passionate husband. It was said of her that she never heard the overture of an opera because she insisted on coming in late, possibly to effect an entrance. The whole audience had to stand for her, and so for many the first act was spoilt. Augusta's love of the arts, the simplicity of her establishment in stark contrast to the affluent show of the Elector, could not but attract Jacob and Wilhelm.

At *Schönfeld* they met on an equal footing the more liberal members of the Hessian gentry and *haute bourgeoisie*, writers and artists, and in 1820 Wilhelm had become tutor in history to the Hereditary Prince, Frederick William. After that, invitations to tea or dinner were frequent. It was even rumoured that Wilhelm might accompany the prince on the Grand Tour. This never happened.

Alas, Wilhelm's pupil did not show much interest in things of the mind. He possessed beautifully bound books which had the appearance of never being opened, and the prince's reading consisted mainly of Hessian almanacs and the *Gotha*. On 14 June 1822, Wilhelm wrote to Arnim:

'. . . as the prince is due to leave on his travels within a day or two, my tutoring is finished for the present. There was talk at one time that I should accompany him, but it was eventually decided to send his military aides only. On the whole, this suits me. The disagreeable would have been sure to outweigh the agreeable, though the undertaking would have decidedly benefited my external position. The prince has a certain mathematical intelligence, a natural respect for what is just, and he is pleasant to his people. These are his good qualities, beyond that he is without feeling, with no inner depth, and given entirely to superficialities . . .'[2]

All the same, when the prince returned he expressed the wish to take up his lessons with *Herr* Grimm, and again Wilhelm was drawn into the life of the little court. He preferred the young princesses to their brother – 'the older one blonde and fragile, the younger one gayer and more easy-going'. He enjoyed their company and that of the ladies-in-waiting who were not at all like ladies-in-waiting 'in books and plays'. There were evenings of reading aloud, particularly the novels of Walter Scott, much appreciated by Wilhelm for their sensitive description of times and people. There was music, and all the ladies brought some needlework. It was well known that the Electress despised idle hands; had she not once remarked of the wife of a high official: 'Surely all her many children need stockings, and still she arrives here without her knitting!' Etiquette was relaxed at these meetings and Wilhelm could write to Jenny von Droste-Hülshoff that 'there is laughter whenever opportunity arises . . .'[3]

The Grimms' friendly relations with the 'rival court' were most certainly a factor in their growing alienation from the Elector.

Meantime work on many projects continued.

Jacob was heavily engaged on his grammar, leaving Wilhelm in almost sole charge of the *Household Tales*. For the second volume of the 1819 edition he had written as an introduction an essay on *Kinderwesen und Kindersitten* – children's beliefs, customs, games and seasonal feasts were made the subject of enquiry. Wilhelm quoted many passages referring to children, from ancient German poetry, interspersing these excerpts with references to tales and legends. He drew attention to the similarity of children's lore in many lands.

A child asking about the source of some information will be told in Germany: '*mein kleiner Finger hat mir's gesagt*' – my little finger told me – while the reply in France is: '*mon petit doigt me l'a dit*'. On burning paper in a fireplace, a mother may watch the sparks against the dark background, telling her children that these are people leaving church, the last spark being the sexton who closes the door. The French mother will say that it is: '*l'abbesse qui fait coucher les nonnains*'. Everywhere children love nursery rhymes: '*Marienwürmchen, fliege weg! fliege weg!*' expresses the same sentiment as: '*Lady-bird, lady-bird, fly and begone! Your house is a-fire and your children at home!*' Games and beliefs, too, are ancient, and vary only slightly in many parts of the world. Blindman's buff, skipping stones on water, mill-toys, kites, hobby-horses and ball games are as universal as the children's oracle of plucking the petals of a marguerite, or the belief that babies come out of a well or from under a cabbage in the kitchen garden.[4]

Wilhelm continued work on the third volume, which was developing into a collection of variants, notes and comments on tales, their motifs and diffusion. He was also revising already published tales for new editions, replacing one variant by another, newly discovered, and perhaps better one. He joined up fragments and made small changes here and there. Everywhere in this reassembly can be traced the imagination of the true poet, and Wilhelm's ear for the way the people talk. More and more, direct speech took the place of reported conversation. Jingles and rhymes were used more freely, together with well known proverbs. In 1860, in the preface to the second volume of *Deutsches Wörterbuch*, Jacob was to describe Wilhelm's ways: '. . . he worked slowly and quietly, but clear-minded and carefully; in our working together he always excelled in gentle and pleasing presentation . . .'.[5]

Wilhelm understood and loved children and perhaps unconsciously, from edition to edition, he told the tales more and more to children.

Wilhelm's letters to Malchen van Zuydtwyk, the ailing daughter of one of the Haxthausen ladies, show the same childlike approach:

8 November 1817

'Dear Malchen,

'Thank you **very** much for the nice little letter with the pretty pictures. Had it not been too late that day, I should have come myself to thank you. Now it is getting so cold here that the flowers cannot stand up because of the frost, and have to lie down. The leaves, too, no longer like sitting high up on the branches, and they just fall. It certainly isn't fun, and I should not like to sit up there at night. And how the wind blows! You cannot imagine what it's like. The wind expects you to raise your hat to it, and recently it tried to lift mine by force, but I clung to it firmly. Wouldn't it be nice if you could come and see me one day. I could show you some pretty things, and might even give you a little white mouse, like the one I have seen not long ago. If we had a dark one as well, they would be the miller and the sweep.

'And now, farewell, my dear child, don't forget me. As a token of my true love I will scatter some blue sand on these lines . . .'[6]

It is interesting to compare one of Jacob's early manuscripts with Wilhelm's final version of *The Sleeping Beauty*:

'. . . and when at the moment the King and his court returned, the whole castle fell asleep, everything even the flies on the walls . . .'[7]

The 'flies on the walls', gave Wilhelm his cue for a long and loving description of the scene:

'. . . and sleep spread over the whole of the castle; the King and the Queen who had just returned and entered the great Hall, fell asleep and the whole court with them. The horses, too, fell asleep in the stables, the dogs in the yard, the pigeons on the roof, the flies on the wall, even the fire flickering on the hearth, went down and fell asleep. The roast stopped frizzling, and the cook who was about to pull the scullery boy's hair because he had done something wrong, let go and fell asleep. The wind dropped, and not a leaf stirred on the trees in front of the castle . . .'[8]

In the second edition of the *Household Tales*, of 1819, the tales were given without notes, now to be included in volume III, eventually published in 1822. The volumes of this second edition had frontispieces from designs by Ludwig Grimm, and the title pages were ornamental. Both, separation of tales from notes and the addition of pictorial material, were gestures to counter earlier criticism and to meet public taste. Possible objections from Jacob were overruled by the fact that in spite of quite a good reception, the first edition of the fairytales had taken some seven years to sell out. In October 1819 their publisher, Reimer of Berlin, had reported that of the one thousand copies of volume II some three hundred and fifty remained in stock.

Popularity therefore had to be courted.

This was even more so when, after the great success of the first English edition in 1823, the brothers decided to select some fifty popular tales for a new German edition, later to become known as the *Kleine Ausgabe*. This smaller and cheaper edition gained entry into thousands of nurseries. It was illustrated.

The presentation was certainly suggested by Edgar Taylor's translations, published as *German Popular Stories*. These were most cleverly adapted to the taste of the nineteenth-century nursery. The 'devil' became a 'giant', 'hell' a 'cave', and when in the story of *The Fisherman and his Wife* the wife aspires to be the Lord himself, Taylor 'softened the boldness of the lady's ambition' by making her ask to become 'the lord of the sun and moon'. George Cruikshank's apt illustrations were much liked by the Grimms. In a letter to Taylor of June 1823 they called them 'light of touch and clever', remarking at the same time that they could not think of a German illustrator of equal gifts, except perhaps the late Chodowiecki.[9]

Wilhelm's work was often interrupted by the return of his old troubles. Suffering from what was sometimes called a *Kardialgie*, nobody quite seemed to know whether heart, nerves or digestion were to blame for his frequent discomforts. He was always surrounded by the family's loving care, even though Jacob grudged the energy wasted on having to run to the doctor's so that he could feel his legs sore for three days after, or – worse still – being polite to the many visiting well-wishers. Draughts of hot milk helped the patient when pills and powders failed.

Physical unease, however, did not stop the working of Wilhelm's eager mind.

A lasting friendship with his fellow-student of Marburg days, Fritz von Schwertzell, made Wilhelm a frequent guest on the family estate in Willingshausen. The von Schwertzells were lively people, and took an interest in all the brothers were doing. One of the daughters, Wilhelmine, had been a keen collector of tales, finding a kindred spirit in Wilhelm. Their ever so slight *amitié amoureuse* lasted over many years. They exchanged scores of letters. About 1817 some ancient mounds, containing burial urns, were discovered on a wooded hillock of the Willingshausen estate, together with a number of stones carrying apparently runic inscriptions. The von Schwertzells drew Wilhelm's attention to these, assuring him that he would be given priority should he decide to investigate the stones and publish his findings. All others would be excluded, even the learned Professor Rommel, who actually came up from Marburg on Christmas Eve 1818. According to a letter,[10] he got 'nothing but a pulled-off biscuit', probably from the Christmas tree. Rommel had reported on the Willingshausen finds in the *Göttingsche Gelehrte Anzeigen* of September 1818, maintaining that the marks on the stones were man-made, and possibly had a magic meaning. Wilhelm carefully examined the stones, and came to the conclusion that the 'inscriptions' were not Gothic runes but casual scribbles. The incident, however, provided the incentive for further work on runes which resulted in a book, *Über deutsche Runen*, published in 1821. In it, Wilhelm expressed the view that the Willingshausen inscriptions were not runes, and science, much later, confirmed this. It was found that the 'runes' were the work of worms – corophiodes – in the soft sandstone of the region. Wilhelm's interest did not flag, and a further book on runes was published in 1828. This was based mainly on the study of manuscripts from the collections of St Gallen, Paris and Vienna.

That Wilhelm had not fallen in with Rommel's theory, and had also been innocently the cause of Rommel not getting further access to the stones, must have irked this ambitious man. No love was lost between him and the Grimms. He was, however, on excellent terms with the Elector who, in 1820, had made him director of the Cassel Court Archives, a position Wilhelm had unsuccessfully applied for. The Elector also granted the professor a decree of nobility. He was now *Herr* von Rommel.

In December 1821 the Grimms were much disturbed by the Elector suddenly having notice served on them to leave their house at the *Wilhelmshöher Tor* within two weeks. The rooms were to be used for administrative offices. They loved the house and its peaceful surroundings: '. . . only the cocks crowed, and every now and then the guard changed at the palaces on the other side of the road . . .'[11] The rent had been low, too. Now all this was to go, and houses were difficult to come by. Eventually permission was granted for the lease to run till Easter. Even then the family only found a poorish apartment, above a blacksmith's workshop, in Cassel's old *Fünffensterstrasse*. It was, said Jacob, 'much worse', and with no view at all. The upheaval seemed awful. Wilhelm found consolation in the fact that visits to the smithy below had already taught him a lot of new expressions, used by the smith in his trade.

Work went on as usual, with short interruptions, either receiving visitors, or paying visits to friends. In the summer of 1823 Jacob saw Steinau again. For twelve days he walked, knapsack on back, through the green hills and dales of Hesse. The weather was fine, and he found the home of his childhood much as he had left it some twenty-five years ago. Though he had wished to stay incognito, he was soon recognized by an old school-fellow. Memories, happy and sad, crowded in, and there was much talk of the good old days.

Soon after the move into their new home, Lotte had married Hassen-pflug, and had settled into her own happy domesticity. The three brothers left in Cassel, Jacob, Wilhelm and Ludwig, led a student existence, with no feminine hand to help.

At Christmas 1820 Jacob had given his brothers and sister an album which carried in print all important family dates. With future events to be noted, the little book was to become a family chronicle. In an intro-duction Jacob asked for lasting affection, considering that their love for one another was the only thing that really mattered.

With much foresight and perception Jacob had included their good neighbour and friend, Dortchen Wild, in the *Hausbüchel*.

Now, on 15 May 1825, a loving friendship of many years was brought to its natural conclusion: the thirty-nine-year-old Wilhelm married Dorothea Wild, by seven years his junior.

'Possessed of a warm heart, natural, sensible and cheerful',[12] *das Dortchen* had long shared joys and sorrows, and it would appear that Wilhelm simply had to ensure her continued presence! Of the great event itself he wrote in his autobiography:

'. . . I have never ceased to thank God for the blessing and happiness of this marriage. I had known my wife ever since she was a child, and my mother had loved her like one of her own, without ever guessing that one day she would be . . .'[13]

Dorothea was, on her mother's side, the great-granddaughter of Johann Matthias Gesner, at one time professor at Göttingen. Ancestors of her father, the late Rudolf Wild, of the *Sonnenapotheke*, had come from Berne, and, indeed, her maternal grandfather was from Basle. So there was quite a lot of Swiss blood in Dorothea. Wilhelm's marriage did not mean separation from the rest of his family. It appeared quite natural to them to continue together, all 'loving' one another, and even sharing all income and expense to manage better.

In 1824 the Grimms had left 'the dark hole', to move into first one and then another flat in the *Bellevuestrasse*. It was a definite improvement, rooms were large and bright, overlooking Cassel's fine parks, the river below and the distant blue hills. The family enjoyed the fresh air, the restfulness after much 'town noise', the bird song and the wide starry sky at night.

Wilhelm's study was on the right, Jacob's on the left, and Ludwig, the painter, had his room to the back where the light suited him.

The family was growing. In 1824 Lotte Hassenpflug had given birth to a boy, to be called Karl, and in December 1825 another child, Agnes, was born. In April of the following year Dortchen and Wilhelm had a son, christened Jacob, after his uncle, who loved the baby dearly. Happiness seemed complete; alas, it was not to last. Agnes and little Jacob both died the same year.

Through all the vagaries of family life the two men kept working.

Jacob had continued his Slavonic studies, and in 1824 he had published a translation of Vuk Stefanović Karadžić's *Serbian Grammar*, with a preface on Slavonic languages and literature. It was admired by Goethe, and contributed to a wider interest in Vuk's own work on Serbian traditions. Jacob also studied Provençal.

In 1825 an anonymous publication, *Fairy Legends and Traditions of the South of Ireland*, had come to the brothers' attention. They recognized the genuineness of the stories, and set out to translate them. They also added a lengthy introduction on fairy lore. Twenty-seven of the thirty-eight traditional tales Thomas Crofton Croker had collected in his Irish boyhood were translated into German. They had an enthusiastic reception, as to many readers these stories were the first bridge from Germanic to Celtic – Scottish-Irish – folk poetry. In return, the 1828 English edition repaid the compliments, and carried a translation of the Grimms' introduction which to this day remains a valuable source of information on different streams of popular tradition.

Wilhelm was busy gathering material for what was to become one of his most important works, *Die deutsche Heldensage*, the German heroic epics. A by-product of his researches was his editing of a hitherto unknown medieval fragment, *Grâve Ruodolf*. *Die deutsche Heldensage* itself was published in 1829. It is a selection of prose and poetry, relevant to the theme, from the sixth to the sixteenth century, together with essays on the subject. For the first time the Germanic epics were taken as seriously as those of Antiquity. The characters of the *Nibelungenlied*, for example, became more widely known, influencing writers, artists and musicians, eventually inspiring Richard Wagner.

In the autumn of 1826 family business took Wilhelm to Steinau, the first time for some twenty years. Approaching the town from a distance everything looked much the same, and childhood days came vividly to mind. Looking closely, however, there were changes: rich gardens and fertile fields had made way for new houses, and some old towers and gates had fallen victims to progress. Wilhelm collected the key of the church, and stood quietly in the place where his grandfather, about a century ago, had preached his first sermon. Through the lofty windows the sun lit the tombstones in the paving, and Wilhelm found the names of two uncles. Between altar and pulpit was the grave of his grandmother, and he meditated how for some twenty years his grandfather must have walked over it, every Sunday on his way to preach.

Marburg University and Castle. Pencil drawing by C. Arnold, 1855.
Landesmuseum, Kassel

Friedrich Karl von Savigny. Pencil and chalk drawing by Ludwig Emil
Grimm. Historisches Museum, Hanau

To both brothers Steinau stood for a feeling of roots and long continuity.

Joy was great when, in 1828, a second son was born to Wilhelm. The happy father watched little Herman in his cradle, 'his round face like that of a marcipan doll'.[14] Uncle Jacob, too, was delighted, telling a friend proudly that 'hardly eight months old, the baby has seven tiny teeth'.[15] Herman was to live and become a well known literary man and loving recorder of memories connected with father and uncle.

In spite of having given up the law as a career, Jacob had kept up a vivid interest in all questions concerning it. He was particularly attracted by the fact that early laws were expressed in metrical form; old customs and usages, too, he thought were close to folk poetry. During a period of exhaustion when he longed for a break from heavy work on his grammar, he turned to a bundle of notes on legal matters. His curiosity revived, and he began collecting material for his *Deutsche Rechtsaltertümer*, published in 1828. Jacob's scientifically trained mind found common origins in early law practices, customs and ways of life, extending to symbols and language. The foundation of any social order was a symbiosis of the ethic and the aesthetic, the right and the beautiful, he thought. In his book he provided a solid study of the society of the Middle Ages in much of Europe. It was to attract jurist, historian and antiquary alike. The *Rechtsaltertümer* remain an important source book to this very day. Early in 1829 the Grimms' colleague, Ludwig Völkel, died. They had worked in great harmony with this able man, and were saddened by his death.

On 2 February the brothers submitted a humble application to the Elector, stating that after giving many years of attentive and loyal service to the library, the happiness of their lives would be complete by now being appointed to this same library as first and second librarian.

The Elector turned the application down within three days.

The brothers were walked over by von Rommel, their old intimate enemy. Rommel might have used his influence to have the brothers advanced, but he was interested only in his own betterment. Almost insultingly, Jacob and Wilhelm were offered an increase in salary of one hundred thalers each. Once and for all the Elector had shown that the work of the Grimms and their growing reputation among scholars meant nothing to him.

In a pathetic little footnote to a letter by Jacob to Johann Smidt, burgomaster of Bremen, a friend of the family, Dorothea explained that she would never wish her little boy to become a librarian, as 'they receive nothing but ingratitude'.[16]

Very typically, Jacob comments on the situation in his autobiography, saying that had Rommel been given the post of director of the museum, with Wilhelm as librarian, he, Jacob, might have become *Archivarius*, and nothing could have made him happier for the rest of his life than being in charge of archives, particularly looking after such rich and little used ones as the Hessian. This might have made the brothers' wish come true, namely to live and die in Hesse.

Fate had decided differently.

Irritated and deeply depressed, Jacob and Wilhelm, encouraged by all their friends, handed in their resignation. It was accepted within twenty-four hours, and the Elector is reported to have uttered the words, often repeated since:

'The *Herren* Grimm propose to leave. A great loss! They have never done anything for me!'

The Elector had ridden roughshod over two men who might have given lustre to his reign.

At this moment of need there came an invitation from Göttingen University for Jacob to become Professor of Philology and librarian and for Wilhelm to serve as librarian. It was suggested that both should lecture. A document, signed by George IV at Windsor Castle, stated that Jacob was to receive one thousand, and Wilhelm five hundred thalers. This was an offer they could not afford to reject.

The brothers had maintained contacts with Göttingen over many years, and the university library had been willing to allow them access to any book they might need for their studies. Jacob had paid several visits to the town, and had received a friendly welcome always. Still, Göttingen seemed 'abroad' to two men who clung to their home like cats. After much heart-searching they took the plunge into the unknown, and accepted.

On 15 November 1829 Jacob wrote to his brother Ferdinand:

'. . . you will have been sorry to hear that we shall leave Cassel and Hessian service. It would have been better for our advancement and our future, if we had done this ten years earlier. However, may God bless this belated, but well considered decision, forced on us in every kind of way. After Völkel's death this year, we did not receive the promotion expected by everybody, and our fair due. This meant that all prospects for the future were cut off. The state of Hanover has now appointed us to Göttingen. I am to be professor in ordinary and librarian, and Wilhelm librarian. This allows us to continue our way of life together; without that we should not have considered the matter. I am to get a thousand, and Wilhelm five hundred thalers, apart from what we can earn by lecturing. We shall both have more work, at least to begin with. Lotte and Hassenpflug are sad about our leaving. Louis would come with us, but for the fact that for the last three months he has been engaged . . .'[17]

At the last minute, very unexpectedly and for reasons quite inexplicable, the Elector's mistress, *Gräfin* Reichenbach, spoke for the Grimms. Advances were made, but too late. The brothers' minds were made up, their sense of honour had gained the upper hand over their attachment to Cassel.

At the end of the year they left for Göttingen. One good friend was awaiting them there, the professor Georg Friedrich Benecke.

Mason's mark from
the Amtshaus
in Steinau

Tile from the
Town Hall
in Steinau

CHAPTER 10

The Move to Göttingen

1830 – 1836

THE Christmas days of 1829 were joyless, spent in an almost empty house, with 'all the usual order gone'. Dortchen, who was expecting another child, was unwell, and little Herman's only treat consisted of a small tree by his mamma's bedside.

On 28 December it was bitterly cold when Jacob and Wilhelm set out, alone, to travel to Göttingen. At the town gates in Cassel, giving their standing as 'Royal Hanoverian librarians', they burnt their boats. An icy wind blew all the time, making the six hours' journey in a carriage, which could only be half closed, a test of endurance. Wilhelm was worried about Jacob, who was suffering badly from the strain of the last few months. He also worried about a little pot plant which Jacob was sheltering under his big coat, perhaps one of their favourite wallflowers or primulas they hoped to save for their new home.

Through Professor Benecke's kindness the brothers found the stoves lit in their temporary lodgings, and some furniture placed in position. On 2 January they began their new work, still alone. With life uncomfortable and everything strange, the brothers were very homesick. Work in the library appeared heavy and boring, and in retrospect Cassel was sheer paradise. Jacob, tense and impatient, wondered whether leaving it had not been 'a silly thing altogether'. Though the famous university of Göttingen, founded in 1737, was a liberal forward-looking institution, and its library one of the finest in Germany, Jacob and Wilhelm did not appreciate their new surroundings. The library was nothing but a treadmill, and working there slavery, with not a moment even to look at all the books. Their immediate superiors seemed self-willed and difficult, attendance at university meetings a waste of time, and to Jacob, standing up to lecture somewhat theatrical.

Both longed for their Hessian solitude, the familiar scenes, the quiet walks just outside their own front door. In Göttingen, Jacob complained, even if one did manage to take a walk, university colleagues would turn up, wanting to chat, and never was one left to one's own thoughts.

The easier Wilhelm was a little less violent. On 8 March 1830 he was to write to Lachmann:

'. . . I don't quite know myself how I like it here . . .'

Lachmann, living in a big city, might not understand and consider it neurotic weakness if he, Wilhelm confessed that the strange countryside, strange hills and strange rooms affected him even more than all the strange faces. In short, it was all like wearing uncomfortable new clothes.[1]

In Cassel little Herman had fallen ill, too, just as Dortchen and the two maids, who were to come with the family to Göttingen, were ready for departure. Anxious days followed, till, by the middle of January, Wilhelm went to collect his family. He found the boy very frail, but with a temporary improvement in the weather the doctor advised travel, in a carriage well supplied with hot-water bottles.

With mother and son still in need of care and rest, the Göttingen household remained far from normal. Dortchen found it difficult to settle. It was all very well to be called *Frau Bibliothekarin* instead of *Frau Sekretärin*, as the strict German etiquette demanded, but there were no old friends round the corner, and life was more expensive too.

In the cold of winter Lotte waited for news.

On 20 January 1830 Wilhelm wrote to his sister:

'. . . You will have heard from Louis, to whom Dortchen sent a message through the coachman, that we have arrived safely. Night fell, and about half an hour's distance from Göttingen a cold wind began to blow, and made the windows of the coach freeze, so that we just arrived in time. The child was exceptionally good all the way in the coach. He played and looked at everything with curiosity, just like the late *Herr* Wild [the boy's grandfather] when he used to stand at his front door. Afterwards he slept quietly and peacefully through the night, and only coughed a little. Today he is so cheerful, fresh and strong, that I cannot thank God enough, and I am filled with great inner joy. Dortchen is working hard getting the house ready, so that I have often to implore her to take care of herself. A joiner has started to polish our favourite cupboard with the green silk curtains . . .'

'The child seems to know definitely that he is in a different place. But he does not know yet how everything can change so completely in one year, just as I feel has happened. As soon as I have settled a little, I will be able to say how I like it here. At the moment I still judge, and only when judging a thing has passed does true insight begin. I can see already that much is good . . .'[2]

For the time being, however, much that was good seemed left behind in Cassel. Jacob, particularly, hated the whole place, and for his inaugural lecture he chose the subject, *De desiderio patriae*. Though first and foremost a discourse on the German language, it revealed his own longing for the

Hessian homeland. Love for one's own country, he said, was something sacred, and deepened by absence.

Fortunately the stars in the sky were the same in Göttingen as in Cassel. There was also the comforting contact with the Cassel relations. Letters flew backwards and forwards, good wishes, presents and freshly baked cakes were exchanged on birthdays.

On 24 February, Ludwig Hassenpflug congratulated his brother-in-law on his birthday:

'. . . Lotte, Karl [their eldest son] and I have started celebrating your birthday today, by clinking glasses, and drinking your health at lunch . . . I am continuing the celebrations by telling you about them. Take my heartiest congratulations, dear Wilhelm. May the sadness about the home you have left – which is bound to overtake you today – be pushed aside by joy in your new circumstances, as I hope and believe it will be. But do keep us in your affection just as if we were still living in the same place. I say this in Lotte's name, too, as headaches, carrying babies about and sewing dresses have worn her out too much to write herself . . .'[3]

Karl Hassenpflug, Lotte's young son, in his own inimitable style wrote:

. . . 16 March 1831
'Dear Uncle Wilhelm,
'I have seen a woman at the fair who had gold on her bonnet. We also have a merry-go-round with small and large horses. Friedrich has ridden twice on a small one, and I just once. Friedrich [Lotte's second son] rode on a small brown, and I on a small white one. They laughed about Friedrich but not about me. I have been to the big hall at the fair. There were pictures inside and many people. There were also lots of toys and cloth and carts, drums and wheelbarrows . . .'[4]

Later that year he reported:

'. . . Dear Uncle Jacob,
'We have a new baby [Louis Hassenpflug], and I wish you could soon come again to Cassel, and I have drawn a picture for you which comes with this letter, and I wish you happiness and that you may be well.
'We are all very well, but my mother has been bitten by the stork, and beaten by its wings . . .'[5]

In March Rudolf, Wilhelm's second son to survive infancy, was born.

Things became a little better after the family had moved into a permanent home, in May of that year. It was in one of Göttingen's finest streets, the *Allee*, close to the library, which could be seen from the windows, and there were a few trees. The house was shared with a colleague, the philologist, Otfried Müller. They used a common lecture room on the ground floor, a circumstance much enjoyed by young Herman. When out for a walk, he could see his uncle standing talking, and nothing in the world would restrain him from shouting: 'Look, there's Apapa!' a name invented by him for Uncle who just seemed another Papa.

Gradually work became a little more attractive, and the liberal atmosphere of Göttingen began to impress itself on Jacob and Wilhelm. It was a contrast to the somewhat oppressive air of Cassel where, as Wilhelm had once remarked to a friend, one daren't throw away the wrappings of a sweet in case a policeman picked it up and read in it a secret message. The brothers became more sociable, and the very invitations and visitors, considered a nuisance earlier on, now became 'vernünftiger und guter Umgang', sensible good company, the mixing with their peers they had often missed in Cassel. They found sympathetic friends in the liberal historian, Christoph Dahlmann, and his wife, Luise. Hoffman von Fallersleben has described Göttingen social life in his autobiography. At a soirée at a professor's house, '... people greeted each other, were introduced and talked a little. Tea was served, later wine . . .', and so the party went on cheerfully. Eventually

Glazed tile

some of the men collected in little groups, telling stories and 'having much fun'. *Herr* Hoffmann von Fallersleben takes much pride in the fact that *tout* Göttingen was still laughing the next day about his own stories which were much repeated.[6]

There were outings, lunches and dinners. At Professor Benecke's house Jacob used to turn up late because he could not stand the smell of cigars, specially as Benecke smoked them – what horror – before dinner. Conversation was animated and intelligent.

All the time political events were clouding the skies. The princes having beaten the French, thought they had beaten the Revolution too. They completely failed to understand the signs of the time. The quiet waters of German *Biedermeier*, with its cosy withdrawal from public affairs into the domestic, were becoming more and more agitated. The man in the street now had an inkling of what liberty meant, and took a growing interest in matters formerly left to his superiors. The young, above all, were disgruntled, and stirring with liberal ideas. For long the universities had been places where youths from all over Germany met, and the thought of German unity was natural to them. In 1815 a new students' society had been founded in Jena, the *Burschenschaft*. Strictly Protestant, liberal, and nationalistic in outlook, it was opposed to the mumbo-jumbo of traditional student life. In 1817 the *Burschenschaft* had gathered at the *Wartburg*, in Thuringia, to celebrate the fourth anniversary of the Battle of the Nations, and the three hundredth of Luther's break with Rome. In their enthusiasm some five hundred students and a few professors had burnt conservative literature and emblems. The authorities were aroused, and when some eighteen months later a weak-minded student, backed by fanatics, assassinated the writer August von Kotzebue, said to be a secret agent in the pay of the Tsar, governments seized the opportunity to suppress all liberal tendencies, and issued the severe Carlsbad Decrees of 1819.

Then, in July 1830, Paris again experienced a revolution. The reactionary King Charles had to flee to make room for his portly Orleans cousin, Louis-Philippe, the *Roi-Citoyen*. Again there were repercussions, with sparks flying everywhere. Castles were burnt down and ministries stormed as the people rebelled against suppression in general and unwanted tolls and taxes in particular. In Cassel an angry mob stormed and looted the bakers' shops, and the Electress, now residing in Fulda to avoid her husband's mistress, had to seek military protection for her palace.

Wilhelm, on a journey, could not proceed to Steinau because of the unrest, and visited his protectress of old in Fulda, admiring her courage in a threatening situation.

Jacob was disturbed by the political turmoil, and his love of freedom offended by the strong measures taken to hold down subversive – demagogic – elements. Universities were closely watched, and books and newspapers censored. Friends of the brothers were involved, among them Jakob Joseph von Görres, fellow-enthusiast for the medieval. Though disillusioned with many aspects of the French Revolution he had once greatly admired, Görres was still a keen champion of liberty. His activities had aroused the displeasure of the Prussian government, and he was about to be arrested when he fled to find refuge among the manuscripts of the Strasbourg library. He then went to Switzerland, and eventually obtained a professorship in Munich under a liberal monarch.

Independent thinking, which after the Wars of Liberation had entered the stuffy atmosphere of the German middle class, took a severe blow. Burghers, frightened by police spies and the threat of imprisonment, returned to their parish pumps. Again, Jacob felt that everything was at stake. He was in despair, often wishing to hide in a quiet place, and live for his researches only.

About a year after their move to Göttingen Wilhelm was ill again. It was thought that the attack had been brought on by a cold he caught while guarding the library against a riotous mob. This time pneumonia was complicating the condition, and his life was in grave danger. Jacob was deeply depressed, dreading the thought of losing his brother when what remained of his own life would be nothing but constant sadness and longing. One day, during a lecture, he simply could not continue, and with great simplicity he apologized to his students, saying: '*Mein Bruder ist so krank*'. The severe sickness of his brother had put every other thought out of his mind.

However, the turn for the better came. Wilhelm recovered very very slowly, and gradually the feeling of health returned. At the height of his illness the sad news of their friend Arnim's death had reached the family. Wilhelm could not be told then, but he was to live to write the introduction to Arnim's complete works.

With the great relief of his brother's recovery Jacob began to feel happier. He dedicated the third part of his grammar to Wilhelm, the brother who knew and understood him well. Jacob also gained in status. The king conferred the title of *Hofrat* on him. His superiors had come to value him, and working conditions were slightly eased. In the autumn of 1831 he made up his mind to travel. He went to the south of Germany, and his reports of the trip sound relaxed and contented:

'. . . so I have once more trundled over a tiny piece of our globe, always sitting in the front of the cabriolet; before me the whole scene, with trotting horses and the postilions, dressed first in red, then blue and then yellow, their horns bobbing up and down on their backs . . .'[7]

The journey through meadows smelling of fresh hay, and woods scented with fallen leaves and pine cones, reminded Jacob of his childhood. As usual, he was satisfied with his own company, and did not mix much with his fellow-travellers, especially the ones from Prussia who might be carriers of the dreaded cholera, then raging there. So far, said Jacob, he hadn't caught it yet!

Staying in Cassel for three days, Jacob felt almost a stranger, visiting all the beloved spots, and spending a quiet hour at his mother's and aunt's graveside. Going further south his keen observation took in everything, from the layout of 'modern' towns to the dresses of the ladies, much influenced by French fashion, he thought. It must be reaching Darmstadt and Karlsruhe quickly from Strasbourg, more quickly than it became available to the good ladies of Frankfurt.

Fashions in Frankfurt must have impressed Jacob all the same, as from that city he sent home a shawl for Dortchen. He explained that it had been carefully chosen, with regard to material, colour, fashion, price and Dortchen's own taste. The Frankfurt ladies had offered advice, and 'black ground, with a pretty border' was at long last decided on.

A true scholar's trip, Jacob's journey was again to help research. He made excerpts in several libraries, and while in the Karlsruhe archives he had to leave his material behind for scrutiny. When he collected his texts later, he found them 'mutilated and brutalized'. Terrified officials had erased many harmless passages. From Kehl Jacob visited Strasbourg where the gates had just been re-opened after a small revolution. He enjoyed seeing a few old friends and some 'Frenchmen in their long red trousers'. At the Lake of Constance Jacob was joined by Werner von Haxthausen, with wife and child, and some Haxthausen relations, among them a Westphalian *Fräulein*. Together they continued to *Eppishausen*, the estate of the learned *Freiherr* Josef von Lassberg whom Jacob had met at the Vienna Congress. A gifted amateur, the *Freiherr* had accumulated a fine collection of books and manuscripts, and scholars were welcome guests at his hospitable home. A stay there would be a delight to Jacob, the passionate copier of all sorts of texts.

To his annoyance, however, some time was to be wasted on a four-day excursion into Switzerland – via Winterthur, Zürich and Lucerne to the Rigi. In the end it all proved very enjoyable. The 'Westphalian *Fräulein*' of the company was Jenny von Droste-Hülshoff, who had come straight from a visit to Cassel where she had missed Wilhelm very much. The tour to the Rigi was to decide her future, for, during it, the much older von Lassberg proposed to her, and was accepted. They were married in 1834, and came to 'lead a quiet, happy life',[8] as she told Wilhelm many years later. It was strange that at this important moment in Jenny's life her first love's brother should be so close.

In 1831 during his grave illness Wilhelm had also been made professor. To secure his possible widow access to a professors' widows' fund had been the chief intent. Now, the dignity brought with it the duty to lecture, putting Wilhelm into the same position as Jacob. He had to combine work at the library with preparation for his students. Wilhelm soon became very popular. His lectures were inspired, and covered a wide range of medieval German writing. Jacob lectured on ancient law, language, grammar and literature. He found it heavy going, and was often glad when there were too few students to continue a course. However, in time he gathered some enthusiastic admirers, among them Georg Gottfried Gervinus, who eventually became a fellow-professor at Göttingen. A few Englishmen also attended his lectures regularly.

Among these was John Mitchell Kemble, who already knew the Grimms through their published works, admired them, and was to become an ardent disciple of Jacob. Born into a famous theatrical family, the son of Charles Kemble, and nephew of Mrs. Siddons, John Mitchell had shown an early interest in the study of law, as illustrating ancient custom, history and language. After work at Cambridge and London, he, like many English students of his day, went first to Heidelberg and Munich and then to Göttingen to study Germanic philology.

Ties to Göttingen became close when Kemble married Natalie Auguste, daughter of Professor Johann Amadeus Wendt, a colleague of the Grimms, whom Jacob, on Kemble's discreet enquiry, had called 'a decent fellow'.[9]

A series of lectures on Anglo-Saxon themes, at Cambridge, and the edition of the *Poem of Beowulf*, in 1833, established Kemble's reputation in England. He dedicated *Beowulf* to the Grimms, warmly praising their work and their friendship. A treatise, published in German in Munich in 1836, *Über die Stammtafel der Westsachsen*, was dedicated to Jacob. In time, Kemble's fervent approval of German methods, together with slighting remarks about Anglo-Saxon studies in England, brought him into disfavour. He was violently attacked by British philologists, who called his work German-Saxon and accused him of being in bondage to Danish and German scholars.

Kemble's warm friendship for the Grimms was reciprocated, and lasted for many years. Jacob never saw the fulfilment of his wish to travel to England, but Kemble spent long periods of his life in Germany, when he was always a welcome and eagerly expected visitor to the Grimm household.

On 15 September 1834 Wilhelm was to write to their friend, Professor Friedrich Blume:

'. . . this Kemble is the first really likeable Englishman I have seen, young, handsome, lively, witty, not arrogant, and very learned in the Anglo-Saxon language . . .'[10]

This was praise indeed, as in the same letter another Englishman had been called 'as dry and stale as snuff' left over in a box!

Jacob's astonishing memory allowed him to lecture without detailed notes, glancing only now and then at a word on a small piece of paper. His delivery remained poor, and he never made an ideal lecturer. All the same, freed more and more from library work, lecturing became less of a drudgery, and he took on more at the death of a colleague. His lectures now included diplomatic for which his life-long study of documents and manuscripts had fitted him well.

In 1832 Jacob went to Heidelberg to work at the university library there. Once before he had found treasures here, mainly concerning animal fables. Visits to Cassel and Frankfurt to see old friends again were made on the way. The past was always alive to the brothers, and they never missed an opportunity to refresh common memories. Once Wilhelm asked his brother to bring a thaler's worth of Frankfurt ginger nuts home. These spiced biscuits may well have been a childhood treat.

In the late summer of 1832 a daughter, Auguste, was born to Wilhelm and Dortchen. The Electress honoured the family by becoming the baby's godmother. For once, life seemed to be running smoothly.

In June 1833 Dortchen and the children travelled to Cassel to find Lotte ill. Influenza and pneumonia were complicated by the premature birth of a daughter. Exhausted, Lotte expected to die at Whitsun, the very day their mother had died of lung trouble so many years ago. But she rallied, lovingly nursed by Dortchen, till Dortchen herself succumbed to illness. Wilhelm stayed by the sick women's bedside, reporting to Jacob, anxiously waiting for news in Göttingen. For days Dortchen's life seemed in danger while Lotte was slightly better. Then came the blow: complications set in, the doctors were helpless, and on the morning of 15 June Lotte Hassenpflug died. The sadness of this closely-knit family was great, only lightened by the need to care for all the young children. Dortchen recovered slowly.

That autumn, Wilhelm, much requiring a change, left to take the waters at Wiesbaden. The romantic scene of the nearby Rhine valley, with its vineyards and ruined castles, once more impressed him and refreshed his spirits. He went to Wiesbaden again in 1834, but this time the 'cure' exhausted him, and the old heart trouble became worse on his return to Göttingen. He was depressed, and could not attend to his work, spending whole days in fits of melancholia. He lost all his usual cheerfulness, retired into himself, taking no obvious interest in anything outside. Jacob and Dortchen stood by, worried, without being able to help. It was almost a year before Wilhelm began working again regularly.

In spite of private and public worries, the brothers continued to publish. Wilhelm immersed in the literature of the Middle Ages, had produced another edition of the *Hildebrandslied*, in 1830, then followed in 1834 a critical edition of *Vrîdankes Bescheidenheit*, a didactic poem, a picture of life and manners during the late thirteenth century, under Fredrick II. This emperor's crusade, in which the poem's author had joined, had occupied Wilhelm for some time. The *Rosengarten* appeared in 1836, and both brothers continued to write for many learned journals.

In 1834 Jacob published *Reinhart Fuchs*, taking High and Low German, Flemish and Latin texts as his sources. The book was well received, and encouraged further research into this particular cycle of beast fables.

For further work on the subject, and with a general interest in Flemish folk literature, Jacob decided on a journey to Belgium. In 1815, on returning from Paris, he had stopped in Brussels, charged with the unpleasant task of claiming, for the Hessian government, manuscripts and art treasures carried off by the French. Now he was paying a private visit. He was fortunate in discovering in Brussels a practically unknown Latin poem on the Fox and the Wolf, in two manuscripts. He copied them.

In a letter of 17 September from Brussels, he described the journey at length. He spent a couple of days in Cassel, walking the familiar streets, renewing old acquaintances, and eventually finding it 'inevitable to pay a few calls'. He enjoyed a drive to Wilhelmshöhe, but was quite glad to leave a town which did not hold pleasant memories only. From Cassel he went through parts of rural Westphalia to Cologne. Alas, it was Sunday, and the libraries were closed. Friends 'dragged' Jacob to the amusement park on the *Rheininsel* where there were great crowds and music. He fled to Aachen, with some quiet walks and an evening at the theatre where he saw Goethe's *Egmont* performed.

Jacob was much impressed by the Belgian coach service, an authorized private enterprise like the French. Coaches were cheaper and more efficient than in Germany. They accommodated twice as many people, including their luggage which was not conveyed separately. Drawn by three horses, the coach took 'only' twenty-two hours from Liège to Brussels, and the journey cost ten francs, not more than the fare from Göttingen to Cassel.

In fine sunny weather Jacob enjoyed the Belgian countryside, with the people looking 'wealthy and gay'. Women sitting in front of their houses in the evening, or walking arm in arm, village fairs, the tinkle of clarions, all seemed pleasant, radiating a Flemish gayness, lacking in the more stolid Dutch. The black hooded cloaks of Brussels women, Jacob believed to be of Spanish origin.

After visiting some libraries in smaller towns, without discovering much of interest, Jacob continued to Paris. A poster in the great library there said: *Vacances*—obviously the French librarians took life easier than their Göttingen counterparts![11]

Jacob returned late in September.

German Christmas and New Year confectionery

While work on the grammar went on, he finished – in 1835 – his important *Deutsche Mythologie*. In it Jacob traced the way the Germanic people had expressed religious feeling, faith and superstition in the myths they invented and told. He demolished the idea of myths being the creations of priests or philosophers. He believed them to be a further extension of 'folk poetry'. The *Mythology* was the beginning of a new era when scholars were to probe the past of the Germanic races in the same way classical scholars had investigated Antiquity.

CHAPTER 11

The Göttingen Seven

1837 – 1838

AFTER seven years of slow adaptation, Göttingen seemed more like home to Jacob and Wilhelm. Established now and happier, they worked with renewed keenness. It was satisfaction to see the appearance of the third edition of the *Household Tales*, a book on which much of their reputation with the general public rested. Wilhelm sent a copy to Bettina von Arnim, recalling how twenty-five years ago Arnim had driven them into publication.

Much had happened since those early Cassel days.

Jacob was completing the fourth and final part of his grammar, comparing himself, in the introduction, to a man making his way home after a day's hard walk. Nevertheless, he thought, his work on the German language was only a beginning.

In September 1837, Göttingen University, the *Georgia Augusta*, celebrated its centenary. It was to be an important gathering. The whole town was *en fête*, and visitors arrived in their hundreds. The Grimm family took an active part, receiving many guests, among them their brother Ludwig with a few Cassel friends. Ludwig gives a lively impression of the festivities, in his memoirs:

'. . . my brothers' house was pretty packed . . . the three of us had to sleep in one small room on the ground floor . . .'[1]

Visitors crowded the streets. Unfortunately, the weather was cool, dull and rainy so that the inns had not enough room for the cold and hungry. No wonder the Grimms' house felt like a dovecot. In the entrance hall a large table had been laid, permanently stocked with cold meats and glasses of red and white wine. Friends and even complete strangers came in and thoroughly enjoyed themselves. There were pageants and a great gala ball, with beautifully dressed ladies. Food and drink was free, and the students drank 'incredibly much'. Champagne glasses, smashed in high spirits, lay about everywhere, and drunks were put into a room specially

111

prepared for them. The king himself joined the party, 'tall, uniformed, white-haired, and with a white moustache'. But to Ludwig, 'his features had nothing agreeable'.

The observant painter of so many portraits had perhaps sensed in the king's face traces of that harshness of character he was soon to display.

On the death of William IV and the accession of Queen Victoria, Hanover was separated from England by virtue of the Salic Law, excluding females from the throne. Ernest Augustus, Duke of Cumberland, fifth son of George III, as the next male heir, had become King of Hanover. A man of strong reactionary tendencies, he considered the 1833 constitution, agreed upon by the king and the States, too liberal. With the connivance of submissive ministers he repealed this constitution in the autumn of 1837. The army as well as all civil servants, including the professors at Göttingen University, were to be released from their oaths.

The country as a whole showed little reaction but there was immediate consternation in university circles. Intrigue was ripe. Confidential audiences were given by the king at his hunting-box, *Rothenkirchen*, near Göttingen, and most professors, though secretly disturbed, appeased. '*Die Charaktere fingen an sich zu entblättern gleich den Bäumen des Herbstes bei einem Nachtfrost.*' In other words, the gentlemen feared for their bread and butter, and sought the expedient way out.

To Jacob and Wilhelm it was inconceivable that an oath should be broken, and that any monarch in the world should force his subjects to do so. The question was a moral, not a political one. Two weeks after the declaration, together with five other professors, they sent a protest to the king, explaining that they considered their oath binding.

Repercussions were not long in coming. On 11 December the king dismissed the seven protesting professors: Albrecht, Dahlmann, Ewald, Gervinus, Weber and the two Grimms. Wilhelm and three of the professors were allowed to remain in Göttingen meantime, while Dahlmann, Gervinus and Jacob, accused of being the ringleaders, and having distributed copies of the protest 'for publication abroad', were ordered to leave the country within three days or go to prison. At a hurriedly conveyed enquiry, the first time Jacob had ever appeared at a court of law, the three agreed that they had sent copies of the protest to friends, but with no thought of publication.

There had, of course, been observers quick in spreading the news. On the very day of the protest the afternoon edition of *Galignani's Messenger*, in Paris, carried this item:

'. . . "Letters from Göttingen", says the *Courier Français*, "state that seven professors in the university of that city refuse to take the oath of fidelity to the new King, and that should the university send a deputy to the States

The nanny at Hassenpflug's, telling fairytales, Christmas 1829. Pen and ink drawing by Ludwig Emil Grimm. Staatsarchiv, Marburg/Lahn

Bettina Brentano, 1809. Pencil drawing by Ludwig Emil Grimm. Brüder
Grimm Museum, Kassel

it will be merely to protest. This courageous determination is likely to exercise considerable influence on the public feeling. The universities of Germany are not only institutions for study, but are also political centres which give an impulse to the rest of the country. On the other side of the Rhine professors are regarded in some sort, as popular magistrates, commissioned to defend the rights of the people as well as the principles of reason.' ''[2]

Göttingen began to take notice. Citizens feared that the reputation of their university as a liberal institution was in danger, and the majority of students were in sympathy with 'The Seven'. Demonstrations were rigorously suppressed, a state of siege was declared, and military reinforcements brought into town. There were street fights, with students arrested in large numbers, and one seriously hurt. But nothing could stop the students from throwing stones into the windows of 'cowards', spontaneously cheering their heroes, indeed keeping up a running warfare with soldiers and police. A meeting on 15 December decided to send an address to the protesting professors, to boycott lectures, and not to ask fees back from the dismissed men.

When it became known that on 17 December Jacob and his companions were to be taken, under an escort of dragoons, to the Hessian border, many students prepared to provide a convoy. A penalty of twenty thalers was to be imposed on all owners of horses and carriages willing to furnish the students with transport. A large number of young men then clubbed together the previous night, and marched for six hours in the cold to the Hanoverian-Hessian border. At the bridge across the Werra in Witzenhausen they awaited the professors' coaches. They arrived at noon to an enthusiastic welcome. The students unharnessed the horses, and drew the coaches to a nearby inn where a cheerful meal followed, with speeches and toasts galore. Some students then returned to Göttingen while others hired carts to accompany the professors to Cassel, their immediate destination.

The 'Witzenhausen Escort' became a legend, and figures of the chief actors were later cast in lead, and sold as a toy: coaches, students and soldiers, with a red-cheeked, smiling Jacob, raising his hat to the crowds.

On the Hessian side of the border an old lady, pointing at Jacob, asked her grandson 'to shake hands with the gentleman, he is a refugee'.

And as 'refugees' the professors entered Cassel. Dahlmann and Gervinus were not allowed to take up residence, while Jacob was given a room in his old home, now his brother's house, in the *Bellevuestrasse*. Ludwig lived in this Böttner property as the husband of Marie, daughter of the late Wilhelm Böttner, *Hofmaler*, and professor at Cassel's art academy.

Dortchen, who had accompanied her brother-in-law, helped him to get settled, before returning to Göttingen alone. The lonely Jacob was grateful for her kindness, and expressed concern lest the journey home, in a rising wind, had done her harm.[3] He began immediately writing a pamphlet on his dismissal, *Jacob Grimm über seine Entlassung*. It was justification and accusation at the same time, and for reasons of censorship had to be published outside Germany, in Basle. Jacob spoke both for himself and his brother with whom, he explained, he had always shared everything. Their temporary separation was one of the hardships of his present situation. The flash of lightning which had struck his quiet existence, he said, was now agitating the hearts and minds of many, and for all who wished to know, matters must be made clear. There was, without doubt, much sympathy with their action, there was also criticism, and for many and varied reasons. Be that as it may. 'The world', continued Jacob – and how extraordinarily modern this sounds – 'is full of men who think and teach what is right. But as soon as they are called upon to act, they are assailed by doubts and fears . . .' All the chaos had been created by one simple fact, namely that an oath was sacred and could not be broken. This truth had to be asserted, and there was no time to look around to see what others were to think or do. It was all the more painful that the encroachment on human rights should have come from a man, brought up under the British Constitution, 'a long established and excellent order', in a country where the permanence of institutions had always been highly respected. Jacob finished by saying: 'As long as there is breath in me, I will be glad of what I have done, certain that whatsoever may survive of my work, will not lose but gain by my action'.

Strangely enough, in most German states the sale of Jacob's pamphlet was not forbidden. It was sold even in Göttingen, then quickly withdrawn. Those who had bought and wanted to keep the brochure were made to sign a declaration to that effect. There were many readers, many who admired the men who, in Jacob's words, 'had a conscience, even when faced with supreme power'. Waves of warmth and sympathy reached the 'exiles'. Whole towns and universities collected money, and expressed their admiration. Admiration for the Göttingen protest spread to all liberally-minded Germans. Old Solomon Heine gave a thousand marks to the funds, and in Cuxhaven a ship was named *Professor Dahlmann*. A *Hilfsverein* was formed to administer money collected.

There were, too, many and unexpected proofs of personal sympathy and affection. In Göttingen the precentor of the Reformed Church who tutored Wilhelm's son, Rudolf, refused to accept the normal school fees. Though not a wealthy man, he kept refusing stubbornly to take money from a dismissed professor. When Dortchen thanked him for his kindness and loyalty, he replied: '*Frau Professorin,* faithful unto death!'

114

For Jacob's quiet taste there were far too many visitors in Cassel, the sympathetic and the curious. What mattered to him most, apart from work, was to keep in close contact with Wilhelm. They arranged to meet halfway, and Wilhelm once came to Cassel. For the rest, letters had to convey all news, big and small. One piece of news at that period gives an indication of the Grimms' simple and lovable domesticity, even in hard times. Jacob reported that, alas, there was a bit of bad news: mould had formed on his favourite cherry preserve, and what could be done about it![4] Little presents were constantly exchanged between Cassel and Göttingen, and once Jacob asked – if this was not too bold a request – for a new pair of braces made of not too coarse a material. He was sorry he could not send a sample, as the ones he was wearing were the only ones he possessed.

Meantime the King of Hanover made light of his professors' dismissal, uttering the inelegant statement that 'dancers, whores and professors could always be got easily for money'.

But there were also well-wishers in quite unexpected quarters. The King of Saxony declared that he was on the side of the seven professors, and would gladly receive them all. In fact, Professor Dahlmann had found temporary refuge in Leipzig, and was anxious that the Grimms should join him there, though not all Dahlmann's experiences were agreeable either. When he decided to publish his own version of the Göttingen affair, the Minister of the Interior created obstacles, and Dahlmann reported to Jacob that his last words at the Ministry had been: 'If your Excellency's views should become generally accepted, it would be better to live in Turkey than in Germany'.[5]

Most German princes were reluctant to make offers to 'The Seven', anxious not to offend Ernest Augustus of Hanover. The *Freiherr* von Lassberg tried to secure the brothers for Zürich University, but the matter was not pursued. The universities of Leyden and Paris also made tentative proposals.

A plan of far-reaching importance was being prepared in Saxony. In the spring of 1838, encouraged by the philologist, Professor Moritz Haupt, the owners of the *Weidmannsche Buchhandlung*, Salomon Hirzel and Karl Reimer, suggested that Jacob and Wilhelm should begin work on a large dictionary of the German language. Though the suggestion was certainly prompted by the wish to help two scholars, the need for a comprehensive German dictionary was very real. There had been minor ones in the past, and the only standard one, Johann Christoph Adelung's *Grammatisch-kritisches Wörterbuch der hochdeutschen Mundart*, 1793-1801, was now inadequate. Work on the dictionary was to make the brothers independent, still able to continue their own researches. It was thought that in time Jacob might also be offered a professorship in Leipzig, and that both would live there.

The matter needed discussion, and as Jacob was not allowed to enter the Kingdom of Hanover, it was arranged to meet Wilhelm at Heiligenstadt. Dortchen and the children accompanied him. Ludwig joined Jacob. Even this 'restless' reunion was enjoyed by the brothers, and on the way back to Cassel, Jacob and Ludwig had an amusing adventure. Stopping at an inn for something to eat, they met two men who were talking about the 'Göttingen Seven', and the 'Witzenhausen Escort'. Suddenly one turned to Jacob, and remarked proudly: '. . . and I saw Grimm there, with my own eyes!'

The suggestions from Saxony appealed to Wilhelm but less so to Jacob, who was not attracted by Leipzig as a permanent residence. Dahlmann was enthusiastic, and insisted that Jacob should at least undertake the journey to Saxony to see the possibilities for himself. In June the Dahlmanns were taking the waters at Kissingen spa, and Jacob joined them there to talk matters over.

He had visited Saxony before, in 1811, when he had searched the Gotha, Leipzig and Dresden libraries for manuscripts. It was then that in Weimar he missed Goethe who had shortly before left for his summer holiday. Dresden had impressed Jacob as a very fine city with much of its old town still intact, its broad new squares and streets full of lively people. Leipzig had not left such a favourable impression.

In a letter to Dortchen, of 12 June 1838, Jacob described his journey:

'. . . at six o'clock on Saturday I arrived safely in Fulda, and came here on Sunday at five. Not to have to wait about in Fulda, I hired a carriage which allowed me to break the journey in fine weather at Brückenau, and take half an hour's walk to the nearby spa. This is delightful country, woods and meadows, and I walked the very paths my aunt Schlemmer and my godfather and uncle – whom I only know from a portrait – must often have taken some fifty or sixty years ago . . . The king has had a splendid pump-room built, with spacious halls . . . The countryside around Fulda and in Franconia is full of lovely rich meadows such as do not exist in Hesse, certainly not in Hanover where there are more ploughed fields which are not so pleasing to the eye.

'But I am sure you would rather hear about people. I put up at the *Kurhaus*, not knowing where the Dahlmanns were staying, and intending to find out from the lists of guests there. I then discovered that they were at the *Kurhaus* itself, on the same floor, just a few doors away from me. They had gone out to the *Kurgarten* to watch a group of tight-rope-walkers. Dahlmann was the first to discover me in the crowd, and there was great joy all round . . .'[6]

As the Kissingen 'cure' was said to be good for everybody, Jacob was persuaded to stay a little for his health's sake. He drank the waters, tasting of iron and sulphur, and did not like them very much. Promenading in the park, he once or twice passed his former employer, the Hessian Elector, who was among Kissingen's guests that summer. Neither gave a sign of recognition. After some two weeks Jacob continued his journey. He first visited Würzburg and Nuremberg where he saw Albrecht Dürer's grave in the old *Johannesfriedhof*. He enjoyed Nuremberg's medieval architecture, and was equally thrilled to travel on the brand-new railway from Nuremberg to Fürth. He much preferred Nuremberg to Fürth 'a new developing town', and after his short but exciting journey, he walked in a spinney of birches to recover from so much modernity, speed and noise!

Jacob then went to Erlangen and Bamberg, admiring that city's beautiful situation and baroque splendour. Everywhere he met friends, was fêted by teachers and students, but carefully avoided public ovations. Via Coburg he eventually reached Leipzig, and reported to the family:

'. . . I am receiving much friendship and marks of respect here, but my general impression of the town is not favourable. It is too fashionable, and taking in the suburbs too big, full of dust and noise . . .'[7]

Houses, he said, were expensive, and the cheaper ones neither pleasant nor comfortable.

In view of much kindness and hospitality Jacob found it difficult to give his decision. Regarding a move to Leipzig it had to be a negative one, about the dictionary itself he was hesitant. He was attracted, but the undertaking was enormous, and he had reservations concerning the time the work would take. Also, never having had a commission, to work 'to order' seemed alien. Jacob parleyed.

In the end both brothers became convinced that it was their duty to accept the proposal. The scheme would provide valuable means towards financial independence which they treasured highly.

In a letter to Lachmann, of August 1838, Jacob explained that the dictionary was to be concerned with the living language but would also go back to the sixteenth, seventeenth and eighteenth centuries. To collect words in use only, would limit the scope, and endanger the work's purpose. He recognised clearly how quickly a language changes, remarking that some expressions and idioms used by Lessing and Wieland were already obsolete. 'All words of beauty and strength since Luther's day'[8] was the ultimate aim, and to present in that way the genuine wealth of the German language.

Negotiations over, Wilhelm and family were now to join Jacob in Cassel,

117

and take up domicile where there were at least traces of former association. Dortchen and Jacob looked at several houses. Then the ground floor of Ludwig's and Marie's house became vacant in October, an opportunity too good to miss. The move was prepared in Göttingen, longingly awaited by Jacob. Ludwig and Marie, he admitted, had been very kind, but Wilhelm, Dortchen and the children alone spelt home to him.

Sugar container belonging
to the Grimm family

Earthenware
baking dish

CHAPTER 12

Exiles in Cassel

1838 – 1840

FEELING like revenants, the brothers began working once more in their familiar surroundings. Wilhelm enjoyed living on the ground floor where for the first time he could shake hands with friends through the window. Jacob was happily engaged in sorting out books and papers. The stillness was beneficial, and they came to believe that leaving the 'Göttingen bustle' had been providential. Jacob always found working in his study and by himself most profitable, and to have exchanged public life for a private one was agreeable to both. They were sick of hearing the Göttingen affair discussed over and over again, and avoided social gatherings more than ever. There was no lack of work, and schemes for the future employed them fully.

To begin with, domestic life was unsettled. Dortchen had hurt her foot in the removal. She was exhausted and limped about the house with difficulty. Bettina von Arnim came to help and comfort. In a letter to a friend Jacob described her visit with mixed feelings:

'. . . in the midst of unpacking (on the 20th), Bettina arrived to pay her long-promised visit, and nothing more was unpacked or put into order. Instead, all kinds of tales were heard, and the most daring plans for our future listened to and discussed . . . her ideas and her talk are always lively, witty and exciting, though at the same time extravagant and uncontrolled. She gives pleasure and comfort, without really being able to help . . .'[1]

As it turned out, Jacob underestimated Bettina's passionate determination to help her old friends. Jacob's and Wilhelm's sympathetic support in the controversy over the publication of her correspondence with Goethe, in 1834, was fresh in her mind. Jacob's favourable review in the *Göttingsche Gelehrte Anzeigen* had done much for the immediate and universal success of Bettina's book.

Wilhelm's children – the boys now at the Cassel *Gymnasium* – and Gustchen, a cheerful little girl, provided pleasant distraction, and with

119

Dortchen's health improving, routine was established at length. In Göttingen Wilhelm had begun working on an edition of the *Rolandslied*, published meanwhile, while Jacob, together with Professor Schmeller of Munich, had edited some Latin poems of the tenth and eleventh centuries.

Now work on the *Wörterbuch* was to begin in earnest.

Hundreds of books would have to be read and excerpts made. It was essential to secure collaborators. The brothers wrote to philologists in many places, and most of them were keen to be associated with a brave venture. Soon some fifty regular contributors could be counted on, and they began working out rules. He laid down the size of paper slips to be used, and the precise way of noting words. All words were to be given in the context of the whole phrase, quoting idioms and proverbs wherever possible. Only in that way would a true picture of the language be conveyed.

Fully aware of the many difficulties ahead, the Grimms began sifting the first material early in 1839. They compared their work to splitting wood for a few hours every day. The more their card indexes became filled, the more the enormousness of the undertaking weighed on their minds. As Jacob was to remember later, 'words seemed to appear from all nooks and crannies', settling on their desks like snow on the countryside in winter. Would this huge mass of words fit into the projected seven volumes, and would the brothers' lives be long enough to finish the task? They began to wonder.

Meantime Jacob was re-thinking his grammar for a third edition of the first volume. He also worked regularly on the *Weistümer*, his collection of ancient law practices which was to provide further source material to the history of Germanic law. Wilhelm edited more medieval texts: Werner vom Niederrhein (1839), and Konrad von Würzburg's *Goldene Schmiede* (1840).

With no clear future in view Jacob and Wilhelm were once more wrapped up in their day-to-day work, done quietly without interference from outside. Now and then the question of academic appointments came up, but, said Jacob, in a letter to John Mitchell Kemble of 23 December 1839, he was 'very contented with the present mistiness'.[2] Not wishing for careers which would separate them, the brothers lacked neither in courage nor firmness. On 11 October 1839 Wilhelm wrote to Professor Dahlmann:

'. . . the greater the tribulations the more reason to pluck up courage, and leave the inevitable to God. I have often seen that He will find ways we have ourselves not thought of . . .'[3]

Two years soon passed.

In September 1840 Wilhelm sent a copy of the new – fourth – edition of the *Household Tales* to Bettina von Arnim, thanking her for the sympathy she had shown ever since 'those fateful days'.

Nobody had certainly worked harder in the interest of the brothers than Bettina. Immediately after the Göttingen protest she began agitating for them in Berlin, stressing that as a member of the *Akademie der Wissenschaften* Jacob had the right to reside and lecture in the Prussian capital, and that both brothers should be officially invited to Berlin. Bettina's chief intermediary was her brother-in-law, von Savigny. After a couple of years in the Chair of Jurisprudence in Landshut, he had come to Berlin in 1810. Apart from his academic appointment, he held a number of State offices.

Savigny was sympathetic but cautious. He had certain reservations about the Göttingen protest, considering the brothers 'innocent but misled'. Bettina continued pressing. At length Savigny tried to obtain a subsidy for the Grimms' work from the *Akademie*. The brothers were reluctant to accept, and their reluctance was interpreted by some as over-sensitivity, even obstinacy. On 11 June 1839 Wilhelm explained in a letter to Bettina:

'. . . responsibility for the temporary refusal to accept a subsidy from the Berlin Academy – of which you have heard – rests not with Jacob but with me. Savigny wrote not to him but to me. I therefore replied according to my own independent judgement, without even asking Jacob. He only expressed his agreement in a postscript. I will now explain the whole matter to you.

'Savigny had asked me for a plan of the *Wörterbuch*, with detailed synopsis, setting out our ideas. He remarked with the most obvious kindness that the *Akademie* possessed funds to assist such scholarly enterprises, and that he hoped to make a successful application. I described our plans in my reply, and continued: ". . . support from the *Akademie* would honour us. That is, provided it can be given by the academy's free and independent decision. Should such a decision, however, need higher consent or even approval, the whole matter would take on a different aspect, and from our point of view difficulties would arise. This is by the way. Moreover, the *Akademie* can only use its funds for schemes the success of which is above all doubt. We have not reached that state yet. Our cause will only merit support when the main bulk of the preliminary work is finished. To accept any help earlier would be an embarrassment . . ."'[4]

Meantime, Wilhelm continued, their immediate needs were catered for. They were working in peace, and what more could they wish for. It would be better to delay an application to the academy though he and his brother were fully aware of the love and friendship that had prompted the thought.

This very typical letter was aimed at those who had criticized the brothers. Savigny, for one, was annoyed. This did not daunt Bettina in the least. On 4 November 1839 she told Savigny that every other nation in the world would have recognized the Grimms' greatness, shown both in their personal integrity and their scholarly achievements. The people of Germany, however, stood by, indifferent, while the academy merely bothered about the brothers being oversensitive.[5] It was time, said Bettina, for Prussia's king to take a lead. She repeated her assault early in December.[6]

In a letter, dated Cassel 26 December 1839, Jacob once more explained to Bettina:

'. . . about our Göttingen protest I need not say much more. To me it seems and has always seemed very easy to understand. Right and wrong, and the voice of conscience are all that need be considered. Neither politics nor expediency should come into it; or put it this way: to act according to what is right and listen to the voice of conscience, will in the end also be right from the point of view of politics and expediency, and justifiable before God. We did not take into account success . . . Without our protest sheer might would have triumphed, and the whole affair been hushed up . . .'[7]

In the end Savigny yielded.

Alexander von Humboldt who had the ear of the Prussian court, and had known and appreciated Jacob in Paris, spoke in favour of the brothers. The Crown Prince had long been among their admirers, and he, too, tried to exert his influence. For the time being, all efforts were doomed. Frederick William III, a kinsman through his late wife, Queen Louisa, of the King of Hanover, was uneasy, fearful to offend him, by appointing members of 'The Seven' to Berlin.

Then, on 7 June 1840, the king died, to be succeeded by his son, Frederick William IV, sometimes called 'a high-minded dreamer', or 'The Romantic on the throne'; he was full of liberal ideas, notwithstanding his firm belief in the God-given right of princes. Soon after his accession he declared an amnesty for political prisoners, setting free many members of a liberal intellectual élite. There were tremendous cheers, and at once rumours started concerning the Grimms. Their possible appointment to Berlin was discussed openly in diplomatic circles, and soon negotiations began. The new king was interested in literature and the arts. He reinstituted Ernst Moritz Arndt and *Turnvater* Jahn, both victims of political persecution, and appointed Dahlmann to a chair at Bonn University.

At the beginning of August 1840, most likely on the instigation of her husband, *Frau* von Savigny stopped in Cassel, on her way to Frankfurt. Praising the new king, she tried to probe the brothers' feelings with regard to Prussian appointments. Jacob let it be understood that he did not feel inclined to make use of his right to establish himself in Berlin as a member of the *Akademie*. The inducement would have to be stronger. After that, things began to move in earnest, and eventually the Prussian Minister of Education, Johann Albrecht Friedrich Eichhorn, was instructed to make an approach to the Grimms. Eichhorn, who knew and respected the brothers highly, had, in fact, befriended Jacob in Paris in 1815 and was now pleased with the opportunity of showing his friendship by conveying the king's message to them.

In recognition of the brothers' untiring labour for German language and literature, the king desired to put them into a position where they could continue their work on the great dictionary in security, with the resources of Prussia's capital at their disposal. The king therefore invited them to come to Berlin, holding out the possibility of academic positions later on. Jacob, as a member of the *Akademie*, had the right to lecture, while Wilhelm as a corresponding member only, would be appointed in time. The brothers were to receive two thousand thalers annually between them, and a subsidy of five hundred thalers towards the cost of removal.

Jacob's reply came quickly. Quietly and with dignity he accepted the king's invitation, with 'grateful and joyous expectation'.

'. . . our lives', he said, 'are past their zenith. All we can wish for is to devote the rest of our days to completing our work concerning the language and history of our beloved country. The king's generosity will allow us the carefree leisure needed for such a task . . .'[8]

They would, he added, as brothers should, divide the salary into two equal parts.

Jacob expressed his intention of travelling to Berlin soon in order to find out whether a move was feasible during the winter. It would then be his pleasure to express his thanks personally, and to receive further instructions from the king.

Sudden security came almost as a shock to the brothers, and the thought of having to live in a big city was bewildering. All the same, satisfaction and 'joyous expectation' prevailed.

On 16 November Jacob wrote to Bettina:

'. . . my eyes are wide open. I shall go to Prussia not expecting heaven. Rather do I forsee more battles before justice and freedom will eventually prevail. However, the king is full of pure and noble intentions . . . What more could we hope for in any German state? . . .'[9]

Early in December Jacob travelled to Berlin, a city he had not visited before. His host there was to be Karl Hartwig Gregor von Meusebach, President of the Court of Appeal, a much respected jurist and scholar and a loyal friend of long standing. By Jacob's judgement he had one vice only, his 'cursed tobacco smoking'! The owner of a fine collection of German sixteenth-century books, Meusebach was a much-loved man with a great sense of humour. This came out in many, sometimes grotesque ways. He had a fondness for making up *Klebebriefe*, documents carefully pasted together from scraps, and only recognisable as such under a magnifying glass. He had once sent one to the Grimms, reading: 'Nursery and House-hold Tales by the Brothers Grimm. Large edition, with two engravings, elegantly bound, four thalers. Children pay half.'

Soon after the Göttingen protest Meusebach had invited Jacob to make his temporary home with him and his wife in Berlin. Jacob had then gratefully declined, but now he was glad to accept Meusebach's generous hospitality. On 8 December he reported to Wilhelm:

'. . . I have arrived here, safe and sound, at a quarter to five this morning. The weather has been bright and mild during the whole journey, turning a little cold only in the early hours of the mornings. During the first night I felt stiff and sore, but was all right during the second. I was tired, however, and in need of sleep. Against my usual habit, I did not manage to close my eyes much in the coach. My arrival in Berlin was something of an adventure. At the posting house I took a carriage to the Meusebachs at Number 36 *Karlstrasse*. It was easy enough to find the street but not the numbers. The moonlight casting heavy shadows, made it impossible to see them. After a lot of groping about and asking night watchmen, we found the house at last. My portmanteau was put down, and I began ringing the bell. But not a soul appeared, and there was no light anywhere. This state had lasted for some half hour when at length someone woke up downstairs. On my enquiry I was told that the Meusebachs did live here. I then climbed two stairs to find another locked door where once more I started ringing. But everybody seemed sound asleep or deaf. So I sat on the stairs till about six o'clock when at last I saw a light appear on the first floor, and I went towards it . . .'[10]

A stranger made coffee for the tired Jacob, handed him the morning paper, and told him that the *Präsidentin* – *Frau* von Meusebach – would still be asleep. At the more polite hour of eight o'clock *Frau* von Meusebach, unaware till then of her guest's early arrival, welcomed him warmly, and led him to his room. He rested for a few hours, and then began the rounds of the capital.

Jacob's main object was to find a suitable house, and for people of moderate means this meant a lease. Looking around took longer than expected, and only shortly before Christmas Jacob could report:

'. . . all last week, . . . in the icy cold, I have run around hunting for a house. I have seen many in several parts of the city, certainly more than twenty, and heard everybody expressing different opinions about them . . .'[11]

In the end, and again with Bettina's help, a house had been found, pleasant and comfortable, 'which all of you will like, and which will make up for much else'. A lease was arranged for two years, starting at Easter 1841, at a cost of about four hundred and seventy-five thalers annually.

There were some ten rooms and a balcony, and the only drawback seemed to be that the children would have a twenty minutes' walk to school. This, however, was more than compensated by the situation of the house, 'quiet, open and cheerful', and much reminiscent of Cassel's parks, with a feeling of the country about it. The learned bachelor did not forget to mention that all immediate household needs were catered for within easy distance.

The Grimms' future home was in the *Lennéstrasse*, its front overlooking the *Tiergarten*. The eastern part of the *Tiergartenstrasse* had been renamed *Lennéstrasse* in honour of Peter Josef Lenné, director of the royal parks, who had re-designed the somewhat neglected *Tiergarten* in the new 'English' manner. Like the gifted *Fürst* Pückler-Muskau, Lenné was one of the early propagators of the *englische Garten* in Germany.

Since the end of the Napoleonic Wars wealthy citizens had built graceful large houses at the edge of Berlin's great park. Many belonged to the intelligentsia, among them old Henriette Herz whose salon had earlier on been the meeting-place of brilliant men and women. Builder and owner of the Grimms' house was Friedrich Hitzig, architect of many fine neo-classical buildings, and later president of the Prussian *Akademie der Künste*.

Friends crowded round Jacob, the salons took him up, and everybody wanted to see him. There was endless sociability and much talk. Bettina was always there, and Alexander von Humboldt, kindly disposed at all times. He advised Jacob to speak to Eichhorn about an increase in the suggested allowance. This was done. Jacob dined at the hospitable home of his publisher, Georg Andreas Reimer, and was pleased to hear that yet another edition of the *Household Tales* would soon be wanted. Savigny and fellow-professors took him about to learned societies, and he heard papers being read at the *Akademie*, some of them 'boring'. Soon Jacob felt exhausted with the running about, visits and endless talk. Once again he longed for quietness, had misgivings, and began to fear Berlin life a little.

The proposed few days in the city had developed into weeks. It took time to settle things, an audience with the king was delayed by court festivities, and the 'restless boredom' continued. It was on 24 December that Jacob could at long last look forward to returning. After an audience with the king, the move could now be fixed definitely for March of the following year. The return journey was planned via Halle and Jena, with

125

only short breaks, to be able soon to knock one morning early at the well known shutters in Cassel. There would be much to tell.

On 25 December, under 'departure of strangers', the Berlin list of visitors could report in its orderly Prussian manner that the *Hofrat* and Professor Jacob Grimm had on that evening departed for Halle.

Early in the new year the brothers received confirmation that their joint salaries were raised to three thousand thalers. For the first time in their lives they were free from financial worries.

On 19 February 1841 the brothers' good friend and protectress, the Electress Augusta, aunt of their new employer, died after a short illness. They were saddened by the loss, and Wilhelm remembered in a letter to a friend how not long ago during a party, the Electress had reminisced about the Berlin of her childhood, when she had seen Frederick the Great in Potsdam.[12]

Soon Berlin was to mean home to Jacob and Wilhelm.

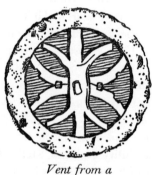

*Vent from a
cellar in Steinau*

*German
earthenware pot*

CHAPTER 13

Finding New Roots

1841 – 1843

AT the middle of March 1841 two huge carts rolled out of Cassel, carrying the Grimms' many boxes of books and all their other belongings. The family followed a day or two later, and took almost a week to reach Berlin, delay being caused by having to avoid roads made impassable by rivers in flood. Another week had to be spent at an inn before the new house was ready for occupation. Again, the brothers' studies were next to each other, and the view of trees bursting into leaf made a happy welcome to a city entered with secret trepidation. In the tremendous change it was comfort to find that Prussia's capital still possessed some semi-rural corners. The city's noisy centre was very different from its periphery near the great park, the one-time hunting-ground of Prussia's rulers.

On 25 April Wilhelm wrote to their friend Dahlmann:

'. . . we live at the *Lennéstrasse* (No. 8), away from the centre, at the edge of the *Tiergarten* which, carefully kept and adorned with flowers and goldfish, has a pleasant and cheerful appearance, particularly now that the first green is out. Also, most days we enjoy country-like peace, while in the city itself the constant rattling of *Droschkes* is disturbing, and the sight of streets, straight as a line, with no visible end to them, makes me quickly tired . . .'[1]

In 1841 Berlin was a rapidly growing city. From some hundred and forty-five thousand inhabitants in 1784, its population had almost doubled. Ever since the seventeenth century the city had expanded from its medieval core. A bigger and bigger garrison, the influx of people from the country and the settling of French Protestants, bringing new trades, had swelled Berlin's population. The *Dorotheenstadt*, begun as a suburb on land belonging to the Electress Dorothea, grew in importance mainly under the influence of the French *émigrés*. Two famous Berliners were of French origin: *Baron* de la Motte Fouqué, of whose romantic writings *Undine* has stood the test of time, and Adelbert von Chamisso, lyric poet,

127

at one time custodian of Berlin's Botanical Gardens, and creator of *Peter Schlemihl*, the man who lost his shadow.

The *Friedrichsstadt*, with its regal streets, 'straight as a line', built by Frederick the Great, gradually became more crowded, and *Unter den Linden*, Prussia's broad lime-planted *Via triumphalis* was laid out. Castles were built and splendid houses for the aristocracy and members of the quickly rising professional and industrial classes. As in all major cities, money and fashion went west, allowing some of the humble, once decent quarters of the north and east to go down in the social scale, and eventually decay into slums.

The city's growth was accompanied by cultural developments. In 1659 the *Preussische Staatsbibliothek* was founded by the Great Elector, then given its own building by Frederick the Great, while the year 1700 saw the start of the *Preussische Akademie der Wissenschaften*, to be followed a little later by an academy of art. There were many schools and teaching centres. The French Revolution and its aftermath of wars had called a halt to expansion. The court went into exile, and the citizens became impoverished through the heavy burden of Occupation and the stagnation of commerce and trade. A few bad harvests caused conditions of near-famine in the countryside.

Only after the collapse of Napoleon's power did things improve again gradually, and then Berlin began to build feverishly. Under the gifted architect, Carl Friedrich Schinkel, churches, theatres, museums, civic buildings, elegant bridges and private houses were erected. Schinkel's inspired neo-classicism created a 'Berlin style', dignified, noble and graceful. After his early death in 1841 his and his disciples' influence made itself felt for another decade or so. Then, his Greek columns, imposing flights of stairs and lofty domes had to yield to unplanned and unrestrained growth. By one of those lucky accidents there was working in Berlin at Schinkel's time the sculptor, Christian Daniel Rauch. A valet to King Frederick William III, he had been helped by a nobleman to study art in Rome, and was then commanded by the king to return to the capital. There he executed monuments and statues of kings and queens, soldiers and poets which suited the mood of Schinkel's buildings to perfection. Also working in the city at that time was Johann Gottfried Schadow, the sculptor remembered best for his quadriga on the Brandenburg Gate.

Between 1813 and 1815 Berlin had played a special part in the national revival. Fichte gave his *Addresses to the Nation* in the old academy. Schleiermacher preached unity and a new responsibility of the individual, while *Turnvater* Jahn showed old and young how to keep physically fit, his stadium, the Berlin *Hasenheide*, becoming a rallying ground for patriots. Literature, science and the arts flourished in the years to follow, suffering

Geb. den 10ten Junius 1762.

Georg Friedrich Benecke, Professor and Chief Librarian at Göttingen.
Pencil drawing by Ludwig Emil Grimm. Historisches Museum, Hanau

View from the Grimms' home at Göttingen. Water-colour (artist
unknown). At one time owned by the Brothers Grimm. Staatsarchiv,
Marburg/Lahn

Lesekränzchen, Cassel, 1827. Pen and ink drawing by Ludwig Emil
Grimm. Brüder Grimm Museum, Kassel

severe setbacks in the reactionary period of the Carlsbad Decrees, when the *Wartburg* Festival of 1817, and the murder of Kotzebue in 1819, had served governments as a pretext to enforce stern measures against all liberal thought. Many outstanding men, among them Wilhelm von Humboldt, Schleiermacher and the Grimms' publisher, Georg Andreas Reimer, were persecuted in true police-state fashion.

In 1810, through the initiative of Wilhelm von Humboldt, Berlin University had been founded, with lectures in the *Prinz Heinrich Palais*. From the beginning it became a gathering-place for men of distinction. After thirty years, and with some two thousand students, it was in the forties one of the most important universities in Germany. Its reputation attracted foreign students, among them Jakob Burckhardt from Switzerland, and the Dane, Sören Kierkegaard, who considered Berlin Europe's foremost university. Outstanding in Berlin's brilliant galaxy were Franz Bopp, the philologist, August Boeckh, classical antiquary and explorer of the Homerian world, the Grimms' friend and colleague, Karl Lachmann, Leopold von Ranke, the historian, and, of course, von Savigny whom the king had made his Minister of Justice in 1842. Hegel, exponent of Germany's idealistic philosophy, had taught here till his death from cholera in 1831, and for a short spell August Wilhelm von Schlegel held the Chair of Literature and Fine Art.

A still active power in Berlin's cultural life was the ageing Alexander von Humboldt. He had managed to combine liberal ideas with being close to the court, and in that way had been in a position to influence many decisions. In the twenties he had lectured on the *Cosmos*, the physical universe, and had been initial in founding the *Gesellschaft für Erdkunde*, after the French, the oldest geographical society. Berlin had become a name in science through men like Dirichlet, the mathematician, the chemists Mitscherlich and Rose, and the astronomer Encke. The year 1841 saw the start of Berlin's zoological park on the site of the *Fasanerie*, the king's former pheasant preserve.

The social life of Berlin's intelligentsia was possessed of genuine culture and grace. A tradition had grown for court circles, aristocracy and the liberal bourgeoisie to mix freely in the salons. In an atmosphere where large public gatherings were sometimes frowned upon or even forbidden, many societies had sprung up. There was the *Mittwochgesellschaft*, famous for its Goethe celebrations, the *Gesetzlose Gesellschaft*, and the *Tunnel über der Spree*, where mainly artists and writers met on a Sunday. In all these associations questions of the day might be discussed which a censored press was not allowed to print, also the aesthetic might provide an escape from at times unpleasant realities.

There were concerts, Paganini had played here, now it was Liszt, and

I   129

music was made in the home. For a short while – on the king's invitation – Felix Mendelssohn-Bartholdy returned to the city of his childhood. The *Opernhaus unter den Linden*, built by Frederick the Great in 1743, was a favourite meeting-place. With Meyerbeer as *Kapellmeister*, it was in time to witness Jenny Lind's success in the composer's *Ein Feldlager in Schlesien*. Hans Christian Andersen was to be in the city then.

The drama, too, flourished, and the success of the 'real' theatre was repeated in the drawing-room, by old and young setting up toy theatres from the popular picture sheets.

Conversation was an art in itself, and went on at all levels. Men sat talking in the many *Weinstuben*. Lutter and Wegner's restaurant was to gain lasting fame for being the locale where the actor Ludwig Devrient met Ernst Theodor Amadeus Hoffman, *Kammergerichtsrat*, and writer of abundant imagination. Their talks were to form the basis for Offenbach's *Tales of Hoffman*.

Cafés attracted new customers by making available to them German and foreign newspapers. Beer gardens served the more extrovert in their gayer and noisier fashion, while the fair sex sipped their coffee on fine afternoons in the pretty *Kaffeegärten* at the back of houses near the *Tiergarten*.

This, then, was the world into which were plunged the two quiet men from Cassel.

It took a while to get used to it all. The solitary Jacob disliked the many social distractions, worried about public appearances, and found academy meetings and committees boring and unproductive. Wilhelm, too, hoped that in time they would find more quietness. All the same, both were grateful for the friendliness shown to them everywhere. They were well received, and to have obtained security was an overwhelming relief. In order to express their gratitude personally, and on von Humboldt's advice, they asked an audience of the king, which was granted.

They were graciously welcomed by a monarch whom they found full of good will, agreeable, natural and intelligent.

On 27 May 1841 Wilhelm wrote to Gervinus:

'. . . our personal position is as happy as we can wish. We are completely free, with the possibility of academic work. Gratefully aware of this, we intend to live as quietly as possible, and hope we will succeed. Life in general is just what I had expected it to be. People are courteous, obliging and friendly, but I could not truthfully say that I have found many to gladden my heart . . .'[2]

The great city's splendour was lacking in depth.

The brothers began their lectures in the spring of 1843. Jacob read on ancient law practices, warning his audience that his lectures would not just harken back to the German past – as lectures on law were wont to do – this past itself was his very subject. He would spread his interests widely, taking in language, literature and religious beliefs. On 8 May the *Augsburger Allgemeine Zeitung* reported:

'Berlin 30 April. Today Jacob Grimm began his lectures on ancient law practices, at the university here. The audience, composed of several hundred students, greeted him with long drawn-out cheers. He thanked them, visibly touched, a state which lasted for a while, and gave his lecture a mild warmth. Fate, he said, had not humbled but uplifted him, and there was reason to praise a fate which had led him into our midst . . .'[3]

On 20 May the same paper wrote about Wilhelm's inaugural lecture:

'Berlin 12 May. Yesterday Wilhelm Grimm began his lectures on the Middle High German heroic epic of *Gudrun*. He, too, was greeted with loud cheers by several hundred students, and thanked them for their sympathetic concern. He continued by saying that flowers growing in the dark are said to open all the more beautiful in the light of the morning. He might well have said the same about himself, had he been younger. What he could assure them, however, was that the nocturnal frosts he had encountered had not done him any harm. He begged his audience's forbearance for not taking them on a highroad, straight as a line, with poplars on both sides hiding the view, and nothing but the destination in sight. His path would lead into open fields, there to survey nature, and find a point from where a panorama of the country's past could be gained. Then Grimm gave an enlightened exposition of the epic and its relation to the *Nibelungen* . . .'[4]

In an essay on the brothers Grimm and Russia, Isidor Levin quotes another contemporary account of the inaugural lectures, probably from the pen of a young Russian, then in Berlin, and published in May 1841 in *Otečestvennyje zapiski*. The excerpts given here are freely translated from Levin's rendering of the Russian text into German.

'. . . Jacob's lecture was the first, in the early days of May or towards the end of April. He made ancient German law practices the subject of his lectures during the summer term. The largest lecture room – No. 17 – was so crowded that there was a shortage of seats. The atmosphere was quite special, and every face showed eager anticipation . . . At last he arrived, and as he entered the door, and settled at his desk, he was received by stormy applause and cheers. He appeared to be taken aback and at the same time deeply moved by this unexpected reception. His voice trembled, and he hesitated as he began: "Thank you, gentlemen, for your applause, but I do not want to accept this honour as due to myself, rather do I see it as arising from a fate which weighed on me heavily, still could not bow me down . . . Now, I am grateful to this very fate which has brought me among you." His eyes rested with an expression of touching gratitude and embarrassment on his keenly listening audience: he was almost unable to breathe, his voice faltered, he smiled, not able to speak for a minute . . . Filled with emotion, he had to rest several times during the lecture. This embarrassment and the pauses were more impressive than any eloquence he might have displayed.

'On 11 May Wilhelm, too, had an imposing reception which could not now be quite as unexpected to him as it had been to his elder brother; and therefore he did not show the same embarrassment, although his face reflected the same emotion and heartfelt gratitude. Standing up there in his old-fashioned frock-coat . . . he looked at the cheering students, listening to their enthusiastic greetings with gentle but dignified modesty. He lowered his head deeply, while his long thick, slightly greying hair, fell forward into his face. When he lifted his head again, there were tears in his eyes. He made the ancient Germanic poem of *Gudrun* the subject of his lecture . . .'[5]

In the late summer of 1841 Wilhelm and Dortchen took a sentimental journey to Hesse, visiting Hanau and Steinau where Wilhelm saw again the very baker's shop which had served the child Lotte, 'dressed in a little white smock', with her breakfast rolls every morning.

Once more childhood memories filled some happy hours.

Dortchen told Jacob in a letter:

'. . . we went round the *Amtshaus*, into the garden; there was still a lime tree in front of the house. Wilhelm says that some barns have been newly built, and a few other things. We visited the hut in the garden. The green-gage tree you planted is no longer there. I should have liked to go inside the house, but Wilhelm thought it would upset him to see it all so changed. We walked around it, and Wilhelm showed me all the windows, also the corner one where you and Wilhelm slept . . .'[6]

Cologne and Wilhelm's beloved Rhine made a fitting end to the holiday.

Early in 1842 Wilhelm fell ill again, causing renewed anxiety. Everybody showed kindness which perhaps helped to make Jacob feel a little closer to their new friends. Wilhelm progressed very slowly, and only when the leaves began to fall was he able to take short walks in the park, leaning heavily on a stick. Jacob, too, had been ordered *Eger* water and daily walks to overcome a certain lassitude, pain in the chest and occasional fits of depression. He often now felt himself doomed, with forebodings of death not far away. He had made his will, leaving all his possessions to Wilhelm or Wilhelm's children. Concerned about so much work on the dictionary undone, he asked that their publishers should be compensated out of his estate.

Walks in the *Tiergarten*, begun as a 'cure', became a habit. For many years they were the brothers' favourite recreation: Jacob walking briskly, Wilhelm more slowly and leisurely, acknowledging each other with a smile and a nod when they met.

They both came to love the freedom of Berlin's park.

On 16 January 1843, Wilhelm wrote to Gervinus:

'. . . the *Tiergarten*, as one says here jokingly, is neither a garden, nor are there any beasts in it. But it still retains somehow the character of a forest, with tall trees, here and there. And even where the park has been embellished to suit present-day taste, the strange and splendid trees and shrubs, carefully tended, are a pleasure to behold. Not far from us thousands of goldfish swim in a long narrow pool, surrounded by high-stemmed roses and intertwining vines, backed again by stately trees . . .'[7]

In their new circumstances the brothers' closeness to each other remained the same. During his serious illness Wilhelm was delirious, and could not be kept quiet. When at one time he insisted on getting out of bed, and could not be managed, Jacob was called in. He sat down quietly at his brother's bedside, looking at him lovingly and intensely. Almost at once the delirium stopped. Wilhelm sank down into his pillow, and fell into a refreshing sleep, an amazing proof of the brothers' attachment.

Even the king recognized it. Through a mistake in the Lord Chamberlain's Office, Wilhelm at one time received an invitation to dine at the palace, but not Jacob. When the king enquired why Jacob wasn't there, Wilhelm explained, and was told that Jacob could have joined his brother without being commanded. Later, Frederick William apologized to Jacob at a meeting of the *Akademie*, and invited him to hear Jenny Lind sing at a court concert.

Inevitably and against their modest inclinations the Grimms were drawn into Berlin's lively society. Their value was recognized and they became highly respected public figures. On 24 February 1843, Wilhelm's birthday, students arranged a torch-light procession, which he described in a letter to Ludwig:

'. . . my birthday has been duly celebrated. We had not invited anybody, but many friends and acquaintances arrived till our rooms were packed. It had become known that we were to be honoured, and everybody wanted to see the students and hear them sing. Without being told, our caretaker had swept the street in front of the house. At half past eight students with torches gathered in a semicircle, a nice picture under the trees, nicer than in the midst of a town. As we came out to the balcony with our friends, the students began to sing. They had been practising for some weeks, and their singing was pure and good. In the stillness (the students did not allow carriages to pass) the songs resounded through the whole length of the street. Neighbours came to the windows or stood on their balconies. After a few songs a deputation came, to hand us a parchment, neatly written and with a gilt heading. It contained a festive song, specially composed and set to music. There was also one in Danish, written by a Norwegian student at the university. The deputation consisted of a Swiss, a man from Offenbach on the Main, and one from Brunswick. All three had pleasant lively faces. One made a speech, and we shook hands with him and thanked him, explaining that we wanted to reply to them all publicly. We asked the students to come up afterwards and spend the evening with us. The deputation left to join in singing the specially composed song and to give us three cheers. Then we – one after the other – spoke to them. After one more song, they extinguished their torches and, marching off slowly, intoned the fine old student's song *Gaudeamus Igitur* . . .'[8]

During a visit to Berlin Princess Caroline, daughter of the late Hessian Electress, called on her old acquaintances, and a little later Jacob and Wilhelm were invited to dine with the king at Charlottenburg. He again showed himself affable, amusing, even gay. The king enquired after Wilhelm's health, discussed the brothers' work, and presented them to his queen. Commands to dinner became frequent. Young Prince Michael of Serbia, together with his tutor, Vuk Stefanović Karadžić, old friend and fellow-philologist, announced himself, and was given a party. Social duties took their toll of badly needed working time, and Wilhelm explained in a letter to Ludwig:

'. . . often I work till the moment they arrive, and then have to act as if I had all the time in the world, and to spare. I am thoroughly pleased when I can spend a night or two at home, quietly . . .'[9]

Frequently the brothers were now included in trainloads of celebrities, conveyed from Berlin to Potsdam to attend a royal performance at the *Neue Palais*. Old Ludwig Tieck had returned to his native city, and Wilhelm was present when Tieck's translation of the *Midsummer-Night's Dream*, with Mendelssohn-Bartholdy's specially composed music, was produced in Potsdam. He has left a pleasing description of the event, in a letter to Professor Hugo of Göttingen. It was written on 30 October 1843.

'. . . the production of the *Midsummer-Night's Dream* on the 14th [October] was, what might be called, an event. For people such as ourselves, it means much effort. I left . . . as early as three o'clock, as the performance was due to begin at five. When we came to the station at Potsdam, there was not a *Droschke* left, and the best inn could not supply a carriage. So, there was nothing for it but to walk to the *Neue Palais*. Fortunately, the weather was good, and the walk, partly through the park at *Sanssouci* – where in places the lawns were still quite green – pleasant. But I am not a good walker, and so I was tired when we arrived at five o'clock . . . The doors had been open for half an hour, and to me the crowd seemed to be bigger than ever. Before the court arrived, Tieck came in. He, too, took his seat outside the semicircle, reserved for the court. Behind it rise, like an amphitheatre, the seats for the other spectators. Tieck is very bent, and he climbed the few steps with difficulty. He would have hardly been able to get to his seat, had not some officers helped him, by actually pushing him up. His eyes shone with delight as he was to see a play by Shakespeare, neither abridged nor changed. At six o'clock the court entered, more brilliant than ever . . . On entering the king greeted the assembled people in a friendly manner as he does usually. He then looked several times at the audience through his opera glasses . . .

'The performance finished about half past ten, and there was a terrific scramble. Not a chance of a carriage, and again we had to walk. But the moon shone magnificently. As I cannot walk quickly I formed the rear, together with some friends. In the semi-dark we lost our way in the park, were eventually shown the direction, but time went by. Had we not been lucky enough to find a *Droschke* in Potsdam, we should have had to spend the night there. As it was, we managed to reach the station at the other side of the Havel, but there was no time to eat. When I complained about being hungry – a state that does not agree with me – a friend offered me a dry rusk . . . I reached home at a quarter to twelve, and when my wife noticed that I was looking for something to eat, she made me some milk soup on the spirit cooker. With this modest food for the body, an evening full of enjoyment for the spirit came to an end . . .'[10]

This performance of the *Midsummer-Night's Dream*, actually fixed for 12 October, was held up by an unforeseen complication.

The parts of the elves in the play were taken by the children of actors and dancers. They did well during the rehearsals, and the king invited them all to stay at *Sanssouci* for a few days before the performance. Naturally, the little troupe enjoyed the freedom of the great park and gardens. The fine grapes on the terraces did not escape the children's notice, and one night in the moonlight the 'elves' jumped out of the windows, and ate their fill of what may have been unripe grapes. The results were awful, and there was no dancing for a day or two after. Hence, the performance had to be postponed. The king, it was said, was greatly amused at the escapade.

Savigny, meantime become Minister of Justice, was now a person of some consequence.

On 23 April 1842 Wilhelm had written to their friend Hugo:

'. . . Savigny visited me a few days ago . . . On the 21st he slept for the first time in his official residence. He is not properly established yet, as some repairs to walls and chimneys have still to be done. The beautiful garden belonging to the house, with a summer house and pond, will be most welcome to him. He has five meetings a week, and if one takes into account the audiences, attendances at court, and other disturbances his position entails, it becomes quite clear that there will be no time for scholarly leisure, and his work will remain unfinished . . .'11

Savigny's home was always open to the Grimms. He had stood the test of troubled times, and had remained a friend though occasionally they missed their former professor's simplicity and informality. He had gone a long way since his Marburg lectures. Wilhelm paints an amusing picture of an evening at the new Prussian Minister of Justice's home, in a letter to Ludwig:

'. . . it's all very grand at the Savignys' these days. The stairs are lit by gas, and decorated with plants and flowers. As soon as one enters the hall, the caretaker rings a bell, and two servants, in blue and silver livery, appear in the anteroom. After taking one's coat they fling open the doors, and through two warm and well-lit rooms lead the way to the *Kabinet*, a large square room, decorated in sky-blue and gold, and hung all over with pictures. Here *Frau* von Savigny is seated on a divan behind a large round table. She does not rise while she waits for her guests, but he comes forward and shakes hands in a friendly manner. People arrive just before nine o'clock, but it is all right to come even half an hour later. Tea is served, and about a quarter past ten all kinds of excellent dishes, their number varying according to the size of the company, are handed round by servants. The table is not laid with a cloth, this not being the done thing. One puts one's plate on the mahogany table while the servants, wearing white gloves, hand round the dishes and pour the wine. Conversation is lively, and *Frau* von Savigny sparkles with wit. Often there are very many people, specially strangers, Englishmen, Frenchmen and Americans. About half past eleven one takes one's leave, while *Frau* von Savigny rises and, with her husband, accompanies her guests to the first door, both making themselves very pleasant and agreeable. Altogether the atmosphere is free and easy. One can stand, or sit down with whoever one wishes to, go away any time one feels inclined without even taking leave. One can join the party any night, but now and then special invitations are sent . . .

'. . . there was great fun a few days ago. We had been specially invited and knew it was to be a biggish party. Dortchen came too. When we arrived at nine o'clock, everything was beautifully lit. Prince August of Württemberg as well as some counts, princes and excellencies were expected. However, the king having Liszt and Rubini perform at the castle the same night, the whole party was commanded to attend the concert, and we were Savigny's only guests. So we had to eat all the lovely dishes ourselves: fricassée of pike, truffle pastries and orange sorbet . . .'12

One can almost hear Wilhelm chuckle at the good feast.

Wilhelm also reported that an English writer, a Miss Austin, 'a lively and clever lady'[13], who with her translations from the German had 'enlightened' her fatherland, was now being received in Berlin society. This was the celebrated Mrs. Sarah Austin, handsome, gay and clever daughter of John Taylor of Norwich, himself a descendant of the famous divine. Married to John Austin, the jurist, she spent years with him in Germany. She had translated into English Ranke's *History of the Popes*, and when one night Ranke joined a party at which Mrs. Austin was present, a lady was heard to whisper: 'Now the original is here, too'.

The spring of 1843 saw the fifth edition of the *Household Tales*. Again Wilhelm dedicated a copy to Bettina, saying:

'. . . before, this book came to you from a distance, now, dear Bettina, I can hand it to you. You yourself have chosen for us this house in which we live, outside the city walls, where at the edge of the forest a new town is rising, sheltered by trees, surrounded by green lawns and beds of roses and other flowers, its peace undisturbed yet by rattling noise. When during last summer's heat I walked in the cool of the morning in the shade of the oaks, a fresh breeze soothing the pressure left from severe illness, I remembered with gratitude how well you had cared for us . . .'[14]

Bettina had certainly cared for her friends, and she still did.

She had made her own home *In den Zelten*, at the northern edge of the *Tiergarten*, in almost country-like surroundings. The Pompeian-red walls of her large drawing-room decorated with antique statues made a fine background for her musical evenings. Grown older, and not always very fit, she had not lost her liveliness and her keen spirits. She adored talk, mixed her guests freely, and delighted in arguments and the occasional clash of temperaments. But equally she liked an evening in the calm atmosphere of the Grimms' home, when she talked wittily, if sometimes too much and for too long, 'till Dortchen's eyes would keep open no longer'. A little wearing at times, yet Bettina was much loved, and the Grimm children considered her almost a double of their own mother, some sort of relation extraordinary. This feeling of kinship was eventually made more real by Herman Grimm marrying Gisela von Arnim, Bettina's daughter.

The Grimms' home attracted many visitors, and all were impressed by the family's harmony and simple contentment. In 1853, the writer, Julius Rodenberg, was to describe in his diary an evening spent at the Grimms:

'. . . from the moment I arrived, I felt warm and comfortable, more than I had ever done since I came here. The *Professorin* is a dear lady, an honest Hessian character, and unpretentious, the most amiable hostess one could wish for . . . Wilhelm came in first, a man with a quietly-contented face, with blue eyes and long grey hair. He looks more a man of feeling than an intellectual. The mildness of his ways is attractive, and he does not intimidate through intellectual superiority. Quite different Jacob, who came in after him. He immediately induces a little nervousness. The liveliness of his eyes is fascinating and compelling, but when his endearing smile lights up his features, and the hasty intenseness of his manners changes to lovable sprightliness, any uneasiness one may have experienced, turns to quite an exceptional feeling of attraction . . . one must love him in the same way one has loved as a child his *Household Tales*. The *Herr Hofrat* did not come easily to me, I rather wanted to call him just Jacob, as did his brother, or 'little Uncle' as Auguste did flatteringly. He is a small man who, in his old-fashioned frock coat, looks like a remnant of the good old days. He has nothing of the bookworm, and even less of the elegant Berlin professor. His high forehead is framed by thick grey hair, and his eyes sparkle . . .'[15]

In 1842 Ludwig had lost his wife, Marie Böttner, and in June of the following year he decided to seek comfort in a visit to his brothers. With his little daughter, Friederike, *das Ideke*, he travelled to Berlin. In his very human and colourful way he has described the journey in his memoirs, once more a document to this brother's loving attachment to Jacob and Wilhelm:

'. . . Berlin for the first time in my life! Thousands of people surrounded our coach. I immediately discovered my dear brother Wilhelm. The child gripped my hand tightly. She had never been in such a crowd. Herman and a Prussian pioneer came to welcome us with open arms. The soldier was Karl Hassenpflug, dear sister Lotte's eldest son, now doing his military service. His father arrived too, and we took a carriage to go to the *Lennéstrasse*, number eight. It is a fine house where Dortchen, Jacob and Rudolf were waiting for us. Augustchen was still at school. At night Bettina and her youngest daughter, Gisela, arrived, and it was all very jolly . . .'[16]

Ludwig's stay in Berlin brought back into the family fold father and son Hassenpflug. The closeness and warmth of former days had faded a little since Ludwig Hassenpflug's reactionary tendencies had become even more pronounced, and his entry into the political scene had made more obvious his dictatorial ways, entirely alien to the Grimms. Risen to the rank of Minister in Hessian service, he had been brusquely dismissed in 1837, following differences of opinion with the Prince Elector. After peregrinations into the administration of the principality of Hohenzollern-Sigmaringen and the Grand-Duchy of Luxembourg, he now served under Prussia's king. Hassenpflug's second marriage – in 1837, to Agnes von Münchhausen – was never quite accepted by Jacob and Wilhelm, who found it hard to picture anybody in the place of their much-loved sister. From Berlin Hassenpflug was to return to Cassel in 1850, as Hesse's Prime Minister. Involved in a life-and-death struggle with the liberals, he became a disappointed and much hated man. He died in Marburg in 1862.

Meantime, Berlin was a splendid place to be in.

Ludwig visited the university, took sightseeing drives through the city, and walks by the goldfish pond in the *Tiergarten*. Social evenings, when he met everyone that counted, alternated with lunch invitations. The Savignys gave a 'splendid lunch' in their *Gartensalon*, when the lady of the house handed round figs, sent specially from Lisbon by her son who served at the German embassy there. Jacob and Wilhelm were patient guides, though Jacob appears to have been in a hurry to get back to his books, as Ludwig complains that he could not always keep pace with him. A fashionable straw hat was bought for Ideke, and Uncle Wilhelm took her to the *Rutschbahn*, the switchback in the city's famous amusement park, the *Tivoli* gardens. Quite naturally, Papa spent much time at museums, galleries and the studios of fellow-painters. At the studio of Peter von Cornelius, known for his illustrations to the *Nibelungenlied* and painter of enormous frescoes, he was shown the sketch for a proposed christening gift from Prussia's king to the Prince of Wales, later King Edward VII.

Ludwig found that Berlin artists talked like 'printed reviews', believing that only they could hit the nail on the head. But Ludwig, though from the provinces did not allow himself to be patronised. He was impressed with a visit to the *Akademie der Wissenschaften* where, he remarked, he saw all the famous Prussian scholars.

He consulted a doctor because of a rheumatic complaint, and was ordered mineral waters and early morning walks. 'Taking the waters' was considered a cure for all evil. One of the Hassenpflug boys once explained to his Uncle Wilhelm that, while with his father in a Thuringian spa, he had to drink sixteen glasses of water a day, and twenty when he was naughty!

After pacing the *Tiergarten* between five and eight in the morning, till he knew every nook and corner, and still not finding much relief, Ludwig decided to try a Bohemian spa. He left his little daughter in Dortchen's care, and departed for Teplitz.

On 3 August another traveller set out from Berlin. Jacob realized a long-cherished dream, he started on his way to Italy.

Earthenware baking dish

CHAPTER 14

Travels and Homecomings:
German Philologists Meet

1843 – 1847

THE change of air of an Italian journey was to 'heal his chest', and Jacob surrendered himself to the adventure of new people and new scenes. He travelled via Frankfurt, Basle and Milan to Genoa. A journey by sea – three days and four nights – then took him to Naples. An excursion to Palermo was cancelled because of the great heat.

From his account,[1] in a speech given to the Berlin Academy the following year, it appears that Jacob Grimm, like many a northerner before him, was deeply impressed by Italy's beauty and grandeur. The feeling of history at every step, and the 'monuments of art', scattered all over the country, were a revelation. Artists and writers had only conveyed a shadowy likeness of the divine reality.

Beneath a radiant sky, 'with not a drop of rain for months', Jacob enjoyed the sail. The sea, now blue, now green, with the foam rising, reflected the brilliant sun by day and the pale light of the moon and millions of glittering stars each night. Travelling by boat 'gliding rapidly along the coast', with the distant mountain ranges always in view, Jacob considered the right way to approach the south. On landing one would be plunged suddenly, and as it were by magic, into the southern scene, whereas many intermediate stops would not allow for the same freshness of impression. Slow country travel might serve well enough for the return journey when the more northerly regions could be enjoyed like mellow autumn after the summer's heat. Indeed, after having turned north for Rome, Jacob did travel by Florence, Venice and Verona, to continue into Austria and Germany.

In Naples, after landing just as the sun rose behind Mount Vesuvius, Jacob began exploring the fragrant countryside. Climbing the heights behind the city, he rejoiced in the famous view over the bay. Plantations of gaunt grey olives, sturdy oaks and slender pines delighted his eyes. Intertwining vines, laden with grapes, compared favourably with German vineyards, where the single vines, each growing against a little wooden

140

pole, made for monotony. He liked the yellow-flowering agaves, with their sharp-pointed leaves, remarking what good and effective fencing they provided, better than railings or walls. Nature, thought Jacob, looked like one big garden, and the gardens again looked natural, so that cultivated and uncultivated land blended pleasantly.

Jacob travelled happily.

In a letter home, of 4 September, he remarked that he had no wish to see all the sights. He liked to take things quietly, with enough time to look at special places, where a beautiful natural scene often held more attraction than a rushed visit to antique remains. In these places the *cicerone* were disturbing, hurrying the visitors along far too quickly.

Visiting the hill-top monastery of Camaldoli, Jacob rode on a donkey, up steep mountain paths, shaded from the hot sun by the thickness of the trees. Trees, shrubs and plants had a stronger scent in the south, and he found it most agreeable. There were wonderful views down deep precipices, across forests and lakes to the far off sea and a cluster of islands. He crept through torch-lit caves, past subterranean waters to visit the grotto of the Sibyl.

Near Naples Jacob called on an old friend, a lady from Cassel married to a silk-manufacturer and now living at the foot of Mount Vesuvius. Her six little girls all knew German, and Jacob thought they might enjoy the *Household Tales*. He promised to send a copy.

He was deeply impressed by Herculaneum and Pompeii, haunted by the thought that the horror of a disaster had been the means of preserving for future generations a clear picture of the life the unfortunate inhabitants led. Many must have been saved by flight, he thought, as comparatively few skeletons were found in the excavations.[2]

Everywhere Jacob found man-made things in harmony with nature, made neither to disturb nor spoil the scene. Seats by the roadside, wells to quench the traveller's thirst, even the very signposts were seemly. The towns were well planned, and every village fitted into its own countryside. After the noisy liveliness of Naples, nature, art and the city's long history seemed to combine to make Rome serene and dignified. Jacob stood in awe before the remains of layer upon layer of past civilizations. The Forum 'with the Capitol behind and the Colosseum in front', was his favourite place. He was less impressed by St Peter's, his Protestant mind set firmly against papal splendour.

Art galleries and collections encouraged doubts. Was it proper to take a sacred painting from its rightful place in a church, or the portrait of an ancestor from the house where it belonged? Relics of past ages had of course to be guarded, but was the craze for collecting and putting on show not going too far? Did it not take away from the true meaning of a work of art, a meaning already doubtful since art no longer was one with myths and religion? A ruin left untouched was a more genuine witness to the past. Jacob disliked the many crosses and Christian symbols superimposed on the buildings of Antiquity. It was unworthy of Christianity, he thought, and to him the ancient gods were still all powerful in the Pantheon.

He loved the Italians, found them friendly, uninhibited and of natural good taste. He loved their costumes, their pageants and the music of their language. Living in a sunny climate, with beauty all around, must have moulded them. On the way north Jacob admired the palaces of Florence, and was inspired by the wonders of Venice.

Back in Berlin, work crowded in again: lecturing, contributing to many journals, editing, and seeing the much enlarged second edition of the *Deutsche Mythologie* through the press. Wilhelm continued publishing the by-products of his medieval studies — Konrad von Würzburg's *Silvester* had appeared in 1841, and in 1844 a new edition of *Grâve Ruodolf* was ready. Both brothers were full of plans, their commitment to the large German dictionary never far from their thoughts.

In February 1844 they became involved, entirely against their wish, in the much discussed *Affäre Hoffmann*. August Heinrich Hoffmann von Fallersleben, the Grimms' friend of many years' standing, had for some time been professor of German at Breslau University, when he was first suspended and then dismissed from his post. This happened on the publication of the second volume of his *Unpolitische Lieder*, a collection of poems considered seditious by the authorities. After some wanderings about Germany he arrived in Berlin, called on the Grimms, and was invited to join a birthday party for Wilhelm. He was told that the students were planning a torch-light procession to celebrate the occasion.

Evening came, Hoffman arrived and so did the students. For a moment Hoffman appeared at a window of the Grimms' house, was recognized and given an ovation. He then went down into the street to thank the students. A few days later he was expelled from Berlin.

Immediately a furious controversy began raging in the papers. There was confusion, rumours snowballed, the brothers were attacked and forced into publicly dissociating themselves from Hoffman, which could not but hurt him. Sides were taken fiercely, and many felt that Jacob and Wilhelm had gone too far in siding with their king, disregarding the feelings of an old friend. Some even maintained that they had sacrificed him in order to flatter their master.

But not all: the king himself, von Humboldt, Dahlmann, Gervinus, Ranke and Savigny took the brothers' side. The passionate Bettina was all for Hoffman, and saddened Jacob and Wilhelm by open enmity, causing a temporary estrangement. They never became quite reconciled with

Hoffman. Jacob eventually made a gesture, but Wilhelm could not forget that in order to gain some small satisfaction, Hoffman had committed an indiscretion. He had abused the hospitality offered him generously and in good faith of two men in office under Prussia's king. When the storm had died down, there was an overwhelming feeling that the Grimms had acted with the same integrity they had shown earlier in Göttingen.

In the autumn of 1844 Jacob saw the Scandinavian north for the first time. He travelled to Copenhagen and Sweden.

The Baltic was grey and less exhilarating than the Mediterranean,

Courtyard of the Amtshaus, Steinau. Drawing by Ludwig Emil Grimm

but it had its own character and attraction. The northern coasts were flat, and vegetation sparse, less abundant even than in Germany. Trees became fewer, the further north Jacob went, till in Sweden oak and beech disappeared completely, leaving only the silver-barked birch and dark green conifers. He was cheered by Sweden's meadows, sprinkled with tiny flowers, and liked the typical brownish-red wooden farm houses, grass and small plants growing in their turfed roofs. Stockholm's position was reminiscent of Genoa or Naples, without the southern heat and brilliance.

The Germanic scholar in Jacob noted the many barrows and rune stones, and took a vivid interest in the languages. He found the Swedes quiet and dignified. In a boat on Lake Mälar, Jacob recalled, people sat quietly, twiddling their thumbs, while in Italy the same boat would have been filled with noisy gaiety. The southern extrovert certainly enjoyed life, but the northerner, turned in upon himself, might experience satisfaction, deeper, and beyond the southerner's comprehension.[3]

In Copenhagen Jacob called on Hans Christian Andersen.

The call had a history.

Not long before, during his travels across Europe, the Danish writer had stayed in Berlin. He was warmly received, enjoyed much hospitality, but met with one great disappointment.

Andersen himself refers to the incident in his autobiography, *The True Story of my Life*.

Speaking of his visit to Berlin in 1845, when 'invitation followed upon invitation, and it took physical strength to endure so much kindness', he continues:

'. . . I had already on the former occasion, visited the brothers Grimm, but I had not at that time made much progress with the acquaintance. I had not brought any letters of introduction to them with me, because people had told me, and I myself believed it, that if I were known by anybody in Berlin, it must be the brothers Grimm. I therefore sought out their residence. The servant-maid asked me with which of the brothers I wished to speak.

' "With the one who has written the most," said I, because I did not know, at that time, which of them had most interested himself in the *Märchen*.

' "Jacob is the most learned," said the servant-maid.

' "Well, then, take me to him."

'I entered the room, and Jacob Grimm, with his knowing and strongly-marked countenance, stood before me.

' "I come to you," said I, "without letters of introduction, because I hope that my name is not wholly unknown to you."

' "Who are you?" asked he.

'I told him, and Jacob Grimm said, in a half-embarrassed voice, "I do not remember to have heard this name: What have you written?"

'It was now my turn to be embarrassed in a high degree; but I now mentioned my little stories.

' "I do not know them," said he; "but mention to me some other of your writings, because I certainly must have heard them spoken of."

'I named the titles of several; but he shook his head. I felt myself quite unlucky.

' "But what must you think of me," said I, "that I come to you as a total stranger, and enumerate myself what I have written; you must know me! There has been published in Denmark a collection of the *Märchen* of all nations, which is dedicated to you, and in it there is at least one story of mine."

' "No," said he good-humouredly, but as much embarrassed as myself; "I have not read even that, but it delights me to make your acquaintance; allow me to conduct you to my brother Wilhelm?"

Dorothea Viehmann, 'The Fairytale-Wife'. Etching by Ludwig Emil Grimm. Staatsarchiv, Marburg/Lahn

Ludwig Achim von Arnim. Original missing since the War

'"No, I thank you," said I, only wishing now to get away; I had fared badly enough with one brother. I pressed his hand and hurried from the house.

'That same month Jacob Grimm went to Copenhagen; immediately on his arrival, and while yet in his travelling dress, did the amiable kind man hasten up to me. He now knew me, and he came to me with cordiality. I was just then standing and packing my clothes in a trunk for a journey to the country; I had only a few minutes' time: by this means my reception of him was just as laconic as had been his of me in Berlin.

'Now, however, we met in Berlin as old acquaintances. Jacob Grimm is one of those characters whom one must love and attach oneself to.

'One evening, as I was reading one of my little stories at the Countess Bismarck-Bohlen's, there was in the little circle one person in particular who listened with evident fellowship of feeling, and who expressed himself in a peculiar and sensible manner on the subject – this was Jacob's brother, Wilhelm Grimm.

'"I should have known you very well, if you had come to me," said he, "the last time you were here."

'I saw these two highly gifted and amiable brothers almost daily; the circles into which I was invited seemed also to be theirs, and it was my desire and pleasure that they should listen to my little stories, that they should participate in them, they whose names will be always spoken as long as the German *Volks Märchen* are read.

'The fact of my not being known to Jacob Grimm on my first visit to Berlin had so disconcerted me, that when any one asked me whether I had been well received in this city, I shook my head doubtfully and said: "but Grimm did not know me".[4]

All was well now, in the memorable winter of 1845.

In September 1846 Germanic philologists held their first conference. They were mainly to discuss problems concerning their own work, but these academic meetings had a much wider significance. In a German Federation still lacking true unity, conferences of scholars provided a forum for the exchange of social and political views. Personal contacts counted for more than the official papers read. Students and professors had for long enjoyed the freedom of the whole of Germany, and the nationalism of these intellectuals now became vocal, a nationalism strongly tinged with liberal thought. They ardently desired a united democratic Germany.

Classical philologists, natural philosophers, doctors and lawyers had all met in recent years – the jurists demanding a unified code of law for all Germany. Now the Germanic philologists assembled in the *Römer*, Frankfurt's ancient town hall. Ludwig Uhland, head of the 'Swabian School' of poets and fellow-investigator of the German past, proposed that

Jacob Grimm should preside over the meeting. It was his pleasure, said Uhland, to propose a man who had done such outstanding work in their field, a field, in some ways, first ploughed by him. The proposal was met with unanimous applause, and Jacob gratefully accepted.

He chaired the meeting with his usual keenness, trying to steer clear of politics. Wilhelm reported on the great dictionary's progress. Contributors – 'from the Swiss mountains to the Baltic, and from the Rhine to the Oder' – were now sending excerpts. With editing to begin soon, it was hoped that 'a natural history' of each word would in time be given.

In 1847 Jacob opened the second meeting at Lübeck, welcoming the change of location which would act against the narrow regionalism sometimes afflicting such conferences. He was again elected chairman, much honoured and applauded.

That year Jacob visited Vienna again.

A few old friends were still there, and in the *Hofbibliothek* he felt that the thirty-two years since he had last set foot into this great library had passed like a dream.

From travels and public appearances the brothers returned to work in their studies. Contemporary descriptions and pictures convey a good idea of what these rooms looked like. Next door to each other, they were similar, and still each expressed in some way, the personality of the owner. Both were kept warm by large tiled stoves, typical of Berlin homes of the time. Both housed many books and piles of papers, but the brothers' 'dear library' was placed on shelves in Jacob's room where also hung the family portraits. Jacob had always considered himself the head of the family, and so the arrangement seemed natural and proper. He appears to have worked in a real 'fortress of books', with a sofa the only concession to comfort. Of his uncle's love for books, Herman Grimm has this to say:

'. . . he loved his books – and this is not too strong a word – with tenderness. He looked after their [the brothers'] common library, and had books bound in different ways, according to his instructions. With this he allowed himself a little extravagance. A more or less precious binding was an indication to what he thought of a book. Presentation copies of small occasional pamphlets he had bound in red velvet. An edition of *Freidank*, printed after my father's death, was given the most expensive binding available. It seemed somehow natural that one who had been a librarian for so long should now treat his own library with respect. He enjoyed pacing along the shelves, taking out a volume here and there, looking at it, opening it, and putting it back into its place. He loved to jump up and find within a second a book someone was looking for. After my father's death when his study was made into a library, Jacob re-arranged the books to a new plan, and put them up by himself. He could trace every volume in the

146

dark, and never made a mistake. He did not like to lend books, as he used to make notes in them or put slips inside. Many [of the brothers' books] have on the last blank page two tables of contents, one written by Jacob, and one by Wilhelm . . .'[5]

Both brothers' studies show the period's delight in hoarding all kinds of objects: ink-wells, letter-stands, bigger and smaller statues. In Wilhelm's room stood large reproductions of the statues of Athene and Apollo of Belvedere, in keeping with the trend towards 'the Classical' in interior decoration. Wilhelm's gentler personality allowed for a few more comfortable chairs and looped muslin curtains. Both brothers loved flowers and pot plants, and were never without them. Herman Grimm recollects that on his father's and uncle's window-sills stood their favourite plants: wallflower and heliotrope on Jacob's, primulas on Wilhelm's. All their lives they felt a closeness to growing things, and were in the habit of gathering on their walks an odd flower or leaf. Many they pressed between the pages of books, sometimes carefully scratching a place and date on a leaf. Others were wrapped in tiny pieces of paper, on which were scribbled further details. There were four-leaved clovers for luck, and leaves gathered on the graves of loved ones. Often they would bring home from their travels a flower picked in a special place, and keep it as a memento.

Increasingly the brothers' work was being recognized at home and abroad. Among others the Philological Society of London made them honorary members. From England there arrived a letter, addressed to Professor James Grimm, to be followed by a similar one to Wilhelm, about a year later:

4 Kings Bench Walk, Temple, London
Aug. 15 1843

'Sir

'I have been instructed by the Council of the Philological Society to inform you, that they have had the pleasure and the honour of enrolling your name as one of their Honorary Members.

'The loose sheets which accompany this note, detail the proceedings of each meeting and contain an abstract of every paper which has been read before the Society. A select number of these papers will hereafter appear in the shape of a Volume of Transactions.

'I have to beg your indulgence for my not having sooner made this communication. A lengthened absence from London occasioned by unexpected business has hitherto prevented me from discharging this, as well as other official duties.

'Allow me to subscribe myself with very high respect, Sir
Your obdt. Humble Servt.
Edwin Guest'[6]

Earthenware
inkstand

Jacob joined the ranks of the *Légion d'Honneur*, and received a letter from François Guizot in which he stated that:

'*le Roi qui se plaît à honorer partout le mérite supérieur a voulu vous donner une marque éclatante de l'estime, qu'il vous porte et du prix qu'il attache à vos travaux . . .*'[7]

He was also one of the first to hold the new order of the *Pour le mérite für Wissenschaft und Künste,* an extension of the military order, for distinguished work in literature and the arts. Alexander von Humboldt had persuaded Frederick William IV to honour an élite of thirty men from all parts of Germany, and thirty foreigners at the same time.

The Grimms were now important enough for leading artists to be anxious to portray them. One of the finest portraits was made by the Danish painter, Elisabeth Jerichau-Baumann, who, married to the sculptor Jens Adolph Jerichau, travelled Europe in search of famous sitters. She is best known for her picture of Hans Christian Andersen, sitting by a child's bedside, reading his stories.

In January 1845 Ferdinand Grimm died in Wolfenbüttel, a strange solitary man who had almost lost contact with the rest of the family. Jacob attended his funeral, and made arrangements for his brother's books and papers to be sent to Berlin. Ferdinand had published several volumes of tales and legends.

With the family growing up, the pleasant house in the *Lennéstrasse* became too small, and in March 1846 the Grimm household moved to *Dorotheenstrasse* number 47, where they were close to the Brandenburg Gate but still within easy reach of the *Tiergarten*. Trouble with an unfriendly landlord necessitated another move the following spring, when comfortable quarters were found at number 7 *Linkstrasse*. This was near the *Potsdamer Platz,* in modern times a centre of activity, but in the mid-nineteenth century a quiet dignified quarter, with well-built houses, inhabited mainly by members of the professions. Nearby was an open market where country wives came to sell their vegetables, fruit, butter and eggs, and perhaps some snowdrops, cornflowers or even mushrooms, gathered in season by their children.

The only disturbing noise was that of the trains from the *Potsdamer Bahnhof*, but not very many came into the station then.

The Grimms remained in the *Linkstrasse* for the rest of their lives.

*Doorknocker
from a house
in Steinau*

CHAPTER 15

March Revolution, Frankfurt Parliament and After

1848 – 1859

THE late forties were unquiet and hungry years. Poor harvests made the price of grain and potatoes go up. The disappearance of many tolls inside Germany, through the Customs Union of 1834, as well as improved roads and an extending railway system, worked for a changeover from a trades-man-based economy to bigger industrial enterprise. Meantime the small man suffered.

Berlin, a growing metropolis, had its own problems. There were more and more demands for social justice. In a book addressed to Prussia's king, Bettina von Arnim had drawn attention to the misery of workers and artisans, crowded together in some of the city's decaying tenements. Many were now sub-let, each single room serving a family as living- and sleeping-quarters. The more sensitive members of society tried to help 'the deserving poor', but under the surface dissatisfaction stirred, increased dissatisfaction with conditions and with a king who had not lived up to his early liberal convictions. Cries for improvement became louder: a con-stitution would be the remedy for all evil.

An incurable romantic, Frederick William firmly believed in the Divine Right of Kings, and his neurotic fear of revolutions prevented him from recognizing the signs of the time. Schemes were proposed while the king wavered. In 1847 he at last summoned a United Prussian Diet to Berlin, but soon made it clear that there would be no constitution. No parchment should ever stand between God Almighty and his country. No rule of paragraphs was to replace the natural bonds of loyalty.

The king did not see reason until it was too late.

In March 1848, about a year after dissolving the Diet, Frederick William was faced with revolution on his own doorstep.

After the abdication of Louis-Philippe in France, waves of rebellion swept Europe. Metternich, the arch reactionary, had to flee Vienna.

All over Germany demands were made for elected representatives and for a constitution. The Prussian capital was uneasy. The king, in fear, now held out promises, but his people, neglected and disappointed, had lost confidence. There was bitterness, and tension rose. On 18 March the people rebelled, mainly against the troops held in readiness. Angry crowds marched to the palace, and there were shouts of: 'Withdraw the troops'. Suddenly in the general pellmell two shots were heard. They may have been accidental, but they sufficed to accelerate the conflict. There was rioting, hatred grew, and hundreds of barricades went up in a few hours. All classes joined the fighting: workmen, artisans, students and professional men.

As all liberal citizens, the Grimms had become disillusioned with their king. Jacob particularly had for long seen the urgent need for a constitution. Now the brothers watched with distress what amounted to civil war.

On 20 March Wilhelm wrote to his brother Ludwig:

'. . . never has there been a day of such anxiety and agitation as was the 18th of the month. At two o'clock the air was full of jubilation about the promises [made by the king], and by three o'clock the wretched fighting had broken out. For fully fourteen hours twenty to twenty-five thousand men fought fiercely against the people in the streets. The rattling of platoon fire and the burst of bullets and shrapnels was quite horrible, particularly at night. Fires broke out in different parts, and when the guns were silent for a moment, the weird sound of the tocsin could be heard . . .'[1]

After a couple of days the king withdrew the troops, not before there had been many dead and wounded. The angry people carried some two hundred bodies into the courtyard of the castle and forced the king and his queen to come down and pay homage to the glorious dead. Many prominent liberals, among them Alexander von Humboldt, took part in the mass funeral.

Only now did Frederick William grant a constitution, declaring that Prussia's interests would in future merge with those of all Germany. Riding at the head of a procession, he wore a sash in the ancient German colours: black, red and gold.

The exuberance was not to last.

Meantime representatives from all German states were elected for the first National Parliament. This 'Pre-Parliament' was to meet at the Frankfurt *Paulskirche*, with the task of preparing – in consultation with their governments – a constitution for a united Germany, a country not yet in existence.

The old Imperial City of Frankfurt received the representatives enthusiastically. There were garlands and gun salutes, and black-red-and-gold bunting fluttering across the narrow streets.

Jacob Grimm was one of the 'men of the *Paulskirche*', elected member for the district of Mühlheim/Ruhr. The finest liberal thinkers of all Germany went to Frankfurt. Among some eight hundred members, there were only a few craftsmen, merchants and men from the country, the rest were academics. All of them were elected for reasons of their personal distinction, but they were not a true cross-section of the entire population. All were possessed of the highest principles, fully aware of the importance of their work, ardent and honest. What they lacked was practical administrative experience. Much time was lost in speech-making, in proposals and counter-proposals and lengthy discussion of theories. It was natural that the learned and very serious gentlemen should want to occupy themselves thoroughly with *Grundrechte* – 'Fundamental Rights' – a concept modelled on the French and American pattern. An overweight of learning played against the need for speedy procedure.

Jacob, not a party man, attended and listened carefully, but did not often speak. His point of view was individual, gained from many years' study of German language and history. He was often impatient with pedantic pomposity.

From the beginning passions were roused at the meetings over the vexed question of Sleswick-Holstein. There existed an age-old relationship between the two duchies and Denmark. While for some seven hundred years Sleswick had been regarded as part of Denmark, Holstein was German in character, belonging first to the Holy Roman Empire and then to the German Federation. The population in both duchies was mainly German. In the fifteenth century the duchies were declared inseparable.

In 1848 when the royal house of Denmark was threatened with extinction, the question of the duchies became topical. The female line of the House of Holstein-Glücksburg was legitimate in succession in Sleswick, but in Holstein, under Salic law, the House of Augustenburg was to succeed. This would mean separation of the duchies, made impossible by the fifteenth-century ruling. When the Danish king proposed to regard Danish law of succession valid for Holstein too, public feeling rose. The German population of the duchies was up in arms. There was fighting, supported by Prussia. But soon the king yielded to an armistice when complications with European powers threatened.

The Frankfurt Parliament passionately maintained that the duchies must remain under one ruler – who in time might be a German prince – and was anti-Danish. Jacob Grimm, in spite of his many Scandinavian friends, was strongly opposed to all Danish claims.

For expediency's sake the Frankfurt assembly had in time to take the side of Prussia's king. Patriots were distressed, and the prestige of the 'Paulskirche men' suffered. Slow deliberations and hair-splitting arguments continued for some time, and it was decided that an emperor should be at the head of the new united Germany.

Paradoxically Frederick William IV was offered the German crown.

He refused. Too engrossed in legitimacy, he would not wear a crown, presented to him by the people.

This refusal, completely in keeping with the king's reactionary inclinations, dealt the Frankfurt Parliament the death blow. Hopes for a liberal and united Germany collapsed like a house of cards, and a great opportunity was missed.

Meantime revolution had been put down in Austria, and everywhere the princes once more established themselves on their shaky thrones. Particularism regained new strength.

More and more disappointed with the *Paulskirche* confabulations, Jacob had become restive by the late summer. Cholera cases were reported from Berlin, and he was worried about not being with the family, in case of danger. His own health was indifferent, and several of his friends and Göttingen associates had already left Frankfurt.

On 8 August he wrote to Dortchen, on holiday with the children at a Baltic resort:

'. . . I have had your letter yesterday, and want to thank you for all your news. As Wilhelm always forwards your letters to me, I have a very clear picture of your life at Heringsdorf and of your little household. There, among the trees, and close to the roaring sea, you live a purer and happier life than I do here, within the walls of the *Paulskirche*, among two thousand roaring people who talk against one another, and quarrel. Seldom only are they satisfied and in good spirits. In nature even unrest has a certain continuity. In fifty years from now the sea will roll against the shore just as it does now, while all these shouting people will be dead and buried, and the fate of our fatherland will have taken quite a different turn from what they imagine, and believe they are bringing about now . . .

'. . . the thought of the cholera approaching, frightens me. Even if it stays away for another few months, it is almost bound to reach Berlin in the autumn. It would be terrible for me, then to be separated from you, and I am still uncertain as to what I shall do or what your plans are. Do come here for six weeks. But if you do not wish to do so (and there will be many an obstacle), I can, as soon as the danger approaches, take two to four weeks' leave, or even give up my position here, to return and share everything with you . . .'[2]

Wilhelm and his family did not come to Frankfurt, and in September Jacob asked to be released from his duties.

Relieved, though unhappy about the frustration of democratic hopes, Jacob left the political scene, to go back to his desk.

The same year his *Geschichte der deutschen Sprache* – a history of the Germanic languages – was published. In the preface to the two volumes Jacob explained that to him the study of language was more than the mere investigation of words. It was a means to exploring man's past. From the word, his studies had always carried him to the actual thing the symbol stands for. 'I did not want only to build houses,' said Jacob, 'I wanted to live in them.'[3]

When in 1851 he read a much-discussed paper to the Berlin Academy, *Vom Ursprung der Sprache* – on the Origin of Language – he took up the subject again, stating that of everything mankind had created and preserved, language remained the noblest possession. Though the universe was full of sound, with the air whistling and howling, the fire crackling, the sea roaring, and every animal making its own specific noise, only man had speech. While primitive expressions of joy and sorrow, laughter, sighs and tears, were common to all mankind, each language was a creation, always changing, always renewing itself, an outcome of man's God-given ability to think.

This paper of Jacob's aroused hostility in some church circles because of the unorthodox views he had expressed. On 18 August 1852 the *Evangelische Kirchenzeitung* in Berlin called it their sad duty to draw attention to the pitiful abuse of an outstanding scientific reputation. It strongly objected to Jacob having doubted the story of the Tower of Babel, and having stated that far from harmful, language being manifold, was a benefit to mankind. Also, Grimm considered the conception of the Deity speaking to Man, the idea of Angels and Demons, images only, and not literal truth, nor did he hold with the creation of one couple, Adam and Eve, only. With other of his contemporaries, including Goethe, he preferred to believe in the creation of several couples as 'original man'.

It seems that the controversy did not attract wide attention and that the matter was allowed to lapse.

In 1853 Jacob, feeling the need for relaxation, once more indulged his love for travel. He went to Switzerland, and by way of Lake Geneva, to Lyons. He continued on the Rhône to Avignon, and saw Nîmes and Montpellier. Suffering from crowds and great heat in Marseilles, he thought this was a place to be avoided. Undaunted, however, he returned by way of Venice, Austria and Prague, a tremendous distance to be traversed by an elderly gentleman.

His observation was as keen as ever.

On 9 August 1853 he reported from Prague:

'. . . from Salzburg the route goes through very pleasant scenery, close to castles and lakes, to Ischl which is an elegant resort, effective less through its waters than the purity of its air. It possesses some palace-like houses, and an enormous hotel, Tallachini. All the villages around are friendly and welcoming, one with a fine Protestant church . . . One travels to the Ebensee, and by boat between rocks to Gemunden, from where a railway goes to Linz. Linz I knew from former days. With a fair going on, it was difficult to find rooms. The town is larger and much improved. The Danube is already quite broad here. From Linz to Budweis in Bohemia, one again travels by rail. These railways, however, are all horsedrawn, and move clumsily. Built originally for the transport of salt only, they were later extended to convey people. From Budweis to Prague, too, the journey has its difficulties. I went by the so-called *Stellwagen*, a kind of omnibus, where one meets a very mixed company. It takes twenty-two hours from Budweis to Prague. In the small Austrian towns food is bad, but they make good coffee, drunk always from glasses. Prague, true to its reputation, makes a grand old-world impression. Its streets are lively and full of people. There is a feeling of history about . . .'⁴

Wilhelm's holiday had been delayed by Dortchen falling ill on the way, in Marburg. After some anxious weeks they were able to continue and to enjoy the vintage on the Rhine in fine autumn weather.

With the necessity of spending long hours at the work of the German dictionary, the brothers had given up lecturing to students. They still read papers to the academy. Wilhelm read one on the history of rhyme, while Jacob concerned himself with many aspects of linguistics. Close to his three score years and ten, he often worked for twelve hours a day. He tackled the letters A to C of the dictionary entirely alone. Then Wilhelm started on the letter D. They now realized that the enormous task could not be completed in their lifetime, but kept their heads above water in 'an ocean of work'. In 1852 a first part of the great dictionary was finished, and in 1854 the complete first volume appeared, sixteen years after the idea had been mooted. It had an excellent reception and was all the talk at the Leipzig Book Fair.

Everywhere the brothers' work was praised, and letters of congratulation arrived from many countries. The Icelandic scholar, Gislason, wrote to Jacob on 18 March 1854:

'. . . from the time when I, at school in Iceland . . . began to learn German, I was mightily attracted by the great nation of which you are an ornament. Even then the name of Grimm was praised and loved on that far off island . . .'⁵

Older works of the brothers were reprinted, and particularly the fairy-tales went from edition to edition. They now stood on many bookshelves next to the Bible, and had become a favourite with children.

To the 1856 edition of the third volume of the *Household Tales*, Wilhelm added a section: *Various Testimonies to the Value of Fairytales*. He took quotations from many sources, far apart in time and place. They began with a chorus from Aristophanes' *Lysistrata*: 'I will tell ye a story', and continued through Antiquity to modern writers, Cervantes, Goethe and Scott among them. The guiding sentiment was perhaps expressed best in Martin Luther's words: 'I would not for any money part with the wonderful stories which I have kept in my memory since my earliest childhood, or have met with in my progress through life'.[6]

An illustration of Jacob's and Wilhelm's popularity as fairytale collectors is the much repeated story of the *Märchengroschen* – the Fairytale-Penny – about which Wilhelm wrote in a letter to Frau von Arnswaldt, née von Haxthausen, on 2 March 1859:

'. . . you will have read about the *Märchengroschen*, a little girl brought us. The story has made the rounds of the newspapers. She was a fine child with beautiful eyes. She saw Jacob first, then Dortchen brought her to me. Carrying the book of fairytales under her arm, she asked: "May I read to you from it?" She then read, well and in a natural manner, the tale which ends: "Whosoever does not believe this, must pay a thaler." "As I do not believe it, I must pay you a thaler. But as I do not get much pocket money, I cannot pay it all at once". From a little pink purse the child then took a *Groschen*, and handed it to me. I said: "I will give the *Groschen* back to you." "No," she answered, "Mamma says that one must not accept money presents." After that she took a courteous farewell . . .'[7]

This young visitor deeply impressed the brothers who themselves preserved a childlike and lovable simplicity till right into old age. It illuminated their home life, and unexpected glimpses of it turn up in their writings.

There is, for example, Jacob's paper, read to the Academy in 1850 to honour Savigny on the occasion of the fiftieth anniversary of his obtaining the degree of Doctor of Law. Jacob recalled an experience of some three years earlier, when he had been invited to lunch at Savigny's house to celebrate the king's birthday.

Walking through the *Tiergarten*, Jacob had contemplated with pleasure his friend's and former professor's achievements. Then, arriving at the *Wilhelmstrasse*:

'. . . through the stream of carriages one walked up broad carpeted steps, flanked by boxes of rare plants. The large carpeted drawing-room, candlelit, was filled with a multitude of splendidly dressed people, most of them unknown to me. It was so crowded that people could only just tend me the tip of a gloved finger. As usual, Dortchen had at my request sewn the decorations on to my coat. They made a little tinkling noise, and were perhaps not quite in their proper places. To anyone like myself, it is troublesome to get out decorations, put them into order, have them sewn on, take them off, and put them away again. Soon everybody took his allotted place, and the meal began, as is the custom, with lavish dishes but only halting, slow conversation. Dishes are served from all directions, but conversation is kept at a low ebb. One is reluctant to bother a strange neighbour with talk, and just barely replies to an indifferent question . . .'

Then, after Savigny had proposed the royal toast, Jacob was itching to get up and say a few words in honour of his friend who, after an interval of some years, had just published the sixth volume of his work on Roman Law.

But:

'. . . a gentleman of rank, whose name I cannot remember, appeared to have noticed my inner as well as outward excitement, and when he looked at me enquiringly, I told him, quite unconcerned of my intention to say something about Savigny's book which had just been published. Kindly enough, my neighbour replied that it was, of course, up to me to do what I liked, but it was not considered proper to toast another person after the royal toast had been given at a meal. Confronted with such authority, my thoughts, prompted by the moment, floated away as – during this month – do the leaves of the trees, one after the other. No doubt there was good reason for this Berlin etiquette. Inside myself, however, I was full of rebellion . . .'[8]

Surely, thought Jacob, it would do no harm to praise after the king somebody whose work was so deserving of praise. Would not in the end all the fashionable company have risen to give honour where honour was due.

Jacob made the paper in praise of his professor an occasion for recalling student days:

'. . . I arrived in Marburg, not knowing any difference between professors, and believing all to be equally good; soon, however, I came to like your lectures best of all . . . I did not just listen, my mind became impressed with your looks and your gestures . . .'[9]

Jacob then remembered that a short while after, in Paris, walking or working beside his teacher, he had kept his eyes fixed on him, looking up to him as a shining example. Eventually their paths had separated, and still he could confess himself Savigny's pupil, though the pupil had grown to be unlike his teacher in almost every way. And yet:

'. . . the breath of your humane instruction wakened my mind to scientific conception, and since all the sciences are basically one . . . your influence has lasted, and your example has provided an impetus even when my desire for learning drove me to fields, untrodden by you . . .'[10]

Jacob pictured his early visits to Savigny's home. In the old town of Marburg, clinging to the hill, crowned by the towering castle of the Landgraves, there had been flights of steps and many steep and narrow lanes. From his rooms the young student had set out daily to climb these lanes, and walking across an ancient cemetery had reached his professor's cheerful house:

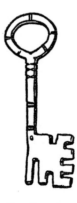

*Small hammer
belonging to the
Grimm family*

Key for chest

'. . . a servant, called Bake, opened the door, and one entered a not too large room, and then, through another door, a smaller one with a sofa . . .'[11]

The rooms were bright and sunny, the whitewashed walls decorated with fine engravings, the floors made of pine wood. The windows gave on the river Lahn below, green meadows and the hazy blue of distant hills. There was enchantment, with the greatest magic in the cupboards, full of rare and interesting books.

Over half a century Jacob remembered with gratitude the master of this treasure house, the professor, only five years older than himself. He was tall, and looked slight, in his grey coat and brown silk waistcoat with blue stripes, his dark hair falling straight over his shoulders. Unforgotten was his encouragement and help, his kindness and the cheerful humour of his free and independent personality. And it was a memorable day indeed when this adored teacher had commented on Jacob's first written essay on a legal question: 'Not only properly judged, but very well presented'. That morning young Jacob had skipped down the steps, back to his rooms.

For Wilhelm life had become more quiet.

With his health far from robust, he no longer attended many official occasions, nor did he travel very far. He paid visits to German watering-places and health resorts, and enjoyed their varying attractions. During a stay in the little town of Friedrichsroda, in the Thuringian Forest, in August 1852 he wrote to their friend Dahlmann about the pleasure of the surrounding pine forests, the pure refreshing air and the tranquillity of the place.[12] In his contacts with old friends the simple domestic kept turning up again and again, as when – on 13 April 1855 – he wrote to Gervinus:

'. . . when you and your wife visited us for the first time in Göttingen, and we saw you down the stairs, we let you peep into our larder, so that you should have seen everything. In it was a shelf of preserves, strawberries, cherries and apricots, and I said: "This is my wife's library, and she keeps nothing but good books". I do wish . . . that memories of us, will now and then present you with such a jar of preserves which you will find agreeable . . .'[13]

In October 1859 Herman Grimm married Gisela von Arnim, Bettina's daughter. It was the last family celebration Wilhelm was to witness.

CHAPTER 16

The Declining Years

1859 – 1863

WILHELM and his family had enjoyed an autumn holiday in Pillnitz on the river Elbe, and had returned to Berlin, happy and refreshed. A few weeks later he fell ill suddenly. A carbuncle on his back had to be lanced, and refused to heal. A high temperature complicated the condition. Then the patient seemed a little easier. He could sit up in bed and look at proofs of a new edition of his *Freidank*. He began laying out presentation copies of another edition of the *Household Tales*, just ready from the press. The family was relieved and hopeful. During the night from the 15th to the 16th of December Wilhelm's temperature again rose alarmingly. He became delirious, but recognized Jacob, who sat on a low stool by his bedside, though he took his brother for a portrait of him, and remarked on the good likeness. He also spoke quietly and clearly about his own life, past and present, almost cheerful in spite of his discomforts.

At three o'clock the following afternoon Wilhelm died.

His enfeebled constitution had not been able to withstand the onslaught. He had lived beyond his early expectations, almost completing his seventy-fourth year.

Fittingly, Wilhelm's coffin, covered with wreaths and flowers, was placed in his study, among his books. Jacob was deeply shocked and saddened, but carried himself with strength and dignity. He was a comfort to the widowed Dortchen, her two sons and daughter. In turn, it was solace to him to know that they would stay together, and the household remain unchanged. In all the world only Dortchen knew Jacob's needs, and though he was the older of the two, she cared for him like a mother.

Herman Grimm later recollected:

'. . . the newspapers printed romantic-sounding reports about Jacob's state after his brother's death. It was said that he roamed the empty rooms in despair, looking for him. None of this is true. He took the event quietly, though he had least expected it. When I wakened him towards morning during the last night, and entered his darkened bedroom, I could hear him

Clemens Brentano. Etching by Ludwig Emil Grimm. Brüder Grimm
Museum, Kassel. Original drawing missing since the War

The Tiergarten, Berlin. Deutsche Staatsbibliothek, Berlin

The Academy, Berlin. Deutsche Staatsbibliothek, Berlin

breathe quietly. "O dear," he said, "I thought all would be well now."
After my father had died, Jacob often went to my father's study, where he
was lying, and looked at him closely. At the funeral, in a strong wind, with
the snow crunching underfoot, he walked sturdily between my brother
and myself, up the small rise of the cemetery. All who then stood by the
graveside, will remember how in the end Jacob's fine fingers groped for a
lump of earth, to throw down into the grave. There appeared to be no
change in him. He at once took up his work again, and carried on the way
he had done always . . .'[1]

Jacob lived on with the steadfastness of a man, grown old and wise, a
man who knows that his own days are numbered, and who finds comfort
in that very thought.

Herman Grimm wrote his father's obituary. After summing up
Wilhelm's life work, he spoke of his father's personal qualities. Those who
had known him, would remember his gentleness and tranquillity, his
fair judgement, and the air of friendliness always about him. His had been
an optimism of the noblest kind. Everywhere, even in the greatest upset
and confusion, he would look for and discover a tendency towards the good.
Faithful to people and places, he enjoyed going back to where he had been
before, walking again the well known paths. He was a loving friend and a
good companion, fond of telling stories, in a manner natural and poetic
at the same time, the very manner that distinguished his literary work,
which would be his lasting memorial.[2]

Wilhelm's enduring love for 'people and places' is shown in the great
many letters to friends he so obviously enjoyed writing all his life. One to
Amalie Hassenpflug, sister of Lotte's husband – of 4 March 1849 – is typical:

'. . . I want to write you a few lines to tell you how pleased I was with you
remembering my birthday. Our hands remain clasped, and sometimes we
can actually clasp them, since the railway has brought us so close to each
other. Very often and quite spontaneously do I remember the old Cassel
days, more than the time at Göttingen. It is like the scent of a flower,
suddenly bringing back a clear impression of bygone days. I then feel as
if I were walking again in the evening through the *Aue*, between solitary
trees, drenched in pale sunlight while all is quiet. I know every step, and
that is why I like it so much, for I am attached to everything I have had for
a long time, and which I have lived with . . .'[3]

On 5 July 1860 Jacob delivered a talk in memory of his brother at the
Berlin Academy. It is a fine record of the brothers' closeness.

'. . . I have been asked to talk about my brother, whom for six months past
now my eyes can no longer see. But at night in my dreams, without any
thought of his having gone, he is still beside me. In his memory I will put
down a bunch of recollections . . .'[4]

Jacob went on to speak about their schooldays when time seemed to move slowly, while:

'. . . we shared one bed and one small room. We sat working at the same table, later, in our student days, there were two beds and two tables in one and the same room. Later again, we had two desks, still in the same room, and up to the very end, we worked in two rooms next to each other, always under one roof . . .'[5]

They had been content to share goods and chattels, including their beloved books. Only when each of them needed a title for constant reference, two copies of a book would be bought. Soon their last beds would be made side by side, too. With such close companionship all through life, it was hard to speak of his brother without speaking about himself also:

'. . . from earliest childhood, I was possessed of unwearying industry, made impossible for him through indifferent health . . .'[6]

Wilhelm's work, however, had been illuminated in a way his – Jacob's – was not. Not given to quick invention, Wilhelm's ways had been slow and deliberate. Working quietly and serenely had given him joy, while Jacob's pleasure had come from work's intensity itself. Shut up in his study, Jacob had spent many a night over his books, while Wilhelm was in cheerful company where people loved him, and listened to his tales with delight. Wilhelm had greatly enjoyed music which had given Jacob only limited pleasure.

But in spite of all these differences, they had shared much. These common qualities would continue to live in their work, culminating in the great dictionary. Wilhelm had been spared to finish his labours on the letter D. Future generations, thought Jacob, might attach special value to his and Wilhelm's work on the fairytales.

'. . . of all our books, the fairytales were closest to his [Wilhelm's] heart, and he never lost sight of them . . . Every time I now take up these fairytales, I am deeply moved, for on every page I see him before me, and recognise his mind at work . . .'[7]

On 26 January 1860 Jacob had given a paper to the Academy: *Über das Alter* – About Old Age. A thin old man, his white locks falling over the collar of his long coat, his eyes as bright as ever, he had stood explaining that old age need not be an affliction but rather a time of serenity, like the cool of the evening after the heat of the day. Nature, a garden, the starry sky at night might mean much to an old man. For the first time during life he might allow himself the leisure for long quiet walks, and speaking of the joy of his own walks in the *Tiergarten*, he referred to the pleasure it had given him to meet Wilhelm suddenly, coming from the opposite direction. They had nodded to each other, and gone on silently. 'That can no longer happen now . . .', he added wistfully. Mental activity need not decline with age, Jacob insisted; it could, indeed, be of high quality.[8]

Jacob himself was a good example of his own pronouncement. He remained committed to his work, so much so that, from time to time, the family had to tempt him away from his desk. Work on the dictionary came first and foremost. He wrote to the publisher, Salomon Hirzel, on 6 February 1860:

'. . . during the next few days I will write a short preface [for the second volume of the dictionary]; I cannot yet get rid of my sad thoughts, and wish I were able to get back to my old ways of working. In Wilhelm's room everything has been left as it was, and we are having a painter make a picture of it . . .'[9]

In the preface to the dictionary's second volume Jacob wrote about his brother who actually should have written this very preface, as most of the volume was his work:

'. . . while I am mourning his passing, it is left for me to speak . . . his talent and his advice, his whole worthy support are now lost to the dictionary . . .'[10]

Work alone could not overcome Jacob's inner loneliness. Though he was now a little deaf, and could not always follow conversation easily, he enjoyed the visits of friends more than in his younger days. He liked to take them on his *Tiergarten* rambles, and they were astonished to see him stride out, left hand on back, with no stick to support him. They sometimes found it difficult to keep up with his quick walk. Jacob maintained an eager interest in everything that happened, putting down his pen the moment the newspapers arrived, ready to scan their pages for news of the day.

There were many changes. In 1858 King Frederick William's growing instability had turned into insanity, making it necessary to appoint his brother, Prince William, regent. On Frederick William's death in 1861, he ascended the throne as William I. Known to be anti-liberal, Prince William had gone through periods of intense unpopularity. He had none of his brother's imaginative qualities, but he soon showed the firmness needed at the head of a Prussia which was grooming itself to play the leading part in uniting Germany.

Jacob, increasingly liberal and democratic, must have been worried over the new 'blood and iron' concept, introduced largely by the power behind the throne, the young squire from Brandenburg, Otto von Bismarck. Jacob recognized with satisfaction the stirrings of genuine national feeling which accompanied the founding of the German *National-verein* and the celebrations of the hundredth anniversary of Schiller's birth.

In 1862 Jacob laid aside his work on the dictionary to get ready for the press a fourth volume of his *Weistümer*, the collection of ancient law practices. It was published in 1863.

On 25 December 1862 Jacob wrote to his Swedish colleague, Anders Uppström, learned editor of the *Codex Argenteus*:

'. . . as my life draws nearer its end, its downhill pace is quickening, and while I keep working steadily, months pass almost like days. My health is declining too, and often gives me trouble, but industry continues, and the wish to go on with what I have begun, remains . . .'[11]

Of this time Herman Grimm writes:

'. . . lately his nights were not as good as before. He woke up and could not go to sleep again. "How nice are the long summer days, to which birds and men look forward! They remind us of our youth when the hours seem to absorb light, and go past slowly. What's left is swallowed soon by the dark of winter and of age. Now I am almost seventy-eight years old, and when I lie awake in bed, the good light comforts me, and calls forth thoughts and memories. 3. June 1862. Jac. Grimm." I found these words, written on a small slip, inside his wallet. He liked to look at the stars, ever since his early days . . .'[12]

In the autumn of 1863 Jacob spent three happy weeks with the family in the Harz mountains, and back in Berlin began work again with real zest. But, unknown to him, life was closing in.

Herman Grimm recollected later:

'. . . it looked as if he [Jacob] might go on for a good many years. When in the spring of 1863 his brother Ludwig Grimm, painter and professor at the Cassel Academy, died, he said: "Now I am the only one left", without thinking that so soon it would be his turn too. He had been given a present of Flourens's book, *Sur la longévité*, as he was collecting material for a revision of his paper about old age. Flourens's book states that the life of a man should be one hundred years. Jokingly he said that it was his intention to reach that age. That now and then he lay down for a little, or, sitting at his desk, let his head sink over his folded arms for a short time, was more a natural need for rest than a sign of declining strength. When he thought it necessary, he could work without interruption. He did not even guess that so suddenly he would be interrupted for ever. There was much in his mind. He wanted to continue with the dictionary, write an introduction to the fairytales, and another volume of *Weistümer* was to be printed, with a lengthy introduction. He also planned a book on German manners and customs. Then there was to be a book on *Ossian*, and he had many more plans only known to himself. The last thing he had printed was a review of Jockbloet's book on *Reinhard*, in the *Göttinger Anzeigen*. Next he might have written a review for the same paper on Goethe's correspondence with Karl August. I found in his desk a newly folded sheet, with the title of the book as a beginning. For this work he wanted to glance through Goethe's correspondence with *Frau* von Stein, and he asked me that if I was to buy the book – which I meant to do – I should do so now. The last thing he read were the proofs, sent to him, of a collection of Greek fairytales. He looked through them with great interest and made some pencil notes. Books sent to him he usually read at once, always pen or pencil in hand. He left a great number of slips with quotations which were all noted down in that way.

'He had before his last illness, as had my father, much benefited from a short autumn holiday. Soon after returning a cold brought about inflammation of the liver. Then it appeared to improve. His days were good, while the nights were restless. During the day he would read in bed for hours, but through the night he had a temperature. He was to get up to sleep better. On a Saturday afternoon when he tried to be up for the second time, sitting at the window next to my sister, she felt him sink towards her. A stroke had affected his right side. He fell into a state of drowsiness, able to move his leg during the moments he was awake, less so his arm, and his tongue was paralysed. He often touched his right arm with the left hand, as if he wanted to find out what was happening to him. This lasted through the night. Sunday, towards morning, he seemed to regain more consciousness, turning his eyes towards us and the friends who were with us, around him. He seemed to understand what we said, and he moved a lot. For a moment we thought him gone, when suddenly he seized a photograph of Wilhelm nearby, and with his sound hand raised it quickly – in his usual manner – close to his eyes. He looked at it for a few moments, then put it down on the bedcover. On Sunday 20 September, at twenty minutes past ten at night, he breathed his last. His bed, as he had predicted, was made beside that of his brother . . .'[13]

Almost to the very end, Jacob had been in good spirits, and the family felt his loss deeply. His niece, Auguste, thanking Fritz Reuter, author, and friend of the Grimms, for his expression of sympathy, wrote, on 9 January 1864:

'. . . Mamma intended to write herself to thank you. But it is too hard for her in her great sorrow. She immediately starts weeping . . . Uncle was always so cheerful and well, that we were apt to forget his age. At times he was in very high spirits, as when last August we were preparing to travel to the Harz mountains, and he sat quite seriously at the dining-room table, wearing Mamma's straw hat with ribbons over his long white locks. And how happy was he when the weather was bad, and he did not have to go for a walk, but could sit at his desk from early morning till late into the night . . .'[14]

The Grimms belonged to the parish of St Matthew, and the brothers were laid to rest in the *Matthäikirchhof*. Jacob had left instructions that nothing but: 'here lies . . .' and the name and dates should be put on their graves. His orders were obeyed when two black marble tombstones were erected later on.

A large company of friends and fellow-philologists followed Jacob's coffin. They had come to pay their respects to a man they all honoured, and many loved dearly. Papers and learned journals were full of appreciation of Jacob's work. They praised the depth and sheer volume of his publications. It was a debatable point how much would remain valid of his investigations, but he himself had been fully aware of constant changes. Indeed, the second and third revisions of some of his books had often had the impact of a completely new piece of work. He was not to be judged by how little he had left for his successors to do, but rather by the impetus he had given.

Everywhere tributes were paid to Jacob's humbleness and his simple way of life, a life that found satisfaction in deep involvement in work for work's own sake. Unassuming and free from pretence, he had never coveted honour or position. This man whom an adverse critic had once called 'a beaver burrowing among his books', had his full share of human understanding and love, a love most deeply expressed for his family, above all Wilhelm, Dortchen and the children whom he counted his very own. He had known devoted students too. Those who had sat at his feet, deriving pleasure from his lectures, and gaining a new love for Germanic studies, would forever cherish the memory of his expressive head, his sharply cut features and penetrating keen eyes.

It was left to future generations to assess fully the significance of Jacob and Wilhelm Grimm's work.

Design on a family gravestone in Steinau Cemetery

CHAPTER 17

The *Nursery and Household Tales* and their influence

WHEN at Christmas 1812 the first slim volume of the *Nursery and Household Tales* appeared on the shelves of German bookshops, nobody, least of all the brothers Grimm themselves, could have foreseen that this collection of tales would in time become one of the greatest successes in the history of publishing, and that some hundred and fifty years later readers would have access to it in over seventy languages.

The book certainly had an immediate response. It was received with pleasure by a good few, but there was criticism too. This was not levelled at the stories being too much 'embellished', rather the contrary, readers found them too stark, and Brentano said openly that he was bored by them. Even the more moderate Arnim had reservations, believing that the presentation of the book did not make it attractive to children. He feared that a 'Leipzig speculator' might make a choice of the most entertaining stories, and publish them with illustrations.

As we have seen, this is exactly what the Grimms did themselves after Taylor's translations had made an English selection very popular. For the *Kleine Ausgabe* of 1825 they chose the fifty best liked tales.

Criticism or no criticism, the *Nursery and Household Tales* were selling. Not many years after publication nine hundred copies of the first volume were sold, and Reimer of Berlin was considering another edition. He was also prepared to take the risk of a second volume which appeared in 1815. A second edition came out in 1819, and a separate volume of notes and commentaries in 1822. Altogether seven editions were published during the brothers' lifetime. The eighth edition, in 1864, was taken care of by Herman Grimm, Wilhelm's son. Also, a one-volume edition gained great popularity at the end of the century.

The first volume of the standard edition contained eighty-six, and the second seventy tales, while the acknowledged canon, now, including children's legends, consists of over two hundred. Tales have been published from the Grimms' manuscripts, and also those printed in early editions and eliminated later for one reason or another. Notable among these publications is a selection by Wilhelm Hansen, *Grimms' Other Tales*, which appeared in English at the Golden Cockerel Press, in 1956. A modern English edition, based on the translation by Margaret Hunt, revised, corrected and completed by James Stern, has the advantage of an excellent introduction by Padraic Colum, and extensive notes on the tales and their collectors. *Die Märchen der Brüder Grimm, Urfassung nach der Original-handschrift der Abtei Oelenberg im Elsass*, by Joseph Lefftz, published in Heidelberg in 1927, and *Die Kinder-und Hausmärchen der Brüder Grimm, vollständige Ausgabe in der Urfassung*, edited by Friedrich Panzer (Wiesbaden 1935), provide ample material for the comparative study of texts. In 1949 the Winkler Verlag of Munich issued a complete edition of the *Household Tales*, containing the foreword of the 1819 edition, a memoir of his father and uncle by Herman Grimm, and a number of fine illustrations by Ludwig Grimm. In 1962 the Eugen Diederichs Verlag reprinted in its series *Märchen der Weltliteratur*, an edition of the *Kinder-und Hausmärchen*, which had appeared originally in 1912, on the occasion of the hundredth anniversary of the collection's first publication. It was edited by the late Professor Friedrich von der Leyen, who arranged the tales in a chronological order of his own making. The Grimms had published their material as it came to hand. Von der Leyen's classification illustrates his theory that the shape of a certain tale is related to the literary style of the age that produced it. He traced the development of the tale in Germany from primitive belief and ancient custom, via the heroic sagas and the Middle Ages, the sixteenth, seventeenth and eighteenth century, up to comparatively modern times. Special types of tales were put together in his edition. Von der Leyen himself did not insist on his arrangement being generally accepted, but it did lead to looking at the tales from a new angle.

There are countless editions in German of the whole collection and of single tales, many are used as school readers.

Only a few years after the first publication of the Grimms' collection, some tales were translated into Danish. There followed a complete edition in Dutch, and Taylor's English translations. Taylor's work was to form the basis for many translations into lesser known languages, and by the end of the last century Grimms' Fairytales were widely read all over Europe and in the United States.

Today the *Brüder Grimm Museum*, in Kassel records translations into the following languages:

Afrikaans, Albanian, Altaic, Armenian, Azerbaijani, Bengali, Bessarabian, Bulgarian, Catalan, Chinese, Cingalese, Croatian, Czech, Danish, Dutch, English, Esperanto, Esthonian, Ewe, Finnish, French, Georgian, Greek, Hebrew, Hindi, Hungarian, Ibo, Icelandic, Irish, Italian, Japanese,

Kazakh, Korean, Latvian, Lithuanian, Luxembourgeois, Macedonian, Malay, Mari, Moldavian, Mongol, Norwegian, Ossetic, Persian, Polish, Portuguese, Rumanian, Russian, Schwyzerdütsch, Serbian, Sikolo, Slovac, Slovene, Spanish, Swedish, Tajiki, Tagal, Thai, Turkish, Turkmanish, Tsova-Tush, Ukrainian, Vietnamese, Volapük, Welsh, Yiddish.

The publication of the *Household Tales* was a fertilizing influence on literature as a whole, but it made a quite special impact on the writing for children. Tales, genuine and spurious, proliferated. Characters from the Grimms' collection appeared in opera, song and ballet, and adapted themselves to film and television.

From the very beginning the *Nursery and Household Tales* inspired artists, with illustrators in almost every part of the world. Ludwig Grimm made many delightful drawings – not all published – for the brothers' collection. His imagery expressed the same keen understanding of oral tradition which his brothers had shown in words. His work succeeds in conveying simplicity and child-like enchantment. Ludwig's fine drawing of the *Viehmännin*, the Fairytale-Wife, became the frontispiece of the 1819 edition. A multitude of illustrators followed in Germany, among

Illustration by George Cruikshank
By courtesy of the *Brüder Grimm Museum*, Kassel

them the very popular Ludwig Richter, whose drawings were in the first place made for Bechstein's collections of tales, published in 1845 and 1856. Tender-hearted, Richter favoured the sweet and sentimental incidents of the tales, and depicted them lovingly. In the nineteenth century, Count Franz Pocci created illustrations in the tradition of the German *Kasperle* puppet shows, slightly grotesque and not unlike the popular Munich broadsheets, printed in the new technique of lithography.

Much can be learnt by looking at illustrators from different countries. Their personal approach may reveal the approach of a whole nation. George Cruikshank, for example, in the illustrations for *German Popular Stories*, stressed the antiquarian, the quaint and the funny, possibly a very English approach to tales at that time. Arthur Rackham, inclined to the spectacular and dramatic, has had a wide appeal. His work still decorates Spanish and Finnish editions of the *Household Tales*.

French artists are apt to emphasize the pretty and elegant – seven charming little beds with puffy muslin curtains, in the house of *Snow-White's* dwarfs. They like formal little gardens, and a well-starched apron on a trim country girl. The Italians tend to stage-like scenes, as when the

Illustration by George Cruikshank
By courtesy of the *Brüder Grimm Museum*, Kassel

170

seven dwarfs march to work in single file across a tree trunk serving as a bridge. In Scandinavian countries figures may take on troll-like appearance. Some remarkable work has been done in Central and Eastern Europe, particularly in Czechoslovakia, Hungary, Poland and Rumania. The Czech artist Trnka's illustrations are outstanding, reminiscent of that country's great puppet tradition.

Even in one and the same country there may be regional distinctions, as in the *Little Red-Riding-Hood* illustrations from Yugoslavia. From the farming region of Slovenia comes a little peasant girl with long plaits, while the big bad wolf wears farmer's boots. In Belgrade, however, *Little Red-Riding-Hood* is a city maiden, complete with mini skirt and sophisticated make-up. In an edition, published in Zagreb, Austrian tradition lingers, with *Riding-Hood* wearing a wide *dirndl* skirt, and the huntsman forester's uniform. And this, with Austrian rule gone for half a century. Some very original work has come from the Soviet Union, with impressive peasants and workmanlike dwarfs, though a tendency remains in Russia to reprint older German illustrations.

Countries of the Middle and Far East sometimes begin by reprinting European illustrations, to commission work by local artists for later editions. Background and figures then take on local colour. There is a charming Japanese edition where the old goat in *The Wolf and the Seven Little Kids* wears a kimono. Often figures revert to European costume, but the strange setting survives.

Also, what is considered shocking in one country may not be so in another. German children, for example, accept the fact that the ass in *The Wishing Table, the Gold-ass and the Cudgel in the Sack* 'spits' gold from its back. The ass is shown in the process in an illustration, the very illustration which has to be redrawn for some countries to show gold coming from the animal's mouth only, the implication of 'gold from the animal's back passage' being considered improper and in poor taste. Translators often have to adapt their wording for similar reasons.

Needless to say, there is a flood of cheap editions here and on the other side of the Atlantic with pictures dwelling on sugariness or violence, and debasing the intrinsic beauty of the tales.

The question of cruelty in fairytales is a perennial one, and a passionate controversy whether they make good reading for children started the moment the Grimms' collection was first published. A story about children playing at 'butcher', where one child kills another, raised many objections, and was in fact omitted in later editions.

As remains from more savage states of mankind, all tales, wherever they may have originated, will present cruel situations and incidents. There never seems to be cruelty for cruelty's sake. Whether these tales are fit entertainment for a child will depend always on the individual child's susceptibility.

It is true also that the traditional tale's simplicity is best suited to the spoken word, and that with a young child, the teller who has 'the feel' of his audience, can adapt or even shorten a frightening tale. A child introduced to tales by having them told to him, later on makes a more understanding reader. Tales by radio or television, lately even by telephone, can never replace stories told by mother or nurse to the child directly.

The late Lisa Tetzner, an experienced collector and storyteller, when considering the question whether, because of their cruelty, fairytales should disappear from the nursery, thought that, sooner or later, the child would meet cruelty in real life. It might therefore be best to learn about it early. Later encounters might well prove more traumatic, and for this very reason some psychologists regard the fairytale as a useful safety valve. It satisfies the child's need for 'black and white', the 'goodies' and the 'baddies'. A child enjoys having his latent feelings of pity, hate and cruelty expressed in a tale. Also, in most tales there is somebody refusing to execute brutal orders, someone who knows mercy, and will engage the child's sympathy. No child, Lisa Tetzner believed, would think it cruel when the bad queen – who tried several times to murder her daughter – has to dance herself to death on red-hot embers.[1]

In the introduction to an English selection from the *Nursery and Household Tales*, published in London in 1868, Ruskin discussed the stories' suitability for children:

'. . . children . . . will find in the apparently vain and fitful courses of any tradition of old time, honestly delivered to them, a teaching for which no other can be substituted, and of which the power cannot be measured; fortifying them against the glacial cold of selfish science, and preparing them submissively, and with no bitterness of astonishment, to behold, in later years, the mystery – divinely appointed to remain such to all human thought – of the fates that happen alike to the evil and the good . . .

'. . . every fairytale worth recording at all is the remnant of a tradition possessing true historical value – historical at least in so far as it has naturally arisen out of the mind of a people under special circumstances, and risen not without meaning, nor removed altogether from their sphere of religious faith. It sustains afterwards natural changes from the sincere action of the fear or fancy of successive generations; it takes new colour from their manner of life, and new form from their changing moral tempers. As long as these changes are natural and effortless, accidental and inevitable, the story remains essentially true, altering its form, indeed, like a flying cloud, but remaining a sign of the sky; a shadowy image, as truly a part of the great firmament of the human mind as the light of reason which it seems to interrupt. But the fair deceit and innocent error of it cannot be interpreted nor restrained by a wilful purpose, and all editions to it by art do but defile, as the shepherd disturbs the flakes of morning mist with smoke from his fire of dead leaves.

'There is also a deeper collateral mischief in this indulgence of licentious change and retouching of stories to suit particular tastes, or inculcate favourite doctrines. It directly destroys the child's power of rendering any

Illustration by Ludwig Richter
By courtesy of the *Brüder Grimm Museum*, Kassel

such belief as it would otherwise have been in his nature to give to an imaginative vision. How far it is expedient to occupy his mind with ideal forms at all may be questionable to many, though not to me; but it is quite beyond question that if we do allow of the fictitious representation, that representation should be calm and complete, possessed to the full, and read down its utmost depth. The little reader's attention should never be confused or disturbed, whether he is possessing himself of fairy tale or history. Let him know his fairy tale accurately, and have perfect joy or awe in the conception of it as if it were real; thus he will always be exercising his power of grasping realities: but a confused, careless, and discrediting tenure of the fiction will lead to as confused and careless reading of fact. Let the circumstances of both be strictly perceived, and long dwelt upon, and let the child's own mind develop fruit of thought from both. It is of the greatest importance early to secure this habit of contemplation . . .'[2]

Sir Walter Scott expressed similar views on popular tales, in a letter, written in Edinburgh, on 16 January 1823.

'Sir, I have to return my best thanks for the very acceptable present your goodness has made me in your interesting volume of German tales and traditions. I have often wished to see such a work undertaken by a gentleman of taste sufficient to adapt the simplicity of the German narrative to our own, which you have done so successfully. When my family were at the happy age of being auditors to fairytales I have very often endeavoured to translate to them in such an extempore manner as I could and was always gratified by the pleasure which the German fictions seemed to convey. In memory of which our old family cat still bears the foreign name of Hinze which so often occurs in the little narratives. In a great number of these tales I can perfectly remember the nursery stories of my childhood, some of them distinctly and others like the memory of a dream. Should you ever think of enlarging your very interesting notes I would with pleasure forward to you such of the tales as I remember. The Prince Paddock was for instance a legend well known to me where a princess is sent to fetch water in a sieve from the Well of the Worlds End [and] succeeds by the advice of the frog who aids her on promise to become his bride.

> Stop with moss and dugg with clay
> And that will weize the water away.

'The frog comes to claim his bride and to tell the tale with effect the sort of splash which he makes in leaping on the floor ought to be imitated singing

> Open the door my hinny my heart
> Open the door my ain wee thing
> And mind the words that you and me spoke
> Down the meadow [by] the well-spring

In the same strain is the song of the little bird:

> My mother me killed
> My father me ate etc, etc.

Independently of the curious circumstances that such tales should be found existing in very different countries and languages which augurs a greater poverty of human invention than we would have expected there is also a sort of wild fairy interest in them which makes me think them fully better adapted to awaken the imagination and soften the heart of childhood than the good-boy stories which have been in later years composed for them. In the latter case their minds are as it were put into the stocks like their feet at the dancing school and the moral always consists in good moral conduct being crowned with temporal success. Truth is I would not give one tear shed over Little Red Ridinghood for all the benefit to be derived from a hundred histories of Tommy Goodchild. Miss Edgworth who has with great genius trod the more modern path is to be sure an exception from my utter dislike of these moral narrations but it [is] because they are really fitter for grown people than children. I must say however that I think the story of Simple Susan in particular quite inimitable. But Waste not, Want not, though a most ingenious tale is I fear more apt to make a curmudgeon of a boy who has from nature a close cautious temper than to correct a careless idle destroyer of whip-cord. In a word I think the selfish tendencies will be soon enough acquired in this arithmetical age and that to make the higher class of character our old wild fictions like our own simple music will have more effect in awakening the fancy and elevating the disposition than the colder and more elevating compositions of more clever authors and composers.

'I am not acquainted with Basile's collection but I have both editions of Straparola which I observe differ considerably – I could add a good deal but there is enough here to show that it is with sincere interest that I subscribe myself

Your obliged servant
Walter Scott'[3]

Scott's letter is addressed to Edgar Taylor, whose translations introduced the Grimms to English-speaking children all over the world.

Taylor, a successful London lawyer, originating from Norwich, spent much of his leisure in literary and linguistic pursuits. His attention may have been drawn to the *Household Tales* by a friend who spent some terms at Göttingen University. Taylor saw his translations mainly as a book for children, but professed to an adult interest in the Grimms' collection.

In the introduction to his *Popular German Stories*, Taylor states that:

'. . . the amusement of the hour was not the translators' only object. The

Illustration by Ludwig Richter
By courtesy of the *Brüder Grimm Museum*, Kassel

175

rich collection from which the following tales are selected, is very interesting in a literary point of view, as affording a new proof of the wide and early diffusion of these gay creations of the imagination, apparently flowing from some great and mysterious fountain head, whence Calmuck, Russian, Celt, Scandinavian and German, in their various ramifications, have imbibed earliest lessons of moral instruction . . .'[4]

Later, commenting on the Grimms' work, Taylor continues:

'. . . the result of their labours ought to be peculiarly interesting to English readers, inasmuch as many of their national tales are proved to be of the highest Northern antiquity, and common to the parallel classes of society in countries whose populations have been long and widely disjointed. Strange to say, "Jack, commonly called the Giant-killer, and Thomas Thumb", as the reviewer observes, "landed in England from the very same hulls and war ships which conveyed Hengist and Horsa, and Ebba the Saxon." Who would have expected that Whittington and his Cat, whose identity and London citizenship appeared so certain – Tom Thumb whose parentage Hearne has traced, and whose monumental honours were the boast of Lincoln – or the Giant-destroyer of Tylney, whose bones were supposed to moulder in his native village in Norfolk, should be equally renowned among the humblest inhabitants of Munster and Paderborn? . . .'[5]

On 6 June 1823 Edgar Taylor sent the first volume of his translations to the Grimms at Cassel. The parcel which also contained a small collection of Nursery Rhymes, was accompanied by a letter:

'. . . Not knowing the precise address of either of you I trust the accompanying packet to a friendly hand hoping it may reach you in safety.
    'It contains a copy of a little work consisting of translations (made by my friend Mr. Jardine lately a student at Göttingen and myself) from your volumes of *Kinder und Hausmärchen*, and we beg your acceptance of it as a small tribute of gratitude for the information and amusement afforded us by your entertaining work as well as by your valuable productions.
    'In compiling our little volume we had the amusement of some young friends principally in view, and were therefore compelled sometimes to conciliate local feelings and deviate a little from strict translation; but we believe that all these variations are recorded in the Notes which were hastily drawn with a view to show that our book had some little pretensions to literary consideration though deep research was out of plan . . .'[6]

The Grimms were delighted with Taylor's work, and the letter started a correspondence lasting through several years.

It is interesting to remember that Taylor's daughter, Jessie, married the German professor Karl Arnold Hillebrand. After being involved in the revolutionary movements in Baden in 1849, Hillebrand was imprisoned and escaped to France. For a while he was secretary to Heinrich Heine,

Wilhelm Grimm's study in Berlin. Water-colour by Michael Hofmann.
Germanisches Nationalmuseum, Nuremberg

Jacob Grimm's study in Berlin. Water-colour by Ludwig Emil Grimm
(destroyed during the War). From a photograph in the Brüder Grimm
Museum, Kassel

and eventually lived in Florence until his death in 1884. There, his widow frequently met Herman Grimm who kept up contacts with the literary community of Florence. In that way the two maintained a friendship, begun by their fathers.

In 1839, shortly before Taylor's early death, there appeared a new selection of tales, *Gammer Grethel*, and seven years later, John Edward Taylor, 'printer of Little Queen Street', published yet another volume of translations from Grimm. The Taylors were the first in an unending line of translators and adaptors who made the German tales completely at home on the shelves of the English nursery.

The first 'scientific' edition, closest to the Grimms' own intent, was that translated and edited by Margaret Hunt, published in London in 1892.

The translator explains in her preface:

'. . . there have been several English translations of the *Household Tales*, and yet this is, I believe, the first which has aimed at presenting them precisely as given by the Brothers Grimm . . . they were not providing amusement for children, but storing up material for students of folk-lore. English translators have, as is not unnatural, hitherto had children most in their minds, and have thought it well to change the devil of the German stories into a less offensive ogre or black dwarf, and so on. In this transla- tion I have endeavoured to give the stories as they are in the German original, and though I have slightly softened one or two passages, have always respected the principle which was paramount with the brothers Grimm themselves. The notes too are now translated for the first time . . .'[7]

The edition carried a long and erudite introduction by Andrew Lang in which he discussed origin and diffusion of tales according to the then fashionable anthropological school.

In summing up Lang concluded:

'. . . as to the origin of the wild incidents in *Household Tales*, let any one ask himself this question: Is there anything in the frequent appearance of cannibals, in kinship with animals, in magic, in abominable cruelty, that would seem unnatural to a savage? Certainly not; all these things are familiar in his world . . .

'. . . as to the *diffusion* of similar *incidents* in countries widely severed, that may be, perhaps, ascribed to the identical beliefs of early man all over the world. But the diffusion of *plots* is much more hard to explain, nor do we venture to explain it, except by the chances of transmission in the long past of human existence . . .'[8]

Looking back over some forty years of collecting tales, Wilhelm wrote in 1856:

'. . . how unique was our collection when it first appeared, and what a rich harvest has sprung up since! At that time people smiled indulgently when we asserted that thoughts and intuitions were preserved in these stories, the origin of which was to be sought for in the darkness of antiquity. Now this is hardly ever denied. Tales of this kind are looked for with full recognition of their scientific value, and with a dread of altering any part of their contents, whereas formerly they were only regarded as worthless amusements of fancy which might be manipulated at will . . .'⁹

Wilhelm's words describe very clearly the change that had come about since the first publication of the fairytales. The brothers' work had provided the impetus for a re-valuation of tales, and the Grimms' method had pointed the way to the systematic collecting of all manifestations of folk tradition: songs, tales, games, riddles and ancient customs. Popular tradition had become respectable and worth serious investigation.

The study of folklore was now firmly established.

The spirit of the time was favourable. Nations anxious to re-discover their identity, keen to go back to grass roots and the heritage of the common people, enthusiastically took Jacob and Wilhelm as their guides. A fervent search for material began in many countries and in all the regions of Germany.

The Slavonic countries showed the first and most notable reaction.

Early on, Brentano had brought back from Bohemia a number of Czech chapbooks which kindled Jacob's interest, and led to a correspondence with Josef Dobrovský, doyen of Slavonic studies, and authority on Bohemian history and literature. Through Dobrovský Jacob had heard much already of Jernej Kopitar, librarian at the *Hofbibliothek* in Vienna, and at one time a student of Dobrovský. Jacob met Kopitar during his stay in Vienna in 1814–15, and the two men became friends.

With his ease for acquiring a new language, Jacob began to study Czech and Serbian, becoming more and more engrossed in Slavonic tradition. Kopitar drew Grimm's attention to a young protégé, Vuk Stefanović Karadžić who was working for a Serbian newspaper, founded in Vienna, after the 1813 rebellion in Serbia. He had just published a collection of Serbian folksongs which Jacob read and admired. Here was genuine *Naturpoesie*. He reviewed the collection favourably for the *Wiener Allgemeine Literaturzeitung*, and encouraged Vuk to turn his attention to folktales. Only in 1853 did Vuk's collection of tales appear. It is certain, however, that he had received the impulse for his life's work from Grimm, and that the triangle, Grimm-Kopitar-Karadžić, was an inspiration to early folklorists in Eastern Europe. Jacob did much to publicise Vuk's work, and eased his way on journeys in Germany.

Karadžić dedicated his Serbian tales to Grimm, and Jacob wrote the introduction for a German edition, published in 1854, a translation by Vuk's daughter Wilhelmina. Welcoming the tales, Jacob looked back with

Illustration by Ludwig Richter
By courtesy of the *Brüder Grimm Museum*, Kassel

satisfaction to the days when he had made it his business to encourage
Vuk, a man versed in all the traditions of his people, to note down narratives
known in his homeland. Since then many collections had been made, not
only in Germany itself, but in Norway, Sweden, Wallachia, recently also
in Albania, Lithuania and Finland. Material was now so varied and plentiful
that in time it would deserve critical investigation. No longer could the
folktale be taken as silly fancy. Once more Jacob expressed his belief that
tales were the debris of ancient myths, and that by moving from people to
people, they had taken on local colour. Important information could be
gained about the relation of countless legends and fables, common in
European countries and in Asia. This community of fable, said Jacob,
could not be explained by isolated and arbitrary borrowings, rather did it
reflect unexpected contacts as occurred also in the history of language and
literature.

Jacob was proud of having been instrumental in helping to preserve

Serbo-Croatian tradition, making the songs and tales of herdsmen, looked down upon by the educated, material fit for literature.[10]

In turn, a people groping its way into nationhood, was proud of Grimm. In 1849 a learned Serbian society made him a corresponding member.

Karadžić, who had spent his childhood in the country, close to the people, was an ideal collector. He also published proverbs, and wrote on ancient customs. His example was followed, and the recording of material got well under way in the southern Slavonic countries.

In Austria itself, Franz Ziska published fairytales in 1822, the Zingerle brothers noted Tyrolian tales, Theodor Vernaleken, a Westphalian, collected Alpine legends, and recorders began work in many regions. Some dedicated their books to the Grimms, and acknowledged their debt to them.

In eighteenth-century Hungary András Dugonics had noted down tales from peasants, herdsmen and horse dealers, often in the midst of noisy fairs. Later the Grimms' work acted as a stimulus. György Gaál, archivist to Prince Eszterházy in Vienna, collected with great care tales, mainly told by soldiers of a Hungarian regiment. He gave these tales his own style, and translated them into German. They appeared in 1822 as *Volksmärchen der Magyaren*. This was the first printed collection. In the introduction Gaál compared one of his storytellers, an old hussar, to the Grimms' Fairytale-Wife. János, Graf Majláth published another collection, much embellished and also in German. It appeared in Brno in 1825. The Hungarian Academy of Science, founded in 1825, of which Jacob Grimm was a corresponding member, issued a successful appeal for the collection of folklore material. János Erdélyi then edited many texts, and a Hungarian mythology was compiled by Arnold Ipolyi, and published in 1853. It was composed from abundant material collected over some thirty years.

Hungary's great poet, János Arany, was very interested in the folktale. When discussing an edition of international tales, he stressed that it was due mainly to the brothers Grimm that the true significance of tales had been recognized, and that their study had become a science. Many more collectors in nineteenth-century Hungary followed in the footsteps of the Grimms.

Stories from the *Household Tales* were eventually re-discovered among Hungarian peasants, some adapted, some unchanged. They had reached distant places through cheap paper editions, and had also found their way into the popular puppet shows.

Czech and Slovak scholars were quite naturally interested in the success of Karadžić's work. His songs were translated into Czech, and inspired native collecting. Palacký collected in Moravia, and Benedikti in Slovenia. A young Slovak, Pavel Jozef Šafarik, who had spent a couple of years at

Jena University, and had there become interested in *Volkspoesie* began recording traditions on his return home. Together with a friend, Jan Kollár, he published some songs. His work, *Slavonic Antiquities*, was much influenced by Jacob Grimm, whom in a letter to a friend he had called 'a giant, an eagle to whose heights it was hard to aspire'.[11] In their letters Šafarik and Grimm exchanged much information on the traditions of their countries. Working songs, children's games, customs at weddings, funerals and seasonal feasts, all held Šafarik's attention. He considered these traditions the key to a nation's history.

In opposition to Kopitar, but in agreement with Jacob Grimm, Šafarik firmly believed in the genuineness of *The Judgement of Libussa* and the *Königinhof manuscript*, two supposedly ancient Czech manuscripts, containing ballads and epic fragments, produced in 1817 by Hanka, a librarian in Prague. At a time of national revival scholars most ardently desired these heroic remains of the past to be real. It is interesting to remember that Jacob Grimm was made an honorary member of the *Museum des Köngreichs Böhmen* mainly because he believed in the genuineness of the ancient manuscripts which are now considered forgeries.

Karel Jaromír Erben, a younger scholar, inspired by the Grimms, was the first to pay serious attention to the Czech folktale. With poetic gifts similar to those of Wilhelm Grimm, he handled his material with imagination. He also published songs, and investigated many aspects of folk tradition.

Research continued, and the Grimms' influence lingered in Prague, a city which had grown into a centre of Slavonic studies.

In Poland, too, rising nationalism created favourable conditions for the study of 'the folk'. Collectors began tramping the countryside; one of them, Kazimierz Wladyslaw Wojcicki, published a collection of tales, much embellished. They were followed by Oskar Kolberg's more 'scientific' recording of songs, tales and customs. Kolberg acknowledged his debt to Jacob Grimm's *Mythologie*. The Grimms' theories on oral tradition were widely quoted by Polish scholars.

In 1831 Anton Dietrich, a German psychiatrist, accompanied a patient to Russia. Interested in tradition, he used his stay in Moscow for the collection of Russian folktales. Dobrovoský had early on drawn Jacob Grimm's attention to Russian tales, and Dietrich found immediate support from him. Grimm helped Dietrich with the editing, found a publisher in Leipzig, and wrote an introduction. In it he expressed the hope that interest in the folktale would increase in the Slavonic countries. In 1841 J. N. Vogl published Russian folktales in Vienna. Both selections were translations into German.

A great collection in Russian was still to come. Vladímir Ivanovitch

Illustration by Ludwig Richter
By courtesy of the *Brüder Grimm Museum*, Kassel

Dalj, son of a Danish doctor, and born in the Ukraine, amassed a lot of traditional material. This, together with tales from the archives of the Russian Geographical Society, formed the nucleus of Aleksander Nikolaevic Afanes'ev's Russian folktales. He was proud to be called 'the Russian Grimm', and schooled himself deliberately in Wilhelm's way of presenting tales. His work achieved great popularity with old and young alike.

In August 1914 *Zivaja Starina*, the folklore journal of the Russian Geographical Society, published a volume in memory of the brothers Grimm, calling them the true begetters of the scientific collecting of tales, and forever associated with the study of tales everywhere.

With their great love for fairytales, the Russians made some of the *Household Tales* their very own. They were found, told by the common people, in distant corners of the USSR. They have also proved popular material for children's films and plays.

From the beginning Jacob and Wilhelm's contacts with the Scandinavian north were of a special nature. There existed a feeling of fellowship with northern scholars, expressed in many letters, a cross-fertilization of ideas between peoples closely related and with a common past.

Just Mathias Thiele's eight-volume edition of Danish legends, published between 1818 and 1823, owes much to Wilhelm Grimm's encouragement. In 1816 Adam Oehlenschläger published a collection of fairytales in Denmark. They were mainly *Kunstmärchen* by German Romantics, with a few tales from the Grimms' collection. The *Household Tales* were translated and published in full in 1821. They served as an example to Mathiaus Winther who collected, and published in 1823, the first genuinely Danish tales. Other mixed collections followed, till in 1854 Svend Grundtvig appealed for recordings from oral tradition. Much material was obtained and some published. In 1904 the *Dansk Folkemindesamling* became the custodian of this rich haul.

In Sweden traditional songs were published first, and between 1839 and 1870 Arvid August Afzelius edited eleven parts of Swedish legends. They were praised by Jacob Grimm. Another fervent admirer and follower of the Grimms, the ethnologist Gunnar Hyltén-Cavallius, also collected Swedish legends.

The finest northern collection of that time – and to the present day – is Peter Christen Asbjørnsen and Jørgen Moe's *Norske Folkeeventyr*, published in Christiania between 1842 and 1844. An enlarged edition of the Norwegian tales, with a detailed introduction, appeared in 1852. It owed its inspiration to the *Household Tales*, and acknowledged it by a dedication to the Grimms.

A friendly correspondence ensued where the exchange of publications and scholarly information was interspersed with scraps of personal news, as when Jacob wrote to Jørgen Moe, on 9 May 1852:

'. . . my brother – whom you thought dead, according to Asbjørnsen's last letter – is, thank God, alive. To be sure, we are both old enough (I am sixty-seven, and he is sixty-five years of age) to make our exits, and some day genuine news of our death will reach you. Do then keep a good memory of us. To matters of our popular tradition which equally attract you, (and in that sense we are one people) we have given our honest attention, unstintingly, and we have achieved a few things which will last . . .

'. . . at the moment I am engrossed, almost buried, in a German dictionary, the end of which cannot be foreseen. But as everything is connected, word and legend, I am enjoying this work very much too, and it leads to unexpected conclusions . . .'[12]

In a letter of 27 June 1856 to Asbjørnsen, Jacob praised Afanes'ev's collection of Russian tales – which he had just received – commenting on their 'genuineness'.[13] On 3 July of the same year Wilhelm sent Asbjørnsen the new edition of the *Household Tales*, Volume 3, as 'a little return present' for his 'excellent collection of fairytales' which he had read with much pleasure.[14]

Illustration by Robert Weiss
By courtesy of the *Brüder Grimm Museum*, Kassel

In August 1859 Jacob expressed his delight – to Asbjørsen – about Dasent's English translation of the Norwegian tales, calling it 'fresh and vivid', while he thought the German edition of 1847 was 'wooden'.[15] Sir George Webbe Dasent's *Popular Tales from the Norse* were published in Edinburgh in 1859. In the introduction he made extensive mention of the Grimms. Deploring that popular tradition had been neglected for so long, he continued:

'. . . there arose a man in Central Germany, on the old Thuringian soil, to whom it was given to assert the dignity of vernacular literature, to throw off the yoke of classical tyranny, and to claim for all the dialects of Teutonic speech a right of ancient inheritance . . . it is almost needless to mention this honoured name . . . there is no spot on which an accent of Teutonic speech is uttered where the name of Jacob Grimm is not a 'household word' . . .

'. . . and the collections of German Popular Tales, which he and his brother William published, have thrown a flood of light on the early history of all the branches of our race, and have raised what had come to be looked on as mere nursery fictions and old wives' fables – to a study fit for the energies of grown men, and to all the dignity of a science . . .'[16]

In Finland where this new science was taken most seriously, culminating eventually in the extensive investigations of the *Folklore Fellows*, the Grimms' work made an impact. Both brothers, Jacob in particular, were interested in Finnish tradition and in the efforts of an awakening nation to bring back the Finnish language, kept alive by oral transmission but generally overshadowed by Swedish. Bards had recited the ancient epics, and some were noted down in the eighteenth century. Then, Elias Lönnrot, a doctor, searched the countryside for old songs and tales. He obtained a wealth of material which he unified and published as the *Kalevala* epic. Jacob was in touch with Lönnrot, and found the doctor's collection a confirmation of his own theory, namely that the common people were the guardians of folk literature.

In 1845 Jacob read a paper to the Berlin Academy, dealing with the *Kalevala*. He had learnt Finnish, and was able therefore to quote parts of the epic, drawing attention to the sound of the original. Jacob's speech was well received, published in Swedish the same year, and in Russian the year after. In the thirties and forties of the nineteenth century many Finnish tales were collected, and the zeal for oral tradition spread to Estonia, Lithuania and all the Baltic countries.

The Netherlands were slow in collecting traditional material, possibly because Dutch Enlightenment frowned heavily on those romantic fancies. Jacob Grimm who corresponded over years with Hendrik Willem Tydeman, the jurist, had sent him his *Märchenbrief* for publication. The appeal was not successful, but in time a few, particularly country parsons, began to note down popular songs. Jacob's mythology created further interest, and the brothers Joost Hiddes Halbertsma, pastor and correspondent of Jacob Grimm, and Eeltje, a doctor, set out, notebook in hand, recording a great deal which otherwise might have been lost for ever. Both brothers were friendly, with an easy approach to the people around them. Still, they encountered the difficulties, known to all field workers: the ordinary man's and woman's fear to be laughed at, and general distrust. The moment the brothers opened their notebooks, people were apt to take them for police inspectors, about to construe 'a case'. Early Dutch material was published in learned journals and anthologies.

In Flanders interest was stirred in the main by the Grimms' friend, Hoffman von Fallersleben, who travelled the Low Countries in search of Germanic traditions. Disappointed in Holland, he found a collaborator in Jan Frans Willems, ardent collector of Flemish material, devoted to the study of songs. With Jacob Grimm he shared an interest in beast fables, particularly the Reynard the Fox cycle.

Johann Wilhelm Wolf, another German, lived for some time in Brussels, and collected tales and legends over the whole of Flanders. In 1842 he published the first results in a journal, called *Grootmoederken*, with the intention of rousing a wider interest in popular tradition. Another journal, *Wodana*, followed, creating a basis for Flemish folklorists to build on.

In France there was a lull after the publication of the many volumes of the eighteenth-century *Cabinet des Fées*. It took a translation of the *Household Tales* to give a fillip to regional recording. Emile Souvestre collected in Brittany, Cénac-Moncaut in Gascony, and Eugène Beauvois in Burgundy. Emmanuel Cosquin, an admirer of Jacob and Wilhelm – though he later on opposed their ideas on the origin of tales – collected in his own countryside, Lorraine, and published his finds with a vast apparatus of notes. Towards the end of the century France witnessed a flood of collections and the founding of a number of folklore journals. The Grimms' theories on origins and diffusion were fiercely attacked by some French scholars.

In Italy, a country boasting early collections of tales, a new wave of recording started during the late nineteenth century. In more recent days Italo Calvino has been called 'the Italian Grimm'. His *Fiabe italiane raccolte dalla tradizione popolare durante gli ultimi cento anni e trascritte in lingua dai vari dialetti*, appeared in 1956. Greece, Spain and other southern European countries all published their own collections, and recording continues.

In the British Isles the main antiquarian interest had been for long ancient customs. Tales and songs were largely disregarded, considered at best quaint material for embellishing. Joseph Ritson, in the late eighteenth century, was an exception when he desired to publish his recordings of ballads and songs exactly as he found them.

The advent of the Grimms led to genuine recording. The publication of John Francis Campbell's of Islay *Popular Tales of the West Highlands* – 1860-1862 – was indirectly due to personal encouragement from Jacob Grimm. Campbell's friend, Sir George Webbe Dasent, had met Grimm in Sweden, when the two men found much common ground. Hoping for an 'English Grimm', Dasent had constantly impressed Campbell with the necessity for recording and publishing while material could still be found. He was well aware that Campbell possessed all the qualities of the true recorder. Much field work has since been done by the School of Scottish Studies in Edinburgh.

In Ireland Thomas Crofton Croker began work about the time of the first publication of the *Household Tales*. His *Fairy Legends and Traditions of the South of Ireland*, taken down from the mouth of the storyteller, were published in 1825. The 'Irish Grimm', Patrick Kennedy, a Dublin bookseller, published three volumes of tales, between 1866 and 1871, giving detailed information about his sources, and speculating on the diffusion of tales. Many more collectors followed, and much valuable material is now in the care of the Irish Folklore Commission.

In England the collecting of tales had a slow start. It appears that English taste preferred legends, humorous or ghost stories to the true fairytale. Ever since Taylor's translations from the *Household Tales* interest grew. Thomas Keightley's *Fairy Mythology*, of 1828, prepared the way, and in time Edwin Sidney Hartland published *English Fairy and other Folk Tales* – 1890 – taken mainly from printed material, and the popular, though much manipulated *English Fairy Tales* by Joseph Jacobs, appeared in the same year. In 1894 *More English Fairy Tales* followed.

Much thought was given to origin and diffusion of tales in Hartland's *The Science of Fairy Tales* – 1891 – taking into account Sir E. B. Tylor's and Andrew Lang's theories of the anthropological school. Hartland was a keen advocate of 'genuine' recording, and serious collectors began in many counties of England.

The impulse given by Jacob and Wilhelm Grimm extended beyond Europe. In America the main link was not a collector of tales, but Francis James Child, the editor of *English and Scottish Popular Ballads* (1857-1859), enlarged and re-issued in 1882-1897. His studies took him to Göttingen and Berlin where he made personal contact with the Grimms, and was much impressed with their work.

The Grimms' conception of oral tradition and their method of collecting continued spreading, reaching countries as different as Japan and Iceland, and people of all colours and creeds.

Much has been discovered since. Theories have changed, and will continue to do so, but Jacob and Wilhelm Grimm laid the solid foundations on which was built the vast edifice of the collection and investigation of oral tradition in general and the folktale in particular.

Abbreviations

Daffis, H. *Inventar der Grimmschränke in der Preussischen Staatsbibliothek Mitteilungen aus der Preuss.* Staatsbibliothek V. Leipzig 1923   Daffis

Grimm:

Briefe der Brüder Grimm, collected by H. Gürtler; ed A. Leitzmann. Jena 1923   Gürtler-Leitzmann

Briefwechsel zwischen Jacob und Wilhelm Grimm aus der Jugendzeit, ed H. Grimm and G. Hinrichs. Weimar 1881   Grimm-Hinrichs

Briefwechsel zwischen Jacob und Wilhelm Grimm, Dahlmann und Gervinus, ed E. Ippel. 2 vols. Berlin 1885-86   Ippel

Briefwechsel zwischen Jenny von Droste-Hülshoff und Wilhelm Grimm, ed K. Schulte Kemminghausen. Münster 1929   Schulte Kemminghausen

Briefwechsel der Brüder Jacob und Wilhelm Grimm mit Karl Lachmann, ed A. Leitzmann. 2 vols. Jena 1927   Leitzmann/ Lachmann

Briefwechsel des Freiherrn Karl Hartwig Gregor von Meusebach mit Jacob und Wilhelm Grimm, ed C. Wendeler. Heilbronn 1880   Wendeler

Briefwechsel der Brüder Grimm mit nordischen Gelehrten, ed E. Schmidt. Berlin 1885   Schmidt

Freundesbriefe von Wilhelm und Jacob Grimm, ed A. Reifferscheid. Heilbronn 1878   Reifferscheid

Unbekannte Briefe der Brüder Grimm, ed W. Schoof in collaboration with J. Göres. Bonn 1960	Schoof-Göres
Private und amtliche Beziehungen der Brüder Grimm zu Hessen, ed E. Stengel. 3 vols. Marburg 1895 and 1910	Stengel
Die Brüder Grimm: Ihr Leben und Werk in Selbstzeugnissen, Briefen und Aufzeichnungen, ed H. Gerstner. Ebenhausen near Munich 1952	Gerstner
Grimm, Jacob, *Kleinere Schriften*. 8 vols. Berlin 1864-1890	Grimm, Jacob, *Kl. Schriften*
Jacob Grimm: Aus seinem Leben, ed W. Schoof. Bonn 1961	Schoof/Jacob
Grimm, Ludwig Emil, *Erinnerungen aus meinem Leben*, ed W. Praesent. Kassel 1950	Grimm (Praesent) *Erinnerungen*
Grimm, Wilhelm, *Kleinere Schriften*, 4 vols. Berlin 1881-1887	Grimm, Wilhelm, *Kl. Schriften*
Wilhelm Grimm: Aus seinem Leben, ed W. Schoof. Bonn 1960	Schoof/Wilhelm
Pissin, R. *Aus ungedruckten Briefen der Brüder Jacob, Wilhelm, Ferdinand, Ludwig Grimm*, in *Preussische Jahrbücher*, Vol 234. Berlin 1933	*Preussische Jahrbücher*
Schoof, W. *Aus der Jugendzeit der Brüder Grimm*, in *Hanauisches Magazin*. Hanau 1934-35	*Hanauisches Magazin*
Schoof, W. *Jacob und Wilhelm Grimm nach der Göttinger Amtsenthebung*, in *Zeitschrift des Vereins für Hessische Geschichte und Landeskunde*, Vol. 58. Kassel 1932	Zeitschrift des Vereins für Hessische Geschichte und Landeskunde
Steig, R. *Achim von Arnim und Jacob und Wilhelm Grimm*. Stuttgart and Berlin 1904	Steig, Arnim/ Grimm
Steig, R. *Clemens Brentano und die Brüder Grimm*. Stuttgart and Berlin 1914	Steig, Brentano/ Grimm
Steig, R. *Goethe und die Brüder Grimm*. Berlin 1892	Steig, Goethe/ Grimm

Notes to Chapters

Introduction

1 Tolkien, J. R. R., *Tree and Leaf,* London 1964, pp. 11-70
2 *The Brothers Grimm* in Hazard, P., *Books, Children, Men,* Boston 1944, pp. 152-157
3 Grimm, Jacob, *Rede auf Wilhelm Grimm,* Berliner Bibliophilen Abend 1965, pp. 23-5

Chapter 1

1 Grimm, Wilhelm, *Kl. Schriften,* Vol I, pp. 4-5
2 Daffis, Appendix, pp. 98-118
3 ibid.
4 Schoof/Wilhelm, pp. 13-14
5 Daffis, Appendix, pp. 98-118
6 ibid.
7 ibid.
8 ibid.
9 *Hanauisches Magazin* 1935; 1/2, pp. 7-8
10 ibid. 1934; 11/12, p 88
11 ibid. 1934; 11/12, p 88

Chapter 2

1 Grimm-Hinrichs, pp 1-2
2 *Hanauisches Magazin* 1935; 1/2, p 11
3 ibid. 1934; 11/12, pp 92-3
4 Grimm (Praesent) *Erinnerungen,* pp 363-4
5 Grimm Sammlung der Murhardschen und Landesbibliothek, Kassel. No. 13
6 ibid. No. 14
7 ibid. No. 14
8 Praesent, W., *Märchenhaus des deutschen Volkes,* pp 83-4. Original letters were destroyed in the war.

9 ibid. p 84
10 Wigand, P., *Denkwürdigkeiten aus einem bescheidenen Leben,* pp 263-7. Ms. Hist. Litt. 4° 33. Murhardsche und Landesbibliothek, Kassel
11 Grimm, Jacob, *Kl. Schriften,* Vol I, p 5
12 Grimm, Wilhelm, *Kl. Schriften,* Vol I, p 12
13 Grimm-Hinrichs, pp 34-6
14 ibid. pp 31-4
15 ibid. pp 16-23
16 ibid. pp 60-4
17 ibid. pp 37-8
18 ibid. pp 5-7
19 ibid. pp 16-23
20 ibid. pp 58-60
21 ibid. p 69

Chapter 3

1 Grimm-Hinrichs, pp 56-8
2 Gürtler-Leitzmann, pp 68-9
3 Grimm, Jacob, *Kl. Schriften,* Vol I, p 10
4 ibid. p 11
5 Schoof/Wilhelm, p 71
6 ibid. p 72
7 ibid. p 75
8 Grimm (Praesent), *Erinnerungen,* p 37
9 *Preussische Jahrbücher,* Vol 234, pp 72-3
10 Grimm, Wilhelm, *Kl. Schriften,* Vol I, pp 15-16
11 Grimm-Hinrichs, pp 76-7
12 ibid. pp 99-102
13 ibid. pp 84-7
14 ibid. pp 112-14
15 ibid. pp 99-102
16 ibid. pp 114-18
17 ibid. pp 118-21
18 ibid. pp 123-8
19 ibid. pp 128-9
20 ibid. pp 137-8
21 ibid. p 172
22 ibid. p 181
23 ibid. pp 181-4
24 ibid. pp 184-6
25 ibid. pp 191-4
26 ibid. pp 202-5
27 Steig, Goethe/Grimm, p 64
28 Schoof-Göres, pp 33-4

Chapter 4

1 Steig, Brentano/Grimm, pp 52-9
2 Bolte, J. und Polivka, G. *Anmerkungen zu den Kinder-und Hausmärchen der Brüder Grimm*, 5 vols, Leipzig 1913-32, Vol IV, p 424
3 Gerstner, p 191
4 Schoof, W., *Ferd. Dümmlers Verlagsbuchhandlung als Grimm Verlag* in *Börsenblatt für den Deutschen Buchhandel*, No. 99, 11.12.1959, pp 1706-8
5 Steig, R., Arnim/Grimm, pp 218-22
6 Grimm, Wilhelm, *Altdänische Heldenlieder, Balladen und Märchen*, Heidelberg 1811, Preface, pp V-XL
7 Brüder Grimm, *Kinder-und Hausmärchen*, Berlin 1812, Vol I, Preface, pp V-XXI
8 Görres, J. von, *Ausgewählte Werke und Briefe*, ed W. Schellenberg, 2 vols in 1, Kempten and Munich 1911, pp 205-6

Chapter 5

1 Reifferscheid, pp 196-7
2 ibid. pp 17-19
3 Schulte Kemminghausen, pp 43-4
4 ibid. pp 45-8
5 ibid. pp 61-3
6 ibid. pp 64-8
7 ibid. pp 73-6
8 Reifferscheid, pp 23-4
9 Brüder Grimm, *Kinder-und Hausmärchen*, Berlin 1815, Vol II, Preface, pp III-XII
10 Grimm-Hinrichs, pp 474-7

Chapter 6

1 Schoof/Wilhelm, pp 136-9
2 Steig, Arnim/Grimm, pp 233-9
3 ibid. pp 230-3
4 Grimm-Hinrichs, pp 215-16
5 ibid. p 217
6 ibid. pp 218-20
7 ibid. pp 221-6
8 ibid.
9 ibid. pp 240-7
10 ibid. p 254
11 ibid. pp 258-61
12 ibid. pp 261-8
13 ibid. pp 286-7
14 ibid. pp 287-91

15 Grimm (Praesent), *Erinnerungen*, p 67
16 Grimm-Hinrichs, pp 339-44
17 ibid.

Chapter 7

1 Grimm-Hinrichs, pp 350-6
2 ibid. pp 386-92
3 ibid. pp 393-4
4 Grimm, Jacob, *Kl. Schriften*, Vol VII, pp 593-5
5 Grimm-Hinrichs, pp 425-7
6 ibid. pp 413-15
7 ibid. pp 397-9
8 ibid. pp 406-13
9 ibid. pp 446-7
10 Grimm, Jacob, *Kl. Schriften*, Vol I, pp 13-14
11 *Grimm-Nachlass* No. 1264. Staatsbibliothek Preussischer Kulturbesitz Handschriftenabteilung, Berlin-Dahlem
12 Grimm (Praesent), *Erinnerungen*, pp 112-13
13 Steig, Arnim/Grimm, pp 331-4

Chapter 8

1 Grimm, Wilhelm, *Kl. Schriften*, Vol I, p 22
2 Stengel, Vol III, pp 190-1
3 ibid. Vol I, pp 162-5
4 Leitzmann/Lachmann, Vol I, pp 439-41
5 *Goethes Briefe an Frau von Stein*, ed A. Schöll, 2 vols, Frankfurt 1885, Vol II, pp 470-1
6 Brüder Grimm, *Deutsche Sagen*, Berlin 1816, Vol I, Preface, pp v-xxvi
7 Reifferscheid, pp 87-9

Chapter 9

1 Grimm, Jacob, *Kl. Schriften*, Vol I, pp 14-15
2 Steig, Arnim/Grimm, pp 514-21
3 Schulte Kemminghausen, pp 69-72
4 Brüder Grimm, *Kinder-und Hausmärchen*, Berlin 1819, Vol II, pp iii-lxviii
5 *Deutsches Wörterbuch*, Vol II, Leipzig 1860, Preface, pp i-vi
6 Reifferscheid, pp 56-7
7 Lefftz, J., *Märchen der Brüder Grimm. Urfassung nach der Originalhandschrift der Abtei Oelenberg im Elsass*, Heidelberg 1927, p 84
8 Brüder Grimm, *Kinder-und Hausmärchen*, 2 vols, Göttingen 1843, Vol I, pp 293-7
9 Hartwig, O., *Zur ersten englischen Übersetzung der Kinder-und Hausmärchen der Brüder Grimm* in *Centralblatt für Bibliothekswesen*, XV Jahrg, Heft 1/2;Jan./Feb.1898, Leipzig 1898, p 8

10 Schoof/Wilhelm, p 166
11 Steig, Arnim/Grimm, pp 547-8
12 Stengel, Vol I, p 238
13 Grimm, Wilhelm, *Kl. Schriften*, Vol I, p 23
14 Reifferscheid, pp 128-30
15 Wendeler, pp 90-1
16 Gürtler-Leitzmann, p 140
17 Schoof-Göres, p 165

Chapter 10

1 Leitzmann/Lachmann, Vol II, pp 854-5
2 Friderici, R., *Harmonie und Dissonanz. Ludwig Hassenpflug und seine Schwäger Jacob, Wilhelm und Ludwig Emil Grimm* in *Brüder Grimm Gedenken* 1963, Marburg 1963, pp 147-201
3 ibid.
4 ibid.
5 ibid.
6 Hoffmann von Fallersleben, A. H. *Leben, Aufzeichnungen und Erinnerungen*, 6 vols in 3, Hanover 1868, Vol I/II, pp 346-7
7 Ippel, Vol I, pp 5-8
8 Schulte Kemminghausen, p 136
9 Gürtler-Leitzmann, p 82
10 ibid. pp 185-7
11 Schoof-Göres, pp 181-6

Chapter 11

1 Grimm (Praesent), *Erinnerungen*, p 296
2 *Galigniani's Messenger*, Paris afternoon edition, Saturday 18.11.1837, p 5
3 Schoof-Göres, pp 191-3
4 ibid. pp 237-9
5 Ippel, Vol I, pp 76-80
6 *Grimm-Nachlass*, Konvolut 413 Staatsbibliothek Preussischer Kulturbesitz Handschriftenabteilung, Berlin-Dahlem
7 *Zeitschrift des Vereins für Hessische Geschichte und Landeskunde*, Vol 58, Kassel 1932, pp 211-34
8 Leitzmann/Lachmann, Vol II, pp 684-91

Chapter 12

1 Gürtler-Leitzmann, pp 23-7
2 ibid. pp 92-4
3 Ippel, Vol I, pp 344-7
4 Gerstner, p 225
5 Bettina Brentano, *Die Andacht zum Menschenbild. Unbekannte Briefe*, ed W. Schellenberg and F. Fuchs, Jena 1942, p 273

6 ibid. p 308
7 Schoof-Göres, pp 301-4
8 Wendeler, pp 298-300
9 ibid.
10 *Grimm-Nachlass,* Konvolut 413. Staatsbibliothek Preussischer Kulturbesitz Handschriftenabteilung, Berlin-Dahlem
11 Schoof/Jacob, pp 352-4
12 Schoof-Göres, pp 291-2

Chapter 13

1 Ippel, Vol I, pp 443-9
2 ibid. Vol II, pp 44-8
3 *Augsburger Allgemeine Zeitung,* 8.5.1841, p 1017
4 ibid. 20.5.1841, p 1117
5 Levin, I., *Das russische Grimmbild* in *Brüder Grimm Gedenken 1963,*
Marburg 1963, pp 380-1
6 Praesent, W., *Märchenhaus des deutschen Volkes,* Kassel 1957, p 23
7 Ippel, Vol II, pp 54-7
8 *Preussische Jahrbücher,* Vol 234, Berlin 1933, pp 75-6
9 ibid. pp 80-1
10 Schoof-Göres, pp 329-34
11 ibid. pp 320-3
12 *Preussische Jahrbücher,* Vol 234, Berlin 1933, pp 78-9
13 Schoof-Göres, pp 325-9
14 Gerstner, pp 258-9
15 Rodenberg, J., *Aus seinen Tagebüchern,* Berlin 1919, pp 34-5
16 Grimm (Praesent), *Erinnerungen,* p 306

Chapter 14

1 Grimm, Jacob, *Kl. Schriften,* Vol I, pp 57-82
2 Schoof-Göres, pp 348-52
3 Grimm, Jacob, *Kl. Schriften,* Vol I, pp 57-82
4 Andersen, H. C., *The true Story of my Life,* London 1847, pp 247-50
5 Grimm, Jacob, *Rede auf Wilhelm Grimm und Rede über das Alter,*
ed Herman Grimm, Berlin 1863, p 33
6 *Grimm-Nachlass* No. 1076. Staatsbibliothek Preussischer Kulturbesitz Handschriftenabteilung, Berlin-Dahlem
7 Schoof-Göres, pp 317-19

Chapter 15

1 *Preussische Jahrbücher,* Vol 234, Berlin 1933, p 83
2 Schoof-Göres, pp 380-1
3 Grimm, Jacob, *Geschichte der deutschen Sprache,* 2 vols, Leipzig 1848,
Vol I, Preface, pp vii-xvi

4 Schoof-Göres, pp 361-2
5 Schmidt, pp 309-11
6 Brüder Grimm, *Kinder-und Hausmärchen*, Vol III, Berlin 1856, pp 271-82
7 Reifferscheid, pp 188-90
8 Grimm, Jacob, *Kl. Schriften*, Vol I, pp 113-44
9 ibid.
10 ibid.
11 ibid.
12 Ippel, Vol I, pp 521-2
13 Gerstner, pp 275-6

Chapter 16

1 Grimm, Jacob, *Rede auf Wilhelm Grimm und Rede über das Alter*, ed Herman Grimm, Berlin 1863, p 26
2 *Vossische Zeitung*, Berlin 24.12.1859
3 Schoof-Göres, pp 392-3
4 Grimm, Jacob, *Kl. Schriften*, Vol I, pp 163-87
5 ibid.
6 ibid.
7 Grimm, Jacob, *Rede auf Wilhelm Grimm* (containing extra pages, at one time believed lost) Berliner Bibliophilen Abend 1965, pp 23-5
8 Grimm, Jacob, *Kl. Schriften*, Vol I, pp 188-210
9 Gerstner, p 305
10 *Deutsches Wörterbuch*, Vol II, Leipzig 1860, Preface, pp i-vi
11 Schmidt, pp 304-5
12 Grimm, Jacob, *Rede auf Wilhelm Grimm und Rede über das Alter*, ed Herman Grimm, Berlin 1863, pp 35-6
13 ibid. pp 36-8
14 Schoof/Jacob, pp 387-9

Chapter 17

1 Tetzner, L., *Aus der Welt der Märchen*, Münster 1965, pp 78-80
2 *German Popular Stories*, Introduction by John Ruskin, London 1868, pp v-xiv
3 *The Letters of Sir Walter Scott*, ed H. J. C. Grierson, 12 vols, London 1932-37, Vol VII, pp 310-13
4 *German Popular Stories*, translated from the *Kinder- und Hausmärchen* collected by MM Grimm, London 1823;1826, 2 vols, Preface, pp iii-xii
5 ibid.
6 *Grimm-Nachlass* No. 1700. Staatsbibliothek Preussischer Kulturbesitz Handschriftenabteilung, Berlin-Dahlem
7 *Grimm's Household Tales*, with the author's notes, translated from the German and edited by Margaret Hunt, London 1884, Preface, pp iii-v
8 ibid. Introduction by Andrew Lang, pp xi-lxxv

9 Brüder Grimm, *Kinder-und Hausmärchen*, Berlin 1856, Vol III, pp 283-414

10 Grimm, Jacob, *Kl. Schriften*, Vol VIII, pp 386-90

11 Horák, J., *Jacob Grimm und die slawische Volkskunde* in *Jacob Grimm. Zur hundertsten Wiederkehr seines Todestages*, ed W. Fraenger und W. Steinitz, Berlin 1963, p 27

12 *Jacob og Wilhelm Grimm's brev til P. Chr. Asbjørnsen og Jørgen Moe meddelt av Anders Krogvig* in *Festskrift til Gerh. Gran*, Christiania 1916, pp 175-88

13 ibid.

14 ibid.

15 ibid.

16 Dasent, Sir George W., *Popular Tales from the Norse*, Edinburgh 1859, Introduction, pp ix-lxxxviii

Selected Bibliography

The translation from the German of letters, diaries and general texts is the author's.

THE MAIN WORKS OF JACOB AND WILHELM GRIMM

Joint publications

Kinder- und Hausmärchen:
  Vol I, Berlin 1812; Vol II, Berlin 1815; (2nd ed, Berlin 1819); Vol III, Berlin 1822 (3rd ed, Göttingen 1837, 4th ed, Göttingen 1840, 5th ed, Göttingen 1843, 6th ed, Göttingen 1850; Vol III 2nd ed, Göttingen 1856, 7th ed, Göttingen 1857, 8th ed, Göttingen 1864).
—*Kleine Ausgabe*. Berlin 1825.
Das Lied von Hildebrand und Hadubrand und das Weissenbrunner Gebet (ed). Cassel 1812.
Altdeutsche Wälder (ed). Vol I, Cassel 1813; Vol II, Frankfurt 1815; Vol III, Frankfurt 1816.
Hartmann v.d. Aue, Der Arme Heinrich (ed). Berlin 1815.
Lieder der alten Edda (ed). Vol I (no further vols published). Berlin 1815.
Deutsche Sagen. Vol I, Berlin 1816; Vol II, Berlin 1818.
Irische Elfenmärchen (trans and edit). Leipzig 1826.
Deutsches Wörterbuch. Vol I, Leipzig 1854; Vol II, Leipzig 1860; Vol III, Leipzig 1864.

WORKS BY JACOB GRIMM

Über den altdeutschen Meistergesang. Göttingen 1811.

Silva de romances viejos. Vienna 1815.

Deutsche Grammatik. Vol I, Göttingen 1819; Vol II, Göttingen 1826; Vol III, Göttingen 1831; Vol IV, Göttingen 1837.

Vuk Stefanović Karadžić. Kleine serbische Grammatik (trans). Leipzig and Berlin 1824.

Deutsche Rechtsaltertümer. Göttingen 1828.

Reinhart Fuchs. Berlin 1834.

Deutsche Mythologie. Göttingen 1835.

Über seine Entlassung. Basle 1838.

Lateinische Gedichte des X. u. XI. Jahrhunderts, ed with A. Schmeller. Göttingen 1838.

Weistümer. Vol I, Göttingen 1840; Vol II, Göttingen 1840; Vol III, Göttingen 1842; Vol IV, Göttingen 1863; Vol V, Göttingen 1866; Vol VI, Göttingen 1869.

Geschichte der deutschen Sprache. 2 vols. Leipzig 1848.

Das Wort des Besitzes. Berlin 1850.

Rede auf Wilhelm Grimm und Rede über das Alter, ed Herman Grimm. Berlin 1863.

Kleinere Schriften. 8 vols. Berlin 1864-1890.

WORKS BY WILHELM GRIMM

Altdänische Heldenlieder, Balladen und Märchen. Translated into German. Heidelberg 1811.

Drei altschottische Lieder. Original and translation. Heidelberg 1813.

Über deutsche Runen. Göttingen 1821.

Zur Literatur der Runen. Vienna 1828.

Grâve Ruodolf. Göttingen 1828.

Die deutsche Heldensage. Göttingen 1829.

De Hildebrando antiquissimi carminis teutonici fragmentum (facs). Göttingen 1830.

Vrîdankes Bescheidenheit. Göttingen 1834.

Der Rosengarten. Göttingen 1836.

Ruolandes liet. Göttingen 1838.

Wernher vom Niederrhein. Göttingen 1839.

Konrads von Würzburg Goldene Schmiede. Berlin 1840.

Konrads von Würzburg Silvester. Göttingen 1841.

Über Freidank. Göttingen 1855.

Kleinere Schriften. 4 vols. Berlin 1881-1887.

THE GRIMMS AND THEIR CIRCLE

DAFFIS, H. *Inventar der Grimmschränke in der Preussischen Staatsbibliothek. Mitteilungen aus der Preuss. Staatsbibliothek V.* Leipzig 1923.

DENECKE, L. *In der Brüder-Grimm Stadt Kassel* in Zeitschrift für Erzberg-bau und Metallhüttenwesen, No. 14. Stuttgart 1965.

DENECKE, L. und GREVERUS, I. M. (ed). *Brüder Grimm Gedenken 1963*.

——*Gedenkschrift zur hundertsten Wiederkehr des Todestages von Jacob Grimm*. Marburg 1963.

FRAENGER, W. und STEINITZ, W. (ed). *Jacob Grimm. Zur 100. Wiederkehr seines Todestages Veröffentlichungen des Instituts für deutsche Volks-kunde*, Vol 32. Berlin 1963.

FRANKE, C. *Die Brüder Grimm*. Dresden and Leipzig 1899.

FRIDERICI, R. *Ludwig Hassenpflug* in Lebensbilder aus Kurhessen und Waldeck 1830-1930, ed I. Schnack. *Veröffentlichungen der Historischen Kommission für Hessen und Waldeck*. Marburg 1955.

GERSTNER, H. *Die Brüder Grimm. Ihr Leben und Werk in Selbstzeugnissen, Briefen und Aufzeichnungen*. Ebenhausen near Munich 1932.

KNODT, H. *Zur Familiengeschichte der Brüder Grimm* in Hessische Heimat, No. 16. Giessen 1963.

PEUCKERT, W. E. (ed). *Die Brüder Grimm. Ewiges Deutschland. Ihr Werk im Grundriss*. Stuttgart 1942.

PRAESENT, W. (ed). *Ludwig Emil Grimm. Erinnerungen aus meinem Leben*. Kassel 1950.

PRAESENT, W. *Märchenhaus des deutschen Volkes. Aus der Kinderzeit der Brüder Grimm*. Kassel 1957.

SCHERER, W. *Jacob Grimm*. Berlin 1865.

SCHNACK, I. (ed). *Die Selbstbiographien von Jacob und Wilhelm Grimm aus dem Juli und September 1830*. Kassel 1958.

SCHÖNBACH, E. *Die Brüder Grimm. Ein Gedenkblatt zum 4. Januar 1885*. Berlin 1885.

SCHOOF, W. (ed). *Lebensweisheit. Aus dem geistigen Vermächtnis der Brüder Grimm*. Kassel 1953.

SCHOOF, W. *Jacob Grimm. Aus seinem Leben*. Bonn 1961.

——*Wilhelm Grimm. Aus seinem Leben*. Bonn 1960.

SCHULTE KEMMINGHAUSEN, K, und DENECKE. L. *Die Brüder Grimm in Bildern ihrer Zeit*. Kassel 1963.

STEIG, R. *Achim von Arnim und Jacob und Wilhelm Grimm*. Stuttgart and Berlin 1904.

——*Clemens Brentano und die Brüder Grimm*. Stuttgart and Berlin 1914.

——*Goethe und die Brüder Grimm*. Berlin 1892.

ZUCKMAYER, C. *Die Brüder Grimm. Ein deutscher Beitrag zur Humanität*. Frankfurt 1948.

LETTERS

GRIERSON, H. J. C. (ed). *The Letters of Sir Walter Scott*. 12 vols. London 1932-1937.

GRIMM, H. und HINRICHS, G. (ed). *Briefwechsel zwischen Jacob und Wilhelm Grimm aus der Jugendzeit*. Weimar 1881.

IPPEL, E. (ed). *Briefwechsel zwischen Jacob und Wilhelm Grimm, Dahlmann und Gervinus.* 2 vols. Berlin 1885-86.

KROGVIC, A. *Jacob og Wilhelm Grimm's brev til P. Chr. Asbjørnson og Jørgen Moe,* in *Festskrift til Gerh. Gran.* Christiania 1916.

LEITZMANN, A. (ed). *Briefe der Brüder Grimm.* Collected by H. Gürtler. Jena 1923.

—(ed). *Briefwechsel der Brüder Jacob und Wilhelm Grimm mit Karl Lachmann.* 2 vols. Jena 1927.

MÜLLER, W. (ed). *Briefe der Brüder Jacob und Wilhelm Grimm an Georg Friedrich Benecke aus den Jahren 1808-1829.* Göttingen 1889.

PISSIN, R. *Aus ungedruckten Briefen der Brüder Jacob, Wilhelm, Ferdinand, Ludwig Grimm,* in *Preussische Jahrbücher Vol. 34.* Berlin 1933.

REIFFERSCHEID, A. (ed). *Briefe von Jacob Grimm und Hendrick Willem Tydeman.* Heilbronn 1883.

REIFFERSCHEID, A. (ed). *Freundesbriefe von Wilhelm und Jacob Grimm.* Heilbronn 1878.

SAUER, A. *Briefwechsel der Brüder Grimm mit slawischen Gelehrten,* in *Prager Deutsche Studien, No. 8, Part 1.* Prague 1908.

SCHMIDT, E. (ed). *Briefwechsel der Brüder Grimm mit nordischen Gelehrten.* Berlin 1885.

SCHÖLL, A. (ed). *Goethes Briefe an Frau von Stein.* 2 vols. Frankfurt 1885.

SCHOOF, W. *Aus der Jugendzeit der Brüder Grimm* (nach ungedruckten Briefen), in *Hanauisches Magazin,* Jahrg, 13.1934/11/12; Jahrg. 14.1935;1/2. Hanau 1934-35.

—(in collaboration with I. SCHNACK) (ed). *Briefe der Brüder Grimm an Savigny.* Berlin 1953.

—(in collaboration with J. GÖRES) (ed). *Unbekannte Briefe der Brüder Grimm.* Bonn 1960.

SCHULTE KEMMINGHAUSEN, K. (ed). *Briefwechsel zwischen Jenny von Droste-Hülshoff und Wilhelm Grimm.* Münster 1929.

STENGEL, E. (ed). *Private und amtliche Beziehungen der Brüder Grimm zu Hessen.*
Vol I, *Briefe der Brüder Grimm an hessische Freunde.* Marburg 1895.
Vol II, *Aktenstücke über die Tätigheit der Brüder Grimm im hessischen Staatsdienste.* Marburg 1895.
Vol III, *Briefe der Brüder Grimm an Paul Wigand.* Marburg 1910.

VASMER, M. (ed). *Kopitars Briefwechsel mit Jacob Grimm.* Berlin 1938.

WENDELER, C. (ed). *Briefwechsel des Freiherrn Karl Hartwig Gregor von Meusebach mit Jacob und Wilhelm Grimm.* Heilbronn 1880.

GENERAL BACKGROUND

ANDERSEN, H. C. *The True Story of my Life.* London 1847.

BENZ, R. *Die deutsche Romantik.* Stuttgart 1956.

BERLIN — *Heimatchronik Berlin.* Vol 25 of *Heimatchroniken der Städte und Kreise des Bundesgebietes.* Cologne 1962.

BOEHN, M. VON. *Biedermeier*. Berlin n.d.

CASSEL — *Cassel und Wilhelmshöhe in alten Stichen und Lithographien*, with text by G. M. Vonau. Kassel 1955.

FRIDERICI, R. *Das Fass auf der Fulda. Ein kleines Kulturbild aus dem Kasseler Biedermeier*. Kassel 1964.

FRIEDELL, E. *Kulturgeschichte der Neuzeit*. Munich 1929.

GÖRRES, J. VON. *Ausgewählte Werke und Briefe*, ed W. Schellenberg. 2 vols in 1. Kempten and Munich 1911.

GRIMM, H. *Das Jahrhundert Goethes*. Stuttgart 1948.

HANAU — *Hanau, Stadt und Land*. Hanauer Geschichtsverein, Hanau 1954.

HAYN, R. *Die romantische Schule. Ein Beitrag zur Geschichte des deutschen Geisteslebens*. Fourth edition by O. Walzel. Berlin 1920.

HOFFMANN VON FALLERSLEBEN, A. H. *Mein Leben, Aufzeichnungen und Erinnerungen*. 6 vols in 3. Hanover 1868.

KOCH, W. A. *Briefe deutscher Romantiker*. Wiesbaden n.d.

PINNOW, H. *Deutsche Geschichte. Volk und Staat in tausend Jahren*. Berlin 1929.

REICH, W. *Bettina von Arnim. Lebensspiel*. Zürich 1953.

RODENBERG, J. *Aus seinen Tagebüchern*. Berlin 1919.

STADELMANN, R. 1848. *Soziale und politische Geschichte der Revolution von 1848*. Munich 1948.

STOLL, A. *Der junge Savigny*. Berlin 1927.

—*Friedrich Karl von Savigny. Professorenjahre in Berlin*. 1810-1842. Berlin 1929.

—*Friedrich Karl von Savigny. Ministerzeit und letzte Lebensjahre*. 1842-1861. Berlin 1929.

WALZEL, O. *Deutsche Romantik*. Leipzig 1908.

WIGAND, P. *Denkwürdigkeiten aus einem bescheidenen Leben*. Ms. Hist. Litt. 4° 33. Murhardsche und Landesbibiliothek, Kassel.

THE *Nursery and Household Tales*

BOLTE, J. und POLIVKA, G. *Anmerkungen zu den Kinder- und Hausmärchen der Brüder Grimm*. 5 vols. Leipzig 1913-1932.

CRANE, T. F. *The External History of the Kinder- und Hausmärchen of the Brothers Grimm*, in *Modern Philology*. Vols 14/15. Chicago 1916-17-18.

DAVID, A. and DAVID, M. E. *A literary approach to the Brothers Grimm*, in *Journal of the Folklore Institute, Vol I, No. 3*. Bloomington 1964.

DIELMANN, K. *Märchenillustrationen von Ludwig Emil Grimm* in *Hanauer Geschichtsblätter No. 18*. Hanau 1962.

German Popular Stories translated from the Kinder-und Hausmärchen by MM Grimm. 2 vols. London 1823; 1826.

German Popular Stories (from E. Taylor's translation). Introduction by John Ruskin. London 1868.

GRIMM. *The Fairy Ring.* Translated by J. E. Taylor. London 1846.

—*Gammer Grethel.* Translated by E. Taylor. London 1839.

GRIMM, BRÜDER. *Kinder-und Hausmärchen.* Vollständige Ausgabe. Munich 1949.

—*Kinder-und Hausmärchen.* Ed F. von der Leyen. 2 vols. Düsseldorf/ Cologne 1962.

—*Grimm's Fairy Tales.* Complete edition, based on the translation by Margaret Hunt, revised, corrected and completed by James Stern. London 1948.

—*Grimm's Household Tales,* with the author's notes; translated from the German and edited by Margaret Hunt. Introduction by Andrew Lang. 2 vols. London 1884.

—*Grimms. Other Tales.* A new selection by W. Hansen translated and edited by R. Michaelis-Jena and A. Ratcliff. London 1956.

HAMANN, H. *Die literarischen Vorlagen der Kinder-und Hausmärchen und ihre Bearbeitung durch die Brüder Grimm.* Berlin 1906.

KARLINGER, F. *Les contes des frères Grimm. Contribution à l'étude de la langue et du style.* Paris-Fribourg 1963.

LEFFTZ, J. (ed). *Die Märchen der Brüder Grimm. Urfassung nach der Originalhandschrift der Abtei Oelenberg im Elsass.* Heidelberg 1927.

LEYEN, F. VON DER. *Das deutsche Märchen und die Brüder Grimm.* Düsseldorf/Cologne 1964.

PANZER, F. (ed). *Die Kinder-und Hausmärchen der Brüder Grimm.* Vollständige Ausgabe in der Urfassung. Wiesbaden 1935.

SCHMIDT, K. *Die Entwicklung der Grimmschen Kinder-und Hausmärchen seit der Urhandschrift.* Halle/Saale 1932.

SCHOOF, W. *Zur Entstehungsgeschichte der Grimmschen Märchen.* Hamburg 1959.

SNYDER, L. L. *Nationalistic Aspects of the Grimm Brothers' Fairy Tales,* in *Journal of Social Psychology,* Vol XXIII. Provincetown, Mass. U.S.A. 1951.

TONNELAT, E. *Les contes des frères Grimm. Étude sur la composition et le style.* Paris 1912.

TONNELAT, E. *Les frères Grimm, leur oeuvre de jeunesse.* Paris 1912.

FURTHER BOOKS CONSULTED

AARNE, A. *Vergleichende Märchenforschung.* Helsinki 1908.

AARNE, A. and THOMPSON, S. *The types of the Folktale.* Helsinki 1961.

BEIT, H. VON, *Symbolik des Märchens.* 3 vols. Berne 1952.

DASENT, SIR GEORGE W. *Popular Tales from the Norse.* Edinburgh 1859.

DÉGH, L. *Märchen, Erzähler und Erzählgemeinschaft.* Veröffentlichungen des Instituts für deutsche Volkskunde. Berlin 1962.

DELARGY, J. *The Gaelic Storyteller.* London 1946.

HARTWIG, O. *Zur ersten englischen Überseztung der Kinder-und Haus-märchen der Brüder Grimm*, in *Centralblatt für Bibliothekswesen, Januar/Februar 1898*. Leipzig 1898.

HAZARD, P. *Books, Children, Men*. Boston 1944.

LEYEN, F. von der, *Das Märchen*. Heidelberg 1958.

—*Die Welt der Märchen*. 2 vols. Düsseldorf 1953.

LOEFFLER-DELACHAUX, M. *Le Symbolisme des Contes de Fées*. Paris 1949.

LÜTHI, M. *Das europäische Volksmärchen*. Berne 1947.

LÜTHI, M. *Märchen*. Second edition. Stuttgart 1964.

RÖHRICH, L. *Märchen und Wirklichkeit*. Stuttgart 1956.

ROUGEMONT, C. . . . *dann leben sie noch heute. Erlebnisse und Erfahrungen beim Märchenerzählen*. Münster 1962.

TETZNER, L. *Aus der Welt des Märchens*. Nach dem Nachlass zusammen-gestellt und bearbeitet von Vilma Mönckeberg-Kollmar. Münster 1965.

THALMANN, M. *Das Märchen und die Moderne*. Stuttgart 1961.

THOMPSON, S. *The Folktale*. New York 1951.

—*Motif-Index of Folk Literature*. 6 vols. Bloomington, Ind. 1955-58.

TOLKIEN, J. R. R. *Tree and Leaf*. London 1964.

WITTGENSTEIN, GRAF OTTOKAR. *Märchen, Träume, Schicksale*. Düsseldorf/Cologne 1965.

```
                                  Friedrich Hermann Georg      Jacob
                                  *12 12 1785                  * 3  4 1826
                                  †16  3 1784                  †15 12 1826

                                  Jacob Ludwig Carl            Herman Friedrich
                                  * 4  1 1785                  * 6  1 1828
                                  †20  9 1863                  †16  6 1901

                                                               ∞25 10 1859
                                  Wilhelm Carl
                                  *24  2 1786                  Gisela von Arnim
                                  †16 12 1859                  *30  8 1827
                                  ∞15  5 1825 ────             † 4  4 1889
                                  Henriette Dorothea Wild
                                  *23  5 1795                  Rudolf George Ludwig
                                  †22  8 1867                  *31  3 1830
                                                               †13 11 1889
                                  Carl Friedrich
                                  *24  4 1787                  Auguste Luise
                                  †25  5 1852                  Pauline Marie
                                                               *21  8 1832
                                  Ferdinand Philipp            † 9  2 1919
                                  *18 12 1788
                                  † 6  1 1845

Philipp Wilhelm Grimm            Ludwig Emil                  Friederike (Ideke) Lotte
*19  9 1751                      *14  3 1790                  Amalia Maria
†10  1 1796                      † 4  3 1863                  *23  7 1833
                                                               †17 12 1914
∞23  2 1783 ────                 ∞(1) Marie Böttner ────
                                  * 9  8 1803                  ∞Rudolf von
Dorothea Zimmer                  †15  8 1842                  Eschwege 19 8 1855
*20 11 1755                                                    *22  1 1821
†27  5 1808                      ∞(2) Friederike Ernst        †24 11 1875
                                  *24 12 1806
                                  †      1894

                                                               Karl
                                                               * 5  1 1824
                                  Friedrich                    †18  2 1890
                                  *15  6 1791
                                  †20  8 1792                  Agnes
                                                               *11 12 1825
                                                               †29 10 1826

                                  Charlotte Amalie             Friedrich
                                  *10  5 1793                  *10  9 1827
                                  †15  6 1833                  †23  1 1892

                                  ∞2  7 1822 ────              Berta
                                                               *27  4 1829
                                  Ludwig Hassenpflug           † 9  6 1830
                                  *26  2 1794
                                  †10 10 1862                  Louis
                                                               * 1 12 1831
                                                               †11 10 1878

                                  Georg Eduard                 Dorothea
                                  *26  7 1794                  *23  5 1833
                                  †19  4 1795                  †24  1 1898
```

(* born   † died   ∞ married)

205

Index